The Literature of Cinema

ADVISORY EDITOR: **MARTIN S. DWORKIN**
INSTITUTE OF PHILOSOPHY AND POLITICS OF EDUCATION
TEACHER'S COLLEGE, COLUMBIA UNIVERSITY

THE LITERATURE OF CINEMA presents a comprehensive selection from the multitude of writings about cinema, rediscovering materials on its origins, history, theoretical principles and techniques, aesthetics, economics, and effects on societies and individuals. Included are works of inherent, lasting merit and others of primarily historical significance. These provide essential resources for serious study and critical enjoyment of the "magic shadows" that became one of the decisive cultural forces of modern times.

Footnotes to the Film

Charles Davy, editor

ARNO PRESS & THE NEW YORK TIMES
New York • 1970

Reprint Edition 1970 by Arno Press Inc.
Reprinted by permission of Peter Davies, Ltd.
Library of Congress Catalog Card Number: 75-124004
ISBN 0-405-01610-7
ISBN for complete set: 0-405-01600-X
Manufactured in the United States of America

Footnotes to
The Film

SNOW WHITE IN THE DWARFS' HOUSE

From Walt Disney's *SNOW WHITE AND THE SEVEN DWARFS*
(R.K.O.-Radio, 1938)

Snow White, sent by the wicked Queen, her stepmother, to die in the forest, is found next morning by the animals. They guide her to the dwarfs' empty house and help her to spring-clean it while the dwarfs are working in their mine.

Footnotes to
The Film

edited by
Charles Davy

Lovat Dickson Ltd
Readers' Union Ltd
London

POINT

THIS edition is not for public sale. It is distributed only to members of Readers' Union, and is possible by co-operative reader demand and by the sacrifice of ordinary profit margins by all concerned. Reader-commentaries on *Footnotes to the Film* will be found in the September issue of *Readers' News*, which is an essential part of Readers' Union and which should always accompany this volume. Membership of Readers' Union can be made at any bookshop or bookstall.

MADE 1938 IN GREAT BRITAIN
TEXT PRINTED BY LOWE & BRYDONE LIMITED, LONDON
DOUBLE-TONE HALF-TONES PRINTED BY JARROLD & SONS LIMITED, NORWICH
FOR READERS' UNION LIMITED
REGISTERED OFFICES, CHANDOS PLACE BY CHARING CROSS, LONDON, ENGLAND

FOREWORD
TO READERS' UNION EDITION

THE choice of this book by Readers' Union means that it will circulate widely in many parts of the world. It may reach readers who live far from any of the big cities where the latest films are shown. Perhaps it will reach readers who have never taken much interest in the cinema and wonder why they should. But is it possible for anyone who looks with intelligent curiosity at contemporary events to ignore the influence of films on human affairs? In the United States there are over 15,000 cinema theatres; in Great Britain, nearly 5,000. They are visited every week by some 40 per cent of the population in this country, and by nearly 70 per cent of the population in the United States. The millions of people who fill these cinema theatres receive constantly a stream of emotional suggestions from the screen; their ideals, opinions, tastes are all more or less affected by the films they see.

Outside the ordinary entertainment field, too, the cinema has many resources, growing from year to year. It can be and is regularly used for education, for news reporting, and for propaganda, direct and indirect, on behalf of all sorts of causes and beliefs. And behind these activities stands a vast industry, employing huge sums of capital and an immense amount of talent and enterprise, searching always for new methods, new ideas, new ways of appealing to public fancy. Not to know something of how and why and where films are made and circulated, something of the men and women who make them and of the audiences who pay to see them, is to remain blind to one of the major forces which for good or evil is shaping the civilisation of to-day and to-morrow. It is by offering a critical survey of a subject of such far-reaching human importance that this book hopes to justify itself.

EDITOR'S PREFACE

A SURVEY of the cinema could start from many different points, but at the centre of it all is the practical work of film-making in the studio. It is here that our book opens with the three chapters of Part One, dealing in turn with the tasks of a director, the technique of screen acting, and the use and misuse of that subtle mechanism, the film camera with its attendant microphone.

The making of a film draws in also the co-operation of specialists from other fields. Writers, musicians, set designers, costume experts—they all contribute. From the comedy film has developed the new art of the animated cartoon. Colour films call for help from the trained eye of the painter. This collaboration of other arts is the main theme of Part Two.

But there would be no films without a film industry. Behind the director stands the producer, and behind him the financier. Here is a source of activities and ambitions and social problems stretching far beyond the limits of the studio and leading inevitably to rival

Editor's Preface

policies and divergent interests. The man with ideas is warned by the man with money not to forget "what the public wants". The close relationship of cinema to theatre makes them both competitors and allies. The social influence of the cinema raises questions: is its business simply to entertain or should the aim of producers be—as John Grierson says in his article—"to build a picture of reality; to bring cinema to its destiny as a social commentator, inspirator and art"? Finally, the film industry is international: what have British films to learn or fear from Hollywood? These are some of the subjects discussed in Part Three.

So at last a film is ready for showing: it is time for the film-goer to speak. What does he—or she—think of the cinema as a recreation? What does the exhibitor think of the crowds pouring into his theatre—or staying away? Then there is the critic who advises film-goers what to see, and the Censor who decides what they may and may not see. This closes Part Four, leaving only a concluding question—Are Films Worth While?

As to the illustrations, they are chosen partly to exemplify the pictorial resources of film production—its use of the most varied settings, indoors and out-of-doors, its command of light and shade and pictorial design, its power to cover wide panoramas and equally to concentrate on a single gesture or a single face—and partly to bring out special aspects of film technique. It should be remembered that stills are not usually enlargements from film negatives; they are taken separately with an ordinary camera. They are not always a reliable guide to the merits of the film from which they come, for it is in terms of movement—

movement within the scene itself and movement from one scene to another—that the pictorial quality of a film must in the end be judged. But stills are the only way of illustrating camera-work in a book; they give at least an idea of the style of a production and show what sort of attention was paid to settings, lighting, grouping and costumes.

Finally—for such a book as this is essentially a co-operative enterprise—acknowledgments are due from the editor to all who have helped to bring it out. My thanks go first to the contributors in several countries, and to the film companies who have helped me generously with information and the loan of photographs. Particularly I owe thanks to Mr Zoltan Tornai, of Berlin, who represents Miss Elsie Cohen of the Academy Cinema and through her good offices kindly procured for me a number of German stills; to Mr W. J. Moss, who placed at my disposal some other German stills he had brought from Berlin; to Mr Paul Rotha for the loan of a rare still from *The Cabinet of Dr Caligari*; to Mr Alberto Cavalcanti, who got me an early still of Charles Ray from Paris; and to Mr Forsyth Hardy, who searched through the library of the Edinburgh Film Guild for certain stills which I could have obtained nowhere else. And, not least, I am grateful to Mr Garfield Howe, of Messrs Lovat Dickson, who conceived the idea of the book and with his firm has stood behind it. To him, also, the book owes many valuable suggestions and the whole work of the index.

C. D.

CONTENTS

	PAGE
FOREWORD TO READERS' UNION EDITION	v
EDITOR'S PREFACE	vii

PART I
STUDIO WORK: HOW A FILM IS MADE

DIRECTION	Alfred Hitchcock	3
FILM ACTING	Robert Donat	16
HANDLING THE CAMERA	Basil Wright	37

PART II
SCREEN MATERIAL: HELP FROM OTHER ARTS

SUBJECTS AND STORIES	Graham Greene	57
COMEDIES AND CARTOONS	Alberto Cavalcanti	71
SETTINGS, COSTUMES, BACKGROUNDS	John Betjeman	87
MUSIC ON THE SCREEN	Maurice Jaubert	101
THE COLOUR FILM	Paul Nash	116

PART III
FILM INDUSTRY PROBLEMS

THE COURSE OF REALISM	John Grierson	137
BRITISH FILMS: TO-DAY AND TO-MORROW	Alexander Korda	162
THE FUTURE OF SCREEN AND STAGE	Basil Dean	172
HOLLYWOOD AND BRITAIN—THREE THOUSAND MILES APART	Maurice Kann	185

PART IV
FILMS AND THE PUBLIC

		PAGE
WHY I GO TO THE CINEMA .	Elizabeth Bowen .	205
WALK UP! WALK UP! *PLEASE*	Sidney L. Bernstein	221
THE CRITIC IN FILM HISTORY .	Alistair Cooke .	238
CENSORSHIP AND FILM SOCIETIES	Forsyth Hardy .	264
ARE FILMS WORTH WHILE? .	Charles Davy .	279
POSTSCRIPT: THE FILM MARCHES ON	Charles Davy .	303
CONTRIBUTORS' WHO'S WHO .	. . .	323
INDEX	. . .	327

LIST OF PLATES

Frontispiece
Snow White and the Seven Dwarfs

Section inserted at Pages 80–81
Two scenes from *Elephant Boy*
Trial scene in *Rembrandt*
Marlene Dietrich in *Knight Without Armour*
Edge of the World
Letzte Rose
Charles Laughton in *Mutiny on the Bounty* and *Vessel of Wrath*
Greta Garbo and Robert Taylor in *Camille*
The Green Pastures: "De Lawd" and the Archangel Gabriel
Paul Muni and Luise Rainer in *The Good Earth*
Open-air Pageantry: *Romeo and Juliet*
Elisabeth Bergner in *Dreaming Lips*
Gracie Fields in *Keep Smiling*
Charles Ray in *The Girl I Love*
Charlie Chaplin in *Modern Times*
Modern Comedy: *Le Dernier Milliardaire*
The Marx Brothers in *A Day at the Races*
Dickens on the Screen: *David Copperfield*
Ginger Rogers practising for *Shall We Dance?*
Studio lighting: *St Martin's Lane*

Footnotes to The Film

Section inserted at Pages 208–209

A group in *La Kermesse Héroïque*
Sous les Toits de Paris
Un Carnet de Bal
Pépé le Moko
Sacha Guitry's hands in *The Cheat*
Russian close-ups: *We from Kronstadt* and *The Circus*
The Documentary Film: *North Sea* and *Olympic Games*
Denham Studios
Pinewood Studios
Alfred Hitchcock directing *The Thirty-nine Steps*
Ordeal by camera: *The Witness Chair*
The March of Time: Father of all Turks
Poetry of Fact: *Song of Ceylon*
The Natural History Film: *Rock Pools* and *Tawny Owl*
Expressionism: *The Cabinet of Dr Caligari*
Silhouette Films by Lotte Reiniger
Things to Come

On Pages 128 and 131

Walt Disney's *Magician Mickey* (United Artists, 1937)
Walt Disney's *More Kittens* (United Artists, 1936)

PART I
STUDIO WORK:
HOW A FILM IS MADE

DIRECTION
By Alfred Hitchcock

MANY people think a film director does all his work in the studio, drilling the actors, making them do what he wants. That is not at all true of my own methods, and I can write only of my own methods. I like to have a film complete in my mind before I go on the floor. Sometimes the first idea one has of a film is of a vague pattern, a sort of haze with a certain shape. There is possibly a colourful opening developing into something more intimate; then, perhaps in the middle, a progression to a chase or some other adventure; and sometimes at the end the big shape of a climax, or maybe some twist or surprise. You see this hazy pattern, and then you have to find a narrative idea to suit it. Or a story may give you an idea first and you have to develop it into a pattern.

Imagine an example of a standard plot—let us say a conflict between love and duty. This idea was the origin of my first talkie, *Blackmail*. The hazy pattern one saw beforehand was duty—love—love versus duty—and finally either duty or love, one or the other. The whole middle section was built up on the theme of love versus duty, after duty and love had been introduced separately in turn. So I had first to put on the screen an episode expressing duty.

I showed the arrest of a criminal by Scotland Yard detectives, and tried to make it as concrete and detailed as I could. You even saw the detectives take the man to the lavatory to wash his hands—nothing exciting, just the routine of duty. Then the young detective says he's going out that evening with his girl, and the sequence ends, pointing on from duty to love. Then you start showing the relationship between the detective and his girl: they are middle-class people. The love theme doesn't run smoothly; there is a quarrel and the girl goes off by herself, just because the young man has kept her waiting a few minutes. So your story starts; the girl falls in with the villain—he tries to seduce her and she kills him. Now you've got your problem prepared. Next morning, as soon as the detective is put on to the murder case, you have your conflict—love versus duty. The audience know that he will be trying to track down his own girl, who has done the murder, so you sustain their interest: they wonder what will happen next.

The blackmailer was really a subsidiary theme. I wanted him to go through and expose the girl. That was my idea of how the story ought to end. I wanted the pursuit to be after the girl, not after the blackmailer. That would have brought the conflict on to a climax, with the young detective, ahead of the others, trying to push the girl out through a window to get her away, and the girl turning round and saying: "You can't do that—I must give myself up." Then the rest of the police arrive, misinterpret what he is doing, and say, "Good man, you've got her," not knowing the relationship between them. Now the reason for the opening comes to light. You repeat every shot used first to illustrate the duty theme, only now it is the girl who is the criminal. The young man is there ostensibly as a detective, but of course the audience know he is in love with the girl. The girl is locked up in her cell and the two detectives walk away, and the older one says, "Going out with your girl to-night?" The younger one shakes his head. "No. Not to-night."

That was the ending I wanted for *Blackmail*, but I had to change it for commercial reasons. The girl couldn't be left to face her fate. And that shows you how the films suffer from their own power of appealing to millions. They could often be subtler than they are, but their own popularity won't let them.

But to get back to the early work on a film. With the help of my wife, who does the technical continuity, I plan out a script very carefully, hoping to follow it exactly, all the way through, when shooting starts. In fact, this working on the script is the real making of the film, for me. When I've done it, the film is finished already in my mind. Usually, too, I don't find it necessary to do more than supervise the editing myself. I know it is said sometimes that a director ought to edit his own pictures if he wants to control their final form, for it is in the editing, according to this view, that a film is really brought into being. But if the scenario is planned out in detail, and followed closely during production, editing should be easy. All that has to be done is to cut away irrelevancies and see that the finished film is an accurate rendering of the scenario.

Settings, of course, come into the preliminary plan, and usually I have fairly clear ideas about them; I was an art student before I took up with films. Sometimes I even think of backgrounds first. *The Man Who Knew Too Much* started like that; I looked in my mind's eye at snowy Alps and dingy London alleys, and threw my characters into the middle of the contrast. Studio settings, however, are often a problem; one difficulty is that extreme effects—extremes of luxury or extremes of squalor—are much the easiest to register on the screen. If you try to reproduce the average sitting-room in Golders Green or Streatham it is apt to come out looking like nothing in particular, just nondescript. It is true that I have tried lately to get interiors with a real lower-middle-class atmosphere—for instance, the Verlocs' living-room in *Sabotage*—but there's always a certain risk in giving your audience humdrum truth.

However, in time the script and the sets are finished somehow and we are ready to start shooting. One great problem that occurs at once, and keeps on occurring, is to get the players to adapt themselves to film technique. Many of them, of course, come from the stage; they are not cinema-minded at all. So, quite naturally, they like to play long scenes straight ahead. I am willing to work with the long uninterrupted shot: you can't avoid it altogether, and you can get some variety by having two cameras running, one close up and one farther off, and cutting from one to the other when the film is edited. But if I have to shoot a long scene continuously I always feel I am losing grip on it, from a cinematic point of view. The camera, I feel, is simply standing there, *hoping* to catch something with a visual point to it.

What I like to do always is to photograph just the little bits of a scene that I really need for building up a visual sequence. I want to put my film together on the screen, not simply to photograph something that has been put together already in the form of a long piece of stage acting. This is what gives an effect of life to a picture—the feeling that when you see it on the screen you are watching something that has been conceived and brought to birth directly in visual terms. The screen ought to speak its own language, freshly coined, and it can't do that unless it treats an acted scene as a piece of raw material which must be broken up, taken to bits, before it can be woven into an expressive visual pattern.

You can see an example of what I mean in *Sabotage*. Just before Verloc is killed there is a scene made up entirely of short pieces of film, separately photographed. This scene has to show how Verloc comes to be killed—how the thought of killing him arises in Sylvia Sidney's mind and connects itself with the carving knife she uses when they sit down to dinner. But the sympathy of the audience has to be kept with Sylvia Sidney; it must be clear that Verloc's death, finally, is an accident. So, as she serves at the table, you see her unconsciously serving vegetables with the carving knife, as though her hand were keeping hold of the knife of its own accord. The camera cuts from her hand to her eyes and back to her hand; then back to her eyes as she suddenly becomes aware of the knife making its error. Then to a normal shot— the man unconcernedly eating; then back to the hand holding the knife. In an older style of acting

Sylvia would have had to show the audience what was passing in her mind by exaggerated facial expression. But people to-day in real life often don't show their feelings in their faces: so the film treatment showed the audience her mind through her hand, through its unconscious grasp on the knife. Now the camera moves again to Verloc—back to the knife—back again to his face. You see him seeing the knife, realizing its implication. The tension between the two is built up with the knife as its focus.

Now when the camera has immersed the audience so closely in a scene such as this, it can't instantly become objective again. It must broaden the movement of the scene without loosening the tension. Verloc gets up and walks round the table, coming so close to the camera that you feel, if you are sitting in the audience, almost as though you must move back to make room for him. Then the camera moves to Sylvia Sidney again, then returns to the subject—the knife.

So you gradually build up the psychological situation, piece by piece, using the camera to emphasise first one detail, then another. The point is to draw the audience right inside the situation instead of leaving them to watch it from outside, from a distance. And you can do this only by breaking the action up into details and cutting from one to the other, so that each detail is forced in turn on the attention of the audience and reveals its psychological meaning. If you played the whole scene straight through, and simply made a photographic record of it with the camera always in one position, you would lose your power over the audience. They would watch the scene without becoming really involved in it, and you would have no means of concentrating their attention on those particular visual details which make them feel what the characters are feeling.

This way of building up a picture means that film work hasn't much need for the virtuoso actor who gets his effects and climaxes himself, who plays directly on to the audience with the force of his talent and personality. The screen actor has got to be much more plastic; he has to submit himself to be used by the director and the camera. Mostly he is wanted to behave quietly and naturally (which, of course, isn't at all easy), leaving the camera to add most of the accents and emphases. I would almost say that the best screen actor is the man who can do nothing extremely well.

One way of using the camera to give emphasis is the reaction shot. By the reaction shot I mean any close-up which illustrates an event by showing instantly the reaction to it of a person or a group. The door opens for some one to come in, and before showing who it is you cut to the expressions of the persons already in the room. Or, while one person is talking, you keep your camera on some one else who is listening. This over-running of one person's image with another person's voice is a method peculiar to the talkies; it is one of the devices which help the talkies to tell a story faster than a silent film could tell it, and faster than it could be told on the stage.

Or, again, you can use the camera to give emphasis whenever the attention of the audience has to be focussed for a moment on a certain player. There is no need for him to raise his voice or move to the centre of the stage or do anything dramatic. A close-up will do it all for him—will give him, so to speak, the stage all to himself.

I must say that in recent years I have come to make much less use of obvious camera devices. I have become more commercially-minded; afraid that anything at all subtle may be missed. I have learnt from experience how easily small touches are overlooked.

The other day a journalist came to interview me and we spoke about film technique. "I always remember," he said, "a little bit in one of your silent films, *The Ring*. The young boxer comes home after winning his fight. He is flushed with success—wants to celebrate. He pours out champagne all round. Then he finds that his wife is out, and he knows at once that she is out with another man. At this moment the camera cuts to a glass of champagne; you see a fizz of bubbles rise off it and there it stands untasted, going flat. That one shot gives you the whole feeling of the scene." Yes, I said, that sort of imagery may be quite good: I don't despise it and still use it now and then. But is it always noticed? There was another bit in *The Ring* which I believe hardly any one noticed.

The scene was outside a boxing-booth at a fair, with a barker talking to the crowd. Inside the booth a professional is taking on all-comers. He has always won in the first round. A man comes running out of the booth and speaks to the barker: something unexpected has happened. Then a cut straight to the

Direction

ringside: you see an old figure 1 being taken down and replaced by a brand new figure 2. I meant this single detail to show that the boxer, now, is up against some one he can't put out in the first round. But it went by too quickly. Perhaps I might have shown the new figure 2 being taken out of a paper wrapping —something else was needed to make the audience see in a moment that the figure for the second round had never been used before.

The film always has to deal in exaggerations. Its methods reflect the simple contrasts of black and white photography. One advantage of colour is that it would give you more intermediate shades. I should never want to fill the screen with colour: it ought to be used economically—to put new words into the screen's visual language when there's a need for them. You could start a colour film with a board-room scene: sombre panelling and furniture, the directors all in dark clothes and white collars. Then the chairman's wife comes in, wearing a red hat. She takes the attention of the audience at once, just because of that one note of colour. Or suppose a gangster story: the leader of the gang is sitting in a café with a man he suspects. He has told his gunman to watch the table. "If I order a glass of port, bump him off. If I order green chartreuse, let him go."

This journalist asked me also about distorted sound —a device I tried in *Blackmail* when the word "knife" hammers on the consciousness of the girl at breakfast on the morning after the murder. Again, I think this kind of effect may be justified. There have always been occasions when we have needed to show a phantasmagoria of the mind in terms of visual imagery. So we may want to show some one's mental state by letting him listen to some sound—let us say church bells—and making them clang with distorted insistence in his head. But on the whole nowadays I try to tell a story in the simplest possible way, so that I can feel sure it will hold the attention of any audience and won't puzzle them. I know there are critics who ask why lately I have made only thrillers. Am I satisfied, they say, with putting on the screen the equivalent merely of popular novelettes? Part of the answer is that I am out to get the best stories I can which will suit the film medium, and I have usually found it necessary to take a hand in writing them myself.

There is a shortage of good writing for the screen, and is that surprising? A playwright may take a year or more writing a play, but in a year the film industry has to make hundreds of films. More and more pictures, one after the other incessantly, with a certain standard to keep up—it throws a great strain on the creative faculties of every one who has to supply the industry with ideas. Of course there must be co-operation, division of labour, all the time. The old saying, "No one man ever made a picture," is entirely true. And the only answer found so far to the writing problem has been to employ a number of writers to work together on the same picture. Metro-Goldwyn, we are told, employ altogether a staff of eighty or ninety writers, so they can draw at any time on a whole group of writers to see a story through. I don't say there aren't drawbacks in this collective method, but it often makes things easier when time is at stake, as it always is in film production. In this country we can't usually afford to employ large writing staffs, so I have had to join in and become a writer myself. I choose crime stories because that is the kind of story I can write, or help to write, myself—the kind of story I can turn most easily into a successful film. It is the same with Charles Bennett, who has so often worked with me; he is essentially a writer of melodrama. I am ready to use other stories, but I can't find writers who will give them to me in a suitable form.

Sometimes I have been asked what films I should make if I were free to do exactly as I liked without having to think about the box-office. There are several examples I can give very easily. For one thing, I should like to make travel films with a personal element in them: that would be quite a new field. Or I should like to do a verbatim of a celebrated trial — of course there would have to be some editing, some cutting down. The Thompson-Bywaters case, for instance. You can see the figures at Madame Tussaud's and the newspapers gave long reports of the trial. The cinema could reconstruct the whole story. Or there is the fire at sea possibility —that has never been tackled seriously on the screen. It might be too terrifying for some audiences but it would make a great subject, worth doing.

British producers are often urged to make more films about characteristic phases of English life. Why, they are asked, do we see so little of the English farmer or the English seaman? Or is there not plenty of good material in the great British industries—in mining or shipbuilding or steel? One difficulty here is that English audiences seem to take more interest in American life—I suppose because it has a novelty value. They are rather easily bored by everyday scenes in their own country. But I certainly should like to make a film of the Derby, only it might not be quite in the popular class. It would be hard to invent a Derby story that wasn't hackneyed, conventional. I would rather do it more as a documentary—a sort of pageant, an animated modern version of Frith's "Derby Day". I would show everything that goes on all round the course, but without a story.

Perhaps the average audience isn't ready for that, yet. Popular taste, all the same, does move; to-day you can put over scenes that would have been ruled out a few years ago. Particularly towards comedy, nowadays, there is a different attitude. You can get comedy out of your stars, and you used not to be allowed to do anything which might knock the glamour off them.

In 1926 I made a film called *Downhill*, from a play by Ivor Novello, who acted in the film himself, with Ian Hunter and Isabel Jeans. There was a sequence showing a quarrel between Hunter and Novello. It started as an ordinary fight; then they began throwing things at one another. They tried to pick up heavy pedestals to throw and the pedestals bowled them over. In other words I made it comic. I even put Hunter into a morning coat and striped trousers because I felt that a man never looks so ridiculous as when he is well dressed and fighting. This whole scene was cut out; they said I was guying Ivor Novello. It was ten years before its time.

I say ten years, because you may remember that in 1936 M.G.M. showed a comedy called *Libelled Lady*. There is a fishing sequence in it: William Powell stumbles about in the river, falls flat and gets soaked and catches a big fish by accident. Here you have a star, not a slapstick comedian, made to do something pretty near slapstick. In *The Thirty-nine Steps*, too, a little earlier, I was allowed to drag Madeleine Carroll over the moors handcuffed to the hero; I made her get wet and untidy and look ridiculous for the purpose of the story. I couldn't have done that ten years ago.

I foresee the decline of the individual comedian. Of course there may always be specially gifted comedians who will have films written round them, but I think public taste is turning to like comedy and drama more mixed up; and this is another move away from the conventions of the stage. In a play your divisions are much more rigid; you have a scene—then curtain, and after an interval another scene starts. In a film you keep your whole action flowing; you can have comedy and drama running together and weave them in and out. Audiences are much readier now than they used to be for sudden changes of mood; and this means more freedom for a director. The art of directing for the commercial market is to know just how far you can go. In many ways I am freer now to do what I want to do than I was a few years ago. I hope in time to have more freedom still—if audiences will give it to me.

FILM ACTING
By Robert Donat

"NOBODY loves the Cinema," one of its most distinguished critics recently wailed, referring to a habit prevalent among my kind to despise it.

Come to think of it, I was recently in high dudgeon myself when the Critics' Circle, inviting me to speak at the Annual Dinner, requested me to respond not to the toast of the Theatre but the Cinema. I was off on my high horse at a gallop at once. Shades of Thespis! Had I sweated at Shakespeare all over the British Isles, had I played in music-hall sketches and curtain-raisers and stop-gap items in cinema intervals and repertory, repertory, repertory once and twice nightly for years and years and years, only to be asked at last to say a few kind words for the Cinema? Finally I contributed a frightful post-prandial about an attempt at actor-management which few of the guests had witnessed. But you could safely bet your best boots and breeches that none of them had avoided seeing *Henry VIII*, *Monte Cristo*, *The Thirty-nine Steps* or *The Ghost Goes West*. If a census had been taken it would go hard if one of these masterpieces had not been encountered during the years of stress in which they were released upon an insatiable and pampered public.

That is the mystery. We love the Theatre—and do not go to it. We despise the Cinema—and flock to it in our millions. Why is this? Is the Theatre so difficult to discover and the Cinema so difficult to avoid? Or can it be that the one is something to be endured, the other not to be resisted? You have heard all the pros and cons—tired business men and queues and high prices and luxurious comfort for people who need extra padding for their seats because their brains are commonly supposed to dwell there. But I am in the wrong queue. I am mingling with the public when I should be pleading for the actors.

I am not taking sides. Nor am I running with the hare and hunting with the hounds. I accepted this job more because I have a cause to plead and an axe or two to grind than because I felt supremely competent to tackle it. I simply seek to show that the cinematic hound and the theatrical hare provide each other with some very healthy exercise, and, far short of the one running the other to death, a lot of superfluous fat has been lost in the chase. For instance, the commercial film, with its excellent standards of entertainment, has made it practically impossible for feeble acting and tawdry plays to exist; theatre-goers will only tolerate the really exceptional play. This alone should justify the commercial film. We are apt to forget that when the theatre is at its healthiest it, too, is commercial. And we are apt to be afraid of success and suspicious of it. For my own part, I can see no reason why the big box-office success—the film of universal appeal—should not be a work of art. Best-sellers are sometimes handed down to posterity as classics, and the book which has the greatest sales of any book happens to be the Bible.

More daft remarks are made in defence of the

Theatre and the Cinema than in any other cause. Why should I defend the Cinema, which has borrowed so blatantly from the Theatre and is so slavishly dependent on it for new recruits? We are apt to forget that even the picture-frame of the cinema screen is pinched directly from the modern picture-frame stage.

And the Theatre? The Theatre, of course, has been in the throes of death ever since films began—and earlier. Silent films having failed in the extermination, Talkies were invented to deal the death-blow. And now Television prepares its fatal draught. Meanwhile the Theatre, announcing its Positively Farewell Performances, is crammed to bursting-point just as often as the fare it proffers proves irresistible to a wayward public.

For myself, I shall return to the stage as often as a good play comes my way. The trouble is, good scenarios are far more plentiful than good plays—by which I mean good entertainment; and I am not ashamed of being voted at the box-office as a good entertainer. In seven years the Theatre has offered me one great play, half a dozen possible plays, two exciting gambles and innumerable duds. Until something really exciting comes along, I go on making films—and enjoy making them enormously. I make my film, seeing it grow day by day until it is finished; then I have shot my bolt and I can look around for new doors to fasten. On the stage one has to try to shoot the same bolt eight times a week for as long as the damn door will remain on its hinges. Few plays are worth that dreadful grind. One of our finest actors recently complained of being in a state of coma towards the end of a run; is it to be wondered that after 400 performances he found it just too hard a wick to keep alight? Even our own Noel Coward collapses after two short seasons playing in some of the most delightful theatricalities ever produced.

There is a certain snobbery among stage actors where filming is concerned; they look upon it as a rather boring, well-paid joke. Their performances in front of the camera, if also rather boring, are not quite so much of a joke. They give rise to the oft-repeated cry: "Where *are* our actors?" Then, too late, they discover they have not gone quite the right way about it. Instead of just acting "a little less" they find out that they must try to act a little better. That is why actors who are successful both on stage and screen are few and far between. It is a very serious business, but increasingly fascinating and worth while.

A stock question is: "What is the difference between Stage Acting and Screen Acting—and which is the more difficult?" I am always inclined to be impatient with this query and reply: "Well, you've paid to see them both, haven't you noticed?" Wouldn't you feel a little annoyed, dear reader, if asked: "How do toffee apples compare with apple fritters?" The only sensible answer is that toffee and puddings cannot be compared—my point being that, ideally, the Cinema cannot demand the same as the Theatre. "The Cinema can do what the Theatre cannot do." This is the champion goat-getter where I am concerned; it is about as bright and useful as comparing the flute to the Mighty Wurlitzer.

I am not belittling the progress of the Cinema; in terms of sheer improvement—mere technical *advance*—the industry has much to crow about. But its technique is limited and I would remind you of that. Speed sometimes describes circles and does not travel very far. The Cinema, as a technique, has travelled quite far enough and is in fine fettle for the artist now. But "Amazing Technical Resources" is just so much bunk. Ever thought about it? The whole history of the Cinema can boast no greater triumph than the theatre's achievement of running *Cavalcade* at Drury Lane for eleven months. It has done similar things, but nothing better. It has wielded larger crowds and used bigger lifts and rotated greater weights and lowered and lifted larger curtains, but what else? The Theatre has had water tanks for years. The one into which my double dived in *Monte Cristo* was bigger and deeper and had a glass side, but these are gadgets which the Theatre has long since scrapped. Nothing will ever erase from my memory the impression of Red Indian after Red Indian in canoe after canoe coming down a water spout as steep as the side of a house at the Manchester Hippodrome. I have seen Niagara on the screen several times since then; comparatively it left me cold.

What can be said of an infant still perversely sprawling in the cradle it has long since outgrown? The Cinema has not chosen its own way of life, like the ultra-modern child at the ultra-modern school. Oh dear, no! It has suffered the most rigorous discipline, the sternest of all restrictions—commercialisation. No child has covered so much ground and progressed so little. In its forty years it has created and discarded a score of fashions but has left us no traditions. Yet the prodigy is so promising we are at a loss which school to put it to! A difficult child, born dumb, it suddenly acquired the gift of speech after thirty years.

When we consider it, this amazing creature has got away with a good deal. Do you realise that quite a good proportion of the early antics were not photographed at all, simply because the cameras could not record them? A merciful thing in some ways, though an alarming idea for the actor to swallow, and rather a shock for the public, too; they were not getting anything like one hundred per cent of the performance they were paying to see. For years it gave us nothing more nor less than conventionalised grimaces based on an alleged emotion which it would be insincere to describe by any other name than "Lurve", and the old stock-in-trade of Melodrama (still its strongest card). Direction was often so inexact that when the hero was supposed to be saying, "Darling, I love you," in actuality he was probably murmuring, "I think you're lousy." By degrees the film-makers rediscovered cruelty, and the public licked its chops over voluptuousness. Then Grief stepped in, in the form of Glycerine. I have no statistics, but it would take the needs of a world war to compete with the quantity that coursed its milky way from the stars. Bill Hart alone—dear William S.—must have kept one factory going.

Then Laughter, holding both its sides, and painfully grimacing under the onslaught of property cream puffs, suddenly held its breath to see a pair of big splayed boots, trousers, a bowler hat and a cane syncopate their impudent and irresistible way while the world discovered Comedy in Mime. Charles Chaplin, the first great artist of the silent screen and the only one to keep its peace, was bred on the English music-hall stage. He is still far and away the greatest of all screen actors and the only legitimate reason for ever permitting the Cinema to subsidise the Theatre—as a thank-offering. Then suddenly some one thought of Thought, and every one was stumped. Nobody had thought of thinking in those days. They had simply Gone After Things in a Big Way. Sometimes, alas, they had Got what they had Gone After. What in hell did Thought look like? And every one wore a puzzled frown. So Thought, in the form of a puzzled frown, made its bow on the screen. For years and years film actors frowned and puckered their brows and looked slightly constipated and you just knew they were thinking.

Face-pulling gradually gave place to something even more dangerous—the Art of Facial Expression. A popular post-War Encyclopedia had a page of photographs illustrating this: Love, Hate, Fear, Doubt, Grief, and so on. It was a good example of its own futility; you cannot label these emotions any more than you can learn them by imitation. Once the titles were covered up the fun began! At a guess, Doubt looked perilously like Love; Grief—just acute disappointment; Fear merely surprise, and I should be accused of extreme vulgarity were I to tell you what Hate looked like. That is why few of the old silent pictures can stand the test to-day; we find them unconvincing and often extremely funny.

There is no such thing as Facial Expression, but there is such a thing as an expressive face. An expressive face helps to convey by natural means the messages of the artist's heart and mind; *helps*—but it cannot tell the whole story. Witness the celebrated wooden-faced comedian who, for some lamentable and apparently unaccountable reason, seldom makes pictures nowadays. Until he arrived, who would have believed that any one could have achieved screen fame by the deliberate avoidance of facial expression? It is the eyes and the voice that matter most.

"Facial" expression is only skin deep; it is superficial and therefore insincere. Your bad actor (invariably a lazy one) visualises surprise, for example, in terms of lifted eyebrows, quivering nostrils, parted lips and popping eyes. Your good actor goes to the very roots of the process and *imagines* (a) the mental state, and (b) the emotional state in which his character is involved at the time of the surprise, (c) the nature of the surprise, and therefore (d) the degree of mental and emotional shock likely to be produced. Also if he is wise (e) he thinks backwards and forwards in continuity to help "place" his acting in proper sequence and size and shape. All these processes are conscious (though very nearly instinctive in a good actor) but the rest of it, the actual putting-over of the message, should be unconscious. The face and eyes will light up, not with a "suitable" expression but with the *only* suitable expression—the real thing. It may be that in his early apprenticeship the good actor studied his own face and made stubborn muscles more pliable by exercise—but woe betide him if he made a habit of it. Your second-rater pulls a face, your first-rater creates a face. Both methods are founded on pretence, the difference being in the use of the imagination.

In the early silent days they could get away with the face-pulling simply because it was new to us and we were fascinated by a novelty. Eyes obscured by bad make-up, and rendered still more indistinct by feeble lighting and faulty projection, mattered little. But as conditions improved and directors gained in experience they began to look about them and, finding inspiration and infinite variety in their fellow creatures, they tried to imitate reality—and gradually sincerity became a necessity. "Type-casting" began —far less an evil than a blessing—because a man who suited the looks of a part had to be able to act it too. Only the spurious character actor suffered; he was ruthlessly weeded out. There is plenty of room for good character actors. The best of them—the Eugene Pallettes and the Jean Hersholts—watch the stars twinkle and fade while they go on for ever.

Just as face-pulling twisted the silents, voice-pulling distorted the talkies—though not for long, for the very good reason that having been forced into the paths of sincerity nothing but sincerity of voice would match. Thus, by the time mechanical improvements had eliminated the tin fog-horn, the all-screeching, all-crooning, all-canoodling voice had disappeared. When Garbo took the plunge into talkies it was inevitable that she should succeed. If she had possessed the voice of a croaking raven it would have been accepted.

How much farther have we travelled since those days? Not so very far, really. It is true we have anchored the camera and put a faster and more delicate motor inside it and more sensitive film in the spools, and we have given the cameraman a host of novelties to play with and more suitable backgrounds to light; but fundamentally the Cinema has given us nothing more than the long-shot, the medium shot and the close-up, plus the variations that a mobile camera can play.

The technical advances of the Cinema simply pay tribute to the age-old leadership of craftsmen in every art. It is always the craftsmen who achieve things. Only the competitive stresses of a great industry could have produced such giant technical strides. The craftsmanship of the chemical laboratory and the camera factory is no whit less highly skilled than the craftsmanship of the medieval wood-carver. The technique of the gear-cutter and lens-maker puts the technique of the average actor to shame. I believe it was Sir Nigel Playfair who once said that if the Theatre gave him an occasional success and an occasional cigar, what more could one expect or deserve? Must we belittle the Cinema because its craftsmen can sometimes afford champagne as well?

We do not really begin to progress until we have the courage to admit and define our limitations; it is futile to pretend they do not exist. The film did not begin to realise its own possibilities until it began to forget them. Then it started throwing away its backgrounds, its crowds, its gorgeous palaces. Something more important had arrived—the scenario, or film story. Ever since that discovery we have simply been trying to tell the story better. Because the film apparently succeeded in doing the things that the stage only pretended to do, it tried to dispense with the arts of pretence altogether. Now it knows better. More and more it is finding its own level in the studio. There, the imitation can be photographed to look more convincing than the real—a paradox discovered by the Theatre ages ago. Its great failing is its dangerous plasticity; it lends itself so readily to interfering fingers.

Cutting is at once a bane and a blessing. More and more it is the actor's own fault if he complains that so much of him lies limply on the cutting-room floor. He should not submit to a script which depends so much on the scissors. A good script is an economical one; it means that the director knows exactly what is wanted. It is up to the actor to study his director as closely as he studies his script; then, when they are actually shooting, they will be aiming together, and the resulting performance will get the cutting it deserves. I had no hand in the cutting of *The Thirty-nine Steps* or *The Ghost Goes West*, but I took what is considered to be a "lively and intelligent interest" in all the proceedings, and I do not think I fared badly at the hands of either Hitchcock or Clair. This kind of submission does not worry me in the least. I know I am in good hands. What I will *not* give in to is the kind of slavery that lands one in any type of part in any type of story for any number of years. Producers know quite well how to handle actors successfully—I do not deny; but a producer's idea of success has a habit of running along the monotonous groove of repetition; I like my pickles mixed. Discipline is good for actors, and we have to thank the commercial film for a healthy dose of ginger. It is the undisciplined egotist, cramming his own films with his own close-ups to the exclusion of others, who finds too late that he is not an exclusive diet and his public is fed up with him. And good riddance! Egotism has played quite enough havoc in the Theatre. There will always be room for the great virtuoso performer provided he finds a good enough vehicle. But the public demands a strong and varied diet. It turned down the play-stealing, fat-part actor-manager soon after the War.

Of this I am quite certain. I am a better actor for my film experience. Two qualities—concentration and sincerity—are even more necessary on the screen than on the stage, and one's work cannot fail to be the richer for their exercise. An American guest—of whom we should be so proud that nothing should ever be permitted to tempt her out of England—recently appeared in the West End of London in a play somewhat miscalled a melodrama. I refer to Miss Constance Cummings. Originally a stage actress, she gained a certain screen reputation and is married to a famous English playwright. It is one of the hopes of our Theatre that Benn Levy will keep her supplied with plays worthy of her rare and exciting abilities. In *Young Madame Conti* Miss Cummings gave a performance made immeasurably superior by her camera experience; so much so, that no young stage actress devoid of film experience could hope to touch it.

Not so very many nights ago I sat in the front row of a London Theatre and watched a distinguished cast wrestle with an undistinguished play. Now, theatrical wrestling can be a joy to watch; in all Theatre there is probably nothing more genuinely creative than this perilous business of skating on the thinnest ice while leading the audience seductively by the nose so that the entire process of skating, the very presence of ice and the danger of its thinness, all go unobserved. But on this occasion I was amazed to find myself conscious for the first time of an alarming series of Psychological Revelations. Let me justify that mouthful. If the Company had taken hands, advanced to the footlights and bawled in unison—"Ladies and Gentlemen, it is uncommonly nice of you to have paid to see us, we do appreciate it, and God knows we are doing our best to give you your money's worth, but this is a bloody awful play, it always was and it always will be, and in addition to that insurmountable fact we have been manhandled by a lazy resourceless producer. So what the hell? It's coming off to-night, anyway"—they could not have more plainly pleaded. Then the lack of discipline; the roving eye, the hesitant speech, the uncertain exit, the sloppy entrance and, worst of all (the only unselfconscious process at work that night), the players' blissful ignorance that all these mistakes were being spilled so extravagantly over the footlights.

Your stage producer rarely directs from the front

row of the stalls; once the play reaches the stage and the curtain is up, you will find him either at the back of the stalls or in the dress circle. The farther rehearsals proceed, the farther away from his actors he tends to get. Filming employs almost the reverse methods. A scene is shot first in long-shot—then medium, then close-up. The film director tends to approach, the stage director to retreat from, the actors. But that is not the only difference. Having been manœuvred practically under the skin of the actors, the camera takes the scene in miniature and later enlarges that miniature. (In this process certain changes occur, but they are not of great importance. For instance, the play of light, cunningly screened and filtered, may transform a made-up face so that film actors' mothers have been known to pay twice before recognising their own progeny. Since we are pursuing comparisons, the theatre has its illusions too, and many of them are shattered at the stage door.)

In the theatre it is the audience which receives; in the studio it is the camera, with this surprising difference—that whereas one can get away with flippancy, sloppiness and insincerity in the theatre, infinite care must be exercised in front of the camera. In the theatre the broad methods necessary to reach topmost galleryite and lowermost pittite sometimes cover a multitude of sins.

Much has been said about the theatre's living response in its audience, but little truth has been spoken. There is nothing to equal the electric give-and-take of a full house, but it is false to describe an audience reaction as "subtle." All mass reaction is collective; its emotions are simple, sometimes crude and often based on hysteria. It is an undeniable stimulus but no more potent than the creative stimulus of actual endeavour. I am certain that my best work has been given either in my own study or at rehearsals where there was no audience at all. The camera, if uncompromisingly critical, is at least unemotional and does not flatter.

With the searching eye of the camera so close upon one, how can one dare to be other than truthful? To say that the average film demands the minimum of veracity is simply a criticism of the average film and no indictment of film acting in itself. Because we are accustomed to seeing displays of pygmy emotion and magazine-story intellect, must we assume that cinematic art has nothing more to offer? Literature is not judged by the penny dreadful.

Somewhere between the tall-brows and the small-brows there is a class of individual affecting to despise anything mechanical. Its distinguishing characteristics are thick ankles (they never walk—being greedy usurpers of mechanical aids), thick speech and thick skulls. "The cinema," they moan, "is a mechanical contrivance for the distribution of canned entertainment." Anything mechanical is dubbed as a Crude Modern Necessity—not the product of dreams and intense thought capable of subtlety. The name of Da Vinci, who found exquisite delicacy in a gear-wheel and searching beauty in a lens, is conveniently forgotten. Not to admit the artistic possibilities of the film seems to me to be as unreasonable and short-sighted as to be doubtful of the ultimate scope of paint upon canvas simply because unruly children, when given a box of paints, are liable to make a mess of them. For a long time the unruly kids had their way, and multitudinous daubs have gone their way round the world; but in the Cinema, be it remembered, nothing holds sway for long (growing pains never last), so cannot we be a little more tolerant of these adolescent joint-crackings?

It is one of the paradoxes of the Cinema that while it is supposed to succeed principally with mass effects it is actually at its best when it handles the little things, the seemingly unimportant. On the screen an apparent triviality can achieve as much pure drama as many a big effect which thrilled its way across the Lyceum footlights in its most theatrical days. Remember our limitations, dear reader. A flicker of doubt in the eyes on the stage is meaningless except to the first few rows of stalls. Contemptuous critics label the filmic process as "simply the real thing photographed." What a compliment—if a veiled one. Let us examine this reality for a moment, and if we bear in mind that technique is needed every bit as much for the overcoming of difficulties as for the actual exercise of the art itself, it may be amusing to recite a few of them.

On the screen, suppose we see a modern young man dangling a leg over a modern office desk with modern New York receding in the background. Suddenly we come closer to him. In other words, the camera moves into close-up. His eyes flash a look of doubt, and that is all. I have purposely chosen something elementary. That flicker of doubt is created in a blaze of light in a dreadful fug under the very nose of that terrifying taskmaster, the camera lens, with a "mike" on a boom hovering overhead, surrounded by the gang of electricians and props boys and faced by the unit staff headed by the director—who is expecting results. Behind him are the plaster walls and an unglazed window with an enlarged black-and-white picture-postcard of New York propped up behind it; above him and everywhere else, lights.

In actual fact, the young man's behind is probably propped up on a couple of cushions or books and the desk raised up on wood blocks to improve matters for the camera, so that his leg dangles at a very unnatural height from the ground, and he must gauge his movements so that at the moment of the close-up his head will be momentarily still and his eyes—almost imperceptibly—will flash their story; not into the lens itself (for the lens, though our most inquisitive neighbour, must be ignored completely if we would win it over completely), not precisely into the lens, then, but at a spot dangerously close. And an exact spot; remember, he is to convey a flicker of doubt—not a flicker of doubt as to where he should look, and so insidiously faithful is the lens that it will blurt out the whole story if given half a chance: "Damn! I'm looking into the lens." "Hell! I looked too low!"

But it is when one sits in the projection theatre at the studio the following day and sees one's previous day's efforts come to life, that the real strength of a mere moment becomes properly significant. Then, when one senses the value of detail and the unique opportunities afforded for perfection, the ultimate possibilities of film-making seem to gain a sort of sanctity. One leaves the stuffy little theatre mellowed and humbled but determined to aim high.

Imagine that I find myself faced with the problem of playing on the screen a part I have already played on the stage. Ideally, this could never exist—a stage play belonging emphatically to the theatre. Here we have the slavish imitations of the film world, the wholesale pinching of ideas. "Dearth of Stories" is simply an admission of the lack of creative talent in film studios, talent which, if worthy of its own medium, should conceive, plan and produce exclusively in filmic terms. The so-called "adaptation," which, at its best, done lovingly with a respect for the original, sends one back longingly to the bookshelf, and at its worst makes one ask whatever gods there be why a good story known and beloved by thousands should be twisted, distorted and disembowelled. Like a recent case I have only too much cause to remember, in which the prologue, epilogue and main theme of a novel were ruthlessly dismembered to make a glamorous holiday; this in itself was lamentable and stupid enough, but the author's slavish submission to such atrocities, and his praise, spoken in my presence, of the butchery, are quite unforgivable. Really, something must be done to protect authors from themselves.

For the sake of investigating the comparison, I will attempt it: James Bridie at last consents to the filming of *A Sleeping Clergyman*. Let me pause to warn you that if ever this does happen it will be neither "freely adapted from" nor "based on" the original; it will follow Bridie's scheme or perish in the attempt. The moment I will choose is the great one in the First Act where the pregnant sweetheart of Cameron the First deliberately smashes his culture tubes. For those so unfortunate as to miss this superb drama, I will explain that Cameron the First anticipated Pasteur's germ theory of disease, and these culture tubes meant so much to him that rather than be separated from them or in any way be hindered in his work he turned a deaf ear to the friends who offered him comparative luxury, sea air and the ravishing proximity of his mistress, and stuck to his combined discomforts in a Glasgow attic. Cameron, who is already half out of bed, seething with fury at the girl's taunts, cries out as she backs away from him into a collision with the table on which his experimental culture tubes repose in their rack. Seeing the mingled horror and love in his eyes—the love which she is denied—she deliberately turns and sweeps them to the floor.

Now so far I have played the purist, rendering unto the Cinema the things which are the Cinema's—and denying any co-operative truck with the Theatre. But I must confess it is a very fascinating comparison, because I have just discovered that the idea which dominated the scene in the reading, but did not dominate in the Theatre, could easily dominate on the screen—the decision being in the scenarist's hands. Which do you wish to predominate, Mr Bridie? The germ theory symbolised by the culture tubes, Cameron's inherent badness, or Cameron's inherent genius? (I haven't forgotten the girl, who, good as her chances are, really carried the baby in more senses than one.) In the reading, the germ theory won the day; in the theatre, Cameron's desperate race against death and his desperate ill-treatment of the girl.

Bridie, who knows the taste and smell of his theatrical onions about as well as any one writing in the Theatre to-day, realising that his little rack of test tubes would be an almost negligible part of the stage setting, built up an edifice of words. Many of these, Mr Bridie, will have to go from our scenario because they will be superfluous. Alternatively, Mr Donat, you will have to sacrifice some of your high-lights too, because those test tubes are going to be given a good deal of footage. Close-up after close-up will plant and re-plant them. Finally, a huge one, as the girl smashes them to the floor, then one of the table, and the awful emptiness where they had been. These things will intensify the drama culminating in Cameron's tragic eagerness to outlive his dream, his bitter hatred of the things that thwart him, his awful agony when he sees his dream destroyed, and his final uncontrollable suicidal rage; intensify it even more than Bridie's theatrical devices built them up for me on the stage. But the camera will now demand the greatest responsibility ever asked of an artist—absolute honesty and integrity. When that relentless eye goggles at us in close-up we may be sure of one thing—we must deliver up to it the finest work of which we are capable; nothing but the truth will do.

And is not that the sum total of any claim we may make for the films? For what does it amount to when all is said and done? Just this: an instrument as subtle, as plastic, as creative and inspired as the technicians we put behind it and the actors we put in front of it. No more; no less.

For the future, it is for the writer, the producer, the director, the technician and the actor to dare to have a conscience, and for the public to discover its own intelligence.

Somewhere above I have hinted that the film actor's most important asset is the eye. Didn't somebody once say that the eye is the window of the soul?

HANDLING THE CAMERA
By Basil Wright

THE cinema camera is a precision instrument, beautifully made. Its metal parts are intricately interrelated with perfect accuracy. They move unerringly at a speed which defeats the eye. Batteries of lenses, filters and other gadget gleams with promises of new movements, new tricks, new means of expression. It is an object to be polished and cleaned continuously, to be transported with the care lavished on a new-born baby, to be guarded jealously against the hands of the incompetent and the careless, the destroyers of delicate machines. It is easy indeed to become so interested in camera-work that bad films are the result.

These notes are not written as a guide to the budding photographer. If they were, a cameraman would have been asked to write them. They are simply a brief attempt to consider some of the possibilities of the camera as a creative instrument in the making of films. In so short a space it will be necessary to omit much and to take much for granted.

In its early days the cinema was sufficiently miraculous in its presentation of photographed motion for the camera to be no more than a passive if vitally important agent. It never moved. It remained a good distance away from the scene. The technique of the stage, of the fixed view-point of the spectator, was sufficient. The camera meekly recorded the self-sufficient actions before it.

One man freed it from this role. D. W. Griffith gave it creative power. He introduced the close-up. He introduced the trucking shot (used with vast effect in the ride of the Ku-Klux-Klan in *The Birth of a Nation*), and the panorama (again in *The Birth of a Nation*, as when the camera moved inexorably from the group of weeping women to the battlefield in the plain below).

From Griffith's early films dates the use of the camera in its own right, as something which—equally with actors and cutters—can add a constructive element to the presentation of an idea in terms of film.

In Germany, during the lean times of the post-War inflation period, the limitations of apparatus and finance brought in a further advance, the use of so-called "camera-angles." A little later, the Russians, under very much the same influences, developed the same ideas, but added to their usefulness by a revolutionary technique of cutting.

Since then, apart from a temporary set-back when sound came in and glued the camera to the floor for a year, there have been no further great changes in the general technique of the camera. The handling of the camera, however—that is, the use of the technique referred to above—has in different hands become more and more interesting.

Let us first review what the camera can do; what are its possibilities, and what its limitations.

First and foremost we must remember that the camera does not see things in the same way as the human eye. The brain behind your eye selects the points of emphasis in the scene before you. You can look at a crowd and see nothing but one umbrella, or you can look at an empty field and see millions of separate blades of grass. Or vice versa. Not so the camera. The lens soullessly records on a sensitised piece of celluloid simply the amount of light of differing values that passes through it. No amount of thinking on the part of the cameraman will achieve any other emphasis. Out of a wide landscape it will not pick out that certain tree. You, as a person, have got to interfere, to place the camera in such a way that the picture it records will somehow give the emphasis you require. Which is simply another way of stating the old adage that all arts exist by exploiting their own limitations.

The camera's main limitation is light. Light is also the cameras *raison d'être*—the core of its existence. All shots are merely the effect of light rays, and under the artificially conditioned circumstances of the film studio the term "cameraman" is probably less correct than the term "lighting expert." Be that as it may, the fundamental issue is that every shot in a film is the result of a period of organised threats, blandishments, and cajolery of light.

The realism of movie photography is in fact achieved by a constant interference with natural forces. A brief glance at the technique of the camera will reveal this—as well as getting this short essay another step towards its doubtful goal.

The average cameraman, then, has the following gadgets at his creative disposal.

He has interchangeable lenses of varying focal lengths. This means—to avoid technicalities—that without moving the camera itself he can take a number of different photographs of any object, ranging from the long-shot to the ultra close-up. For example, he sets up his camera opposite a church. With a one-inch lens he photographs the entire church and part of the surrounding landscape. With a two-inch lens he takes in the church only; with a four-inch lens he reveals only half of the church. With a six-inch lens he gives a close-up of part of the tower—and so on right down to the forty-inch lens which reveals no more than a notice pinned on the church door.

Now, as he could get exactly the same series of shots with, say, a solitary two-inch lens, by moving the camera itself nearer and nearer to the church, the battery of lenses might seem to be merely an encouragement to laziness, did we not remember that in many cases the camera cannot be placed near a given object (e.g., a ferocious wild elephant or a face at a window on the twelfth storey).

But that by no means exhausts the value of a series of lenses. From the creative point of view, they can actually produce very important and varying effects. These are all distortions, in the sense that they endow the scene with spatial relationships different from those presented to the human eye.

The aspect given by the two-inch lens corresponds most nearly to the focussed area of the human eye-sight.

Camera lenses of less than two-inch focal lenses distort scenes by exaggerating distances. A one-inch lens can make a box-room look like a ballroom. It can also make a man's fist plunged at the audience loom in such exaggerated perspective that it seems as big as his whole body. In fact, it extends space and enlarges distances.

Similarly, space can be reduced and concertina-ed by using lenses of more than two-inch focal lengths. In these, the longer the focal length, the closer together are brought the foreground and background of the picture, so that, in extreme cases, you can see people going through all the actions of running, but yet apparently—like the famous scene in "Through the Looking Glass"—staying in the same place. Scenes like this are frequently to be noted in news-reel shots of cricket matches.

Further interference with nature is possible by placing things to interfere with light before it reaches the lens—things such as coloured glass filters to accentuate or eliminate certain colour values; gauzes to soften the outlines of a scene; even smears of vaseline to distort the outlines. Also "masks," cut to give the effects of keyholes, binoculars, hearts, or what you will.

The normal cine-camera runs at a speed of twenty-four pictures a second. Film is invariably projected at this speed in the cinema. The cameraman can therefore get special effects by taking fewer or more pictures per second (the speed of projection remaining constant at twenty-four pictures a second). On the minus side he can even go so far as to take only one picture an hour or even a week. It is in this way that the plant-growths in *Secrets of Nature* films are recorded. On the plus side, he can at present go as far as some 3,000 pictures a second, which will give you a slow-motion film of a bullet leaving a gun.

Between these two extremes are a great variety of possible effects. They are usually directed either to melodramatic, comic or scientific ends. The Hollywood motor-car chases, with their carefully calculated hairbreadth escapes, are a typical example of speeded-up motion, but on occasions these tricks of speed have been used in a more interesting manner. In *Zéro de Conduite*, for instance, Vigo shot a procession of boys during a dormitory riot entirely in slow motion. In *The General Line* Eisenstein used speeded-up office activities to indicate the urgency of the Five Year Plan.

Pudovkin has enumerated various plans for varying camera speed within a given sequence to increase the visual emphasis. He suggested, for example, that in filming a man wielding a scythe, the use of slow motion on some of the actions—such as the swathe of grass falling when the scythe has cut through, and the back stroke of the scythe itself—would produce a cinematic interpretation of the movements most closely akin to the emotions of a sympathetic spectator witnessing the actions in real life.

The cameraman can also make pictures fade-in and fade-out by the simple process of progressively diminishing or increasing the amount of light reaching the film. He can make "dissolves"—the gradual mingling of one picture into another—which are, to put it simply, the "fade-in" of one shot superimposed on the "fade-out" of the previous shot. Superimpositions can be used in their own right to present the spectator with a double image. These are easily accomplished by winding back the exposed film and shooting a further image on the scene already imprinted on it.

It may be noted here that there is an increasing tendency to transfer these tricks to the optical sections of the processing laboratories—but as they are originally very much of the camera, they are mentioned here.

There are many other special effects still to be catalogued. Multiple-prism lenses can cover the screen with a mass of exact duplicate images of the object photographed. They are beloved of Busby Berkeley.

By means of various forms of back-projection, scenes played in the comparative peace of the studio can be combined with a background of Africa's wildest jungle, a raging Pacific, or the swiftly passing landscape seen from train or plane.

We can conclude by listing the use of cartoon, animated diagrams, and various colour systems, and so pass to yet another set of possibilities.

The camera must stand on a solid base, as the slightest rocking or vibration will be transferred, enormously intensified by enlargement, to the screen. So we must consider the tripod as a vital part of the camera. The top, or head, of the tripod, is usually made to move on a ball-bearing or gyroscopic principle which gives it a horizontal swing (or "pan") of 360 degrees and a vertical tilt (up and down) of about 90 degrees. A single bar projecting from the tripod head operates both these movements, which can therefore take place simultaneously, and enable the cameraman to follow accurately such things as the erratic and unpredictable flight of a bird.

But the tripod can also be put on wheels, and travel forwards, backwards or sideways. Or the camera may be on a crane even more free in its movements. And while the truck or the crane is whisking the camera through space, it may also be performing the pans or tilts as explained in the previous paragraph.

Such are the powers at the disposal of a cameraman. With a little imagination you can visualise him as a small but omnipotent figure, standing beside the apparatus as a thousand-ton crane swings it up and forward through a vast hall lit by an incalculable amperage, while the camera itself in its dizzy flight is moved at his will horizontally and vertically on its own axis, shooting now in slow motion, and now with telescopic vision finally denying the genuineness of anything on earth.

Whereas, in point of fact the good cameraman is as sparing as possible in the use of elaborate stunts. After all, the technique of the camera has been evolved by the demands of men making films for their own specific purpose. The apparatus should be subservient to the idea.

There was an early talkie in which the obsession with camera tricks was so great that the hero could not speak to the heroine without the camera leaving his face, and, following as it were his winged words right round their luxurious apartment, finally coming

Handling the Camera

to rest on the heroine in time for her to reply. This was excessively tedious. Also, note you, it was shot by one of the best cameramen living.

This brings us to the vital point of the whole affair—the relationship of the camera to the other factors of equal or greater importance which go to make up the finished film.

If we are not careful, this will lead to an enormous disquisition on direction. The relation between cameraman and director therefore must be here considered in its narrowest sense, to avoid such an unwieldy digression. The essential point is that the camera is an instrument of expression and is there to do the director's will. The cameraman is, therefore, as it were, the Genie of the Lamp (and the Slave of the Director). His expert technical knowledge should be such that he can carry out the director's demands economically and expeditiously. This, however, is not necessarily to deny creative ability or creative personality to the cameraman. By his very knowledge of camera-work he may be able to carry into practice the vague desires of the director. "For God's sake make this wrinkled harridan look more like Manon," screams the director. With lenses, soft lighting, clever angles and what not, the cameraman achieves the miracle.

Any one who remembers the camera-work of, say, *Zoo in Budapest*, will realise this point (speaking generally, of course, and not about the heroine).

But camera-work is not all, and most people prefer bad camera-work plus good direction to good camera-work plus bad direction. It is interesting to note that most cameramen famous for their artistic ability tend in the end to become directors themselves. And, in the solitary case of Robert Flaherty, you find a great director who has made of himself a great cameraman.

The ultimate need, in any case, is for a close sympathy to exist between director and cameraman. This teamwork aspect crops up again and again in all branches of cinema, and nowhere is it more vividly seen than in such partnerships as that of Eisenstein and Tissé, or Lang and Wagner. This give-and-take collaboration, in which the director, of course, always has the last word, is the ideal but all too rare state. The next best thing is for the cameraman to be supremely gifted as to technique, but without much artistic conscience of his own. In this case, the director evolves all the effects himself and is limited only by the competence of the cameraman or the physical possibilities at the disposal of a modern camera. In any case, a director seldom takes No for an answer.

Everything the director does is seen by his ultimate audience through the eye of the camera. He can operate only on what the lens sees. He must think of every scene, every action, in terms of the lens, in terms of what the camera can do. That is why so many directors can be seen with their eyes glued to the viewfinder during a rehearsal—to make sure. In the same way, the impetus for camera movements or tricks of various sorts comes from the director via the shooting script.

This is no place to discourse on scenario and script

Handling the Camera 47

work, but it should be remembered that camera-movements are nearly always to be found indicated in the script. Sometimes, indeed, the result of the demands made by the script is the signing-up of a specialist in some particular field of camera-work.

Then, of course, there is the Art Director. His work means a lot to the cameraman, for on him rests the ultimate responsibility of lighting the completed set. It is absolutely essential for the designs to allow of the set being amply lit from above, for top-lighting supplies from three-quarters to two-thirds of the general illumination of a set. There must also be opportunities for side and front lighting. All this frequently makes it desirable for the set to be sectional, so that certain parts of it can be removed for special shots to allow the cameraman to re-arrange his lighting. It is, for instance, particularly important for the cameraman to keep *continuity of lighting* while shooting different shots on the same set. If the lighting effect is not the same in the close-up as it is in the long shot the cutting department will find itself in a jam and will rightly blame the cameraman. The studio electricians are, or should be, intimately acquainted with each cameraman's idiosyncrasies. The chief electrician frequently carries out the general illumination of a set before the cameraman arrives. This should not cause a dust-up. The relation between camera department and lighting department must be as intimate and cordial as possible.

It is also necessary to remember that, in the studio at any rate, most shooting is synchronous. The cameraman is therefore somewhat dependent on the work of the Sound Department, which is in itself a branch of camera-work devoted to the photography of sound waves. The Sound men demand as much freedom in the placing of their microphone as does the Picture man in the placing of his camera. And during the shooting, both Picture and Sound cameras are operated by a master switch. Here again the situation demands the maximum of co-operation and amiability.

These facts may indicate that the cameraman is not an Almighty God, but merely a member of a semi-democratic Olympus, presided over by a directorial Jupiter of uncertain temper. And behind it all moves the bony and relentless hand of Finance Omnipotent.

So much for technique and organisation. Next comes a more nebulous but also more interesting consideration—the artistic approach of the cameraman. The reference here is not a highbrow one, but an attempt to analyse the more personal approach to the taking of any shot, in fact an analysis of camera-sense, or "a feeling for the subject."

This is more difficult, and is bound to some extent to be coloured by the personal feelings of the writer. It is, on the other hand, the most vital consideration in regard to the camera. It will be necessary in this case to consider the camera *per se*, and to forget about directorial control or the requirements of a script. The question is simply this: How does one approach the taking of a movie shot?

The number of positions from which a camera may take a shot of any given subject has to be regarded as unlimited. All points of the compass are available.

Handling the Camera

Any degree of distance is possible. The camera may be poised in the heaven above or the pit below. From this illimitable field the most telling position (or positions) must be chosen. We are considering, in fact, the angle from which the object is to be photographed.

The first instinct, and the most natural, is to place the camera in the same position as the eyes of a spectator standing facing the object, at a distance which allows the object to be seen in its entirety. This could be regarded as the norm from which all variations proceed.

The first variation arises probably from the instinct to exploit the camera's genius for giving detail or intimacy. In other words, to approach more nearly to the object, either by moving in the camera itself or by using a longer focus lens from the same camera position. These alternatives—as has already been indicated—are not merely a matter of convenience, but also of the instinct of the cameraman. One man may prefer to use a lens of wide angle, with the camera near the object, in order either to emphasise the action by exaggerating the spatial relationships, or to retain a depth of focus as between the object and its background. Another—Flaherty is an example—may wish to achieve a greater spontaneity by taking a close-up of a person without the embarrassing presence of a camera right on top of him. For him, the telephoto-lens is the answer. Personal experience shows that there is seldom any hesitancy on the cameraman's part in making such a choice. His own instinct arrives at a foregone conclusion without his indulging in mental arguments of any kind.

He could also get another effect by "trucking" the camera in on its trolly so that the spectator witnessed every change of distance, from long shot to close-up. This he would probably do only if he wished to put heavy emphasis on the object to be seen in the final close-up position. Otherwise he would merely be using the apparatus for its own sake, with dreariness and waste of footage as an inevitable result.

The next step involves a change of angle as opposed to a mere change of distance. That is, the camera may be lower or higher than the norm we have already suggested. It may be put low down and tilted upwards, either for practical reasons (it may be the only way to show the size and extent of a tall building), or because the unusual view-point gives a special emphasis; for instance, a policeman shot from a low angle may look more impressive, more important, more monumental—especially if in addition to the camera position, the effect is increased by the use of a wide-angle lens.

It is pointless to elaborate too much on the actual possibilities of camera angles. The mere multiplication of examples is of no value. What is fundamentally important is to realise that where the camera is put must depend, not on an attempt to make the shot "striking" or "interesting" at all costs, but on the urgency of expression affecting the man behind the camera. By taking a movie shot the cameraman is not merely trying to reproduce something; he is trying also to comment on it, or to relate it to a specific idea, of which one shot may merely be an

Handling the Camera 51

item. But in cinema many items build up the coherent statement. If you like you can regard the standard long-shot of an object as the noun. Pans, changes of angle and distance, trick shots or what you will, these are the verbs, adjectives, adverbs, prepositions and so on which when put altogether make up a coherent sentence. In cinema, a flowery style is not an advantage. The more succinct the statement, the better. Two good shots, carefully chosen as regards distance and angle, are better than twenty taken either carelessly or with an eye only to the unusual.

In point of fact, if you ask any competent cameraman to take three shots of any occurrence, he will not go into any special huddle with himself. Experience has taught him the sort of position which will give him the best effects, and he will know within a foot or so the three most likely angles for his purpose. The *exact* angles are a matter for more care, and you may find him trying out various lenses and so on before he finally shoots.

There are certain fundamental points which still remain to be considered. They may be roughly grouped under one word—Composition.

It is vital to remember that the composition of a picture on the movie screen contains one element entirely denied to the art, say, of painting. Screen composition is fluid; it is perpetually in motion.

Now it is obviously the aim of any cameraman to achieve with each shot a balanced and good-looking composition (at the least). But if he tries to base his shooting entirely on the great painters, or for that matter on the great still photographers, he will probably fail.

The movements of any persons or objects within the frame of the cinema screen are the prime factor of the composition. One may go further, and point out that even motionless objects may have a movement imparted to them by the panning, tilting or trucking of the camera. In other words, a movie shot of a group of statuary or a landscape may produce an aesthetic effect quite other than that possible in any other medium, arising simply from the carefully calculated movement of the camera itself.

Like most painters, good moviemen try for a composition which will get away as far as possible from the two-dimensional limitations of the screen. But they are not limited entirely to attempts to produce perspective by relationship of mass to mass within their composition.[1] They can also achieve it by the relationship of movement to movement, or of movement to mass, or both. That this is not mere theory can be easily proved by going to any cinema and analysing the effects by which good or bad composition is achieved, shot by shot, in the film which happens to be running. Various points will at once emerge. For instance, it will be seen that movements *to and from* the camera are more emphatic, and give a greater perspective, than movements *sideways or across* the camera. Or again, the use of some solid mass in the foreground of the picture will give point and emphasis to what otherwise would have been a

[1] As yet, however, they lack one advantage which the painter exploits—controlled colour relationships.

very uninteresting pictorial presentation. (The *reductio ad absurdum* of this last is to be found in certain cameramen on "interest" films, who used to carry a small branch of a tree around with them in order to get an artistic effect by placing it in the foreground as a frame or halo to any uninteresting village or church tower they had to shoot.)

These principles of composition are the subconscious stand-by of the cameraman, and they produce those idiosyncrasies which enable us to distinguish at a glance between a shot by Flaherty and a shot by James Wong Howe. They are truly the fundamentals of the cameraman's art, and it is his sensibilities in this regard which make him either more or less of a genius in the manipulation of the apparatus at his disposal.

To these principles he subordinates his command over light—lenses, filters, fades, dissolves; his command over speed—fast motion or slow motion; his command over movement—pans, tilts, truck-shots, crane shots; in a word, his ability to use the intricate, difficult, but entirely fascinating reproductive mechanism which makes possible the art of cinema.

PART II
SCREEN MATERIAL:
HELP FROM OTHER ARTS

SUBJECTS AND STORIES
By Graham Greene

THERE is no need to regard the cinema as a completely new art; in its fictional form it has the same purpose as the novel, just as the novel has the same purpose as the drama. Tchehov, writing of his fellow novelists, remarked: "The best of them are realistic and paint life as it is, but because every line is permeated, as with a juice, by awareness of a purpose, you feel, besides life as it is, also life as it ought to be, and this captivates you." This description of an artist's theme has never, I think, been bettered: we need not even confine it to the fictional form: it applies equally to the documentary film, to pictures in the class of Mr Rotha's *Shipyard* (one remembers the last sequence of the launching: the workers who have made the ship watching from the banks and roofs the little social gathering, the ribbons and the champagne) or Mr Wright's *Song of Ceylon*: only in films to which Tchehov's description applies shall we find the poetic cinema. And the poetic cinema—it is the only form worth considering.

Life as it is and life as it ought to be: let us take that as the only true subject for a film, and consider to what extent the cinema is fulfilling its proper function. The stage, of course, has long ceased to fulfil it at all. Mr St John Ervine, Miss Dodie Smith, these are the popular playwrights of the moment: they have no sense of life as it is lived, far less even than Mr Noel Coward, and if they have some dim idea of a better life, this is expressed only in terms of sexual or financial happiness. As for the popular novel, Mr Walpole, Mr Brett Young, Mr Priestley, we are aware of rather crude minds representing no more of contemporary life than is to be got in a holiday snapshot: Mr Walpole the house and garden, Mr Brett Young the village street, the old alms-houses and the vicar, Mr Priestley the inn, the forge, the oldest inhabitant.

I think one may say that *Dodsworth* represents about the highest level to which this type of writer can attain on the screen. *Dodsworth* as a book was far less readable than as a picture it was seeable. The dimmest social drama can be given a certain gloss and glitter by a good director and a good cameraman. No one, I think, could have been actively bored by *Dodsworth*. It had the great virtues of natural acting and natural speech; it did in its way, its too personal and private way, fulfil one of the functions we have named; it at least presented life as it presumably appears to an American millionaire, unhappily married to a wife who is determined to climb socially: perhaps one is rash in making even that claim, for the number of people who can judge its truth must needs be strictly limited. But as for life as it ought to be, the nearest *Dodsworth* comes to that is a quaint Italian villa on the bay of Naples and the company of a gentle, refined and flower-like widow. It is alas! still true of the theatre what Mr Ford Madox Ford wrote in 1911, in an essay on the functions of the arts in the republic, "that, in this proud, wealthy and materially polished civilisation, there was visible no trace, no scintilla, no shadow of a trace of the desire to have any kind of thought awakened." In those days before the great four years' deluge Mr Ford found that "it is to the music-halls we must go nowadays for any form of pulse stirring," the popular entertainment of that day. The cinema has to a large extent killed the music-hall, but has it absorbed its virtues or "the sinister forms of morality" Mr Ford found in the theatre?

Writing this in the third week of February, 1937, I turn to the list of films now to be seen in London (perhaps it may amuse a few readers when this book appears to try to recall these films, and if a few do still stick obstinately in the memory, to try to recall their subjects, a few sequences): *Ernte, Maid of Salem, Magnificent Obsession, Mazurka, This'll Make You Whistle, The Great Barrier, Devil Takes the Count, The Texas Rangers, Beloved Enemy, Dreaming Lips, O.H.M.S., Aren't Men Beasts, Ramona, The Plainsman, Girls' Dormitory, His Lordship, Accused, La Kermesse Héroïque, Good Morning Boys.* It is not on the whole such an unfavourable week. I think three of those films may be remembered in a year's time. But how many of them show any inkling of the only subject-matter for art, life as it is and life as it ought to be, how many even fulfil what Mr Ford defines as the functions of merely inventive literature, of diverting, delighting, tickling, of promoting appetites? Only, I think, the three I have mentioned: *La Kermesse Héroïque, The Texas Rangers, The Plainsman.* The first had at least an adult theme, that the sexual appetite is a great deal stronger than patriotism: it did present life—in fancy dress for safety—as it is; it had the characteristic personal exaggeration that Mr Ford demands of the imaginative writer: it was a Feyder film. The other two had good, if less interesting and more obvious themes: that when you have settled a new country, you must make it safe for the unarmed and the weak, themes which do contain of their very nature the two halves of Tchehov's definition.

But I am afraid in the plots of the others you will get the more representative film. *Mazurka*: fallen woman shoots her seducer to save her child from a similar fate; *Magnificent Obsession*: a woman loses her eyesight when a drunken young plutocrat smashes his car, the drunken young plutocrat turns over a new leaf, studies medicine, becomes the greatest eye surgeon of his day in time to cure and marry the girl while both are young; *Dreaming Lips*: a young wife falls passionately in love with a musical genius; unable to choose between the genius and the boy husband, she kills herself; *Girls' Dormitory*: an innocent and dewy schoolgirl falls in love with her headmaster, writes an imaginary love letter which is discovered by a prying mistress, is expelled for immorality, runs away in the rain pursued by the headmaster who then discovers the truth.

It is difficult to see what critical purpose is served by subjects like these. (I say *critical* purpose because the sense of life as it should be must always be a critical one. An element of satire enters into all dramatic art.) Is it possible that the glittering prizes the cinema offers defeat their purpose? The artist is not as a rule a man who takes kindly to life, but can his critical faculty help being a little blunted on two hundred pounds a week? A trivial point perhaps, but one reason why we do not look first to Hollywood or Denham for films of artistic value, for the poetic cinema.

I use the word poetic in its widest sense. Only of quite recent years has the term poet been narrowed down to those who write according to some kind of metrical or rhythmical scheme. In Dryden's day any creative writer was called a poet, and it would be difficult to justify any definition which excluded James or Conrad, Tchehov or Turgenev from the rank of poets. Mr Ford Madox Ford has given us the most useful definition for the quality which these prose writers have in common with Shakespeare and Dryden: "not the power melodiously to arrange words but the power to suggest human values."

So we need not consider, I think, the various screen adaptations of Shakespeare. It isn't that kind of poetry we are seeking (the poetry made tautological by the realistic settings), nor will we find in the smart neat *Dodsworths* and *Dreaming Lips* the power to suggest human values. We come nearer to what we seek perhaps in a picture like *Hortobagy*, the film of the Hungarian plains acted by peasants and shepherds. The photography was very beautiful, the cutting often superb, but photography by itself cannot make poetic cinema. By itself it can only make arty cinema. *Man of Aran* was a glaring example of this: how affected and wearisome were those figures against the skyline, how meaningless that magnificent photography of storm after storm. *Man of Aran* did not even attempt to describe truthfully a way of life. The inhabitants had to be taught shark-hunting in order to supply Mr Flaherty with a dramatic sequence. *Hortobagy* did at least attempt to show life truthfully: those wild herds tossing across the enormous plain, against the flat sky, the shepherds in their huge heavy traditional cloaks galloping like tartar cavalry between the whitewashed huts, the leaping of the stallions, the foaling of the mares shown with meticulous candour, did leave the impression that we were seeing, as far as was humanly possible, life as it is. It was documentary in the finest sense: on the documentary side it has been unsurpassed: but Mr Basil Wright's *Song of Ceylon*, faulty in continuity as it was, contained more of what we are looking for, criticism implicit in the images, life as it is containing the indications of life as it should be, the personal lyric utterance.

It was divided, it may be remembered, into four parts, and opened with a forest sequence, huge revolving fans of palm filling the screen. We then watched a file of pilgrims climb a mountain-side to the stone effigies of the gods, and here, as a priest struck a bell, Mr Wright used one of the loveliest visual metaphors I have seen on the screen. The sounding of the bell startled a small bird from its branch, and the camera followed the bird's flight and the bell notes across the island, down from the mountain side, over forest and plain and sea, the vibration of the tiny wings, the fading sound. Then, in a rather scrappy and unsatisfactory movement, we saw the everyday life of the natives, until in the third movement we were made aware of the personal criticism implied in the whole film. As the natives followed the old ways of farming, climbing palm trees with a fibre loop, guiding their elephants against the trees to be felled, voices dictated bills of lading, closed deals, announced through loud-speakers the latest market prices. And lest the contrast between two ways of life should be left too indecisively balanced, the director's sympathy was plainly shown in the last movement: back on the mountain-side with the stone faces, the gaudy gilded dancers, the solitary peasant laying his offering at Buddha's feet, and when he closed the film with the revolving leaves, it was as if he was sealing away from us devotion and dance and the gentle communal life of harvest, leaving us outside with the bills of lading and the loud-speakers.

Here, of course, with the director who acts as his own cameraman and supervises his own script, with the reduction of credits to a minimum, and the subsidised film, we are getting far from the commercial picture. The *Song of Ceylon* will always stand outside the ordinary cinema. We are getting closer to the poetic and yet commercially possible cinema with a picture like *The Song of Freedom*, an inexpensive picture made by a small British company, full of muddled thought and bad writing: the story of a black dockhand who becomes a famous singer and goes back to his ancestral home to try to save his people from the witch-doctors. Full of muddled thought and absurdities of speech, it is true, yet this film had something which the *Dodsworths* lacked. A sense stays in the memory of an unsophisticated mind fumbling on the edge of simple and popular poetry. The best scenes were the dockland scenes, the men returning from work free from any colour bar, the public-house interiors, dark faces pausing at tenement windows to listen to the black man's singing, a sense of nostalgia, of what Mann calls "the gnawing surreptitious hankering for the bliss of the commonplace."

The commonplace, that is the point. The poetic drama ceased to be of value when it ceased to be as popular as a bear-baiting. The decline from Webster to Tennyson is not a mere decline in poetic merit—"Queen Mary" has passages of great beauty—but a decline in popularity. The cinema has got to appeal to millions; we have got to accept its popularity as a virtue, not turn away from it as a vice.

Only the conviction that a public art should be as popular and unsubtle as a dance tune enables one to sit with patient hope through pictures certainly unsubtle but not, in any real sense, popular. What a chance there is for the creative artist, one persists in believing, to produce for an audience incomparably greater than that of all the "popular" novelists combined, from Mr Walpole to Mr Brett Young, a genuinely vulgar art. Any other is impossible. The novelist may write for a few thousand readers, but the film artist *must* work for millions. It should be his distinction and pride that he has a public whose needs have never been met since the closing of the theatres by Cromwell. But where is the vulgarity of this art? Alas! the refinement of the "popular"

Subjects and Stories

novel has touched the films; it is the twopenny libraries they reflect rather than the Blackfriars Ring, the Wembley final, the pin saloons, the coursing.

> I'm not the type that I seem to be,
> Happy-go-lucky and gay,

Bing Crosby mournfully croons in one of his latest pictures. That is the common idea of popular entertainment, a mild self-pity, something soothing, something gently amusing. The film executive still thinks in terms of the "popular" play and the "popular" novel, of a limited middle-class audience, of the tired business man and the feminine reader. The public which rattles down from the North to Wembley with curious hats and favours, tipsy in charabancs, doesn't, apparently, ask to be soothed: it asks to be excited. It was for these that the Elizabethan stage provided action which could arouse as communal a response as bear-baiting. For a popular response is not the sum of private excitements, but mass feeling, mass excitement, the Wembley roar; and it is the weakness of the Goldwyn Girls that they are as private an enjoyment as the Art Photos a business man may turn over in the secrecy of his study, the weakness of Bing Crosby's sentiment, the romantic nostalgia of "Empty saddles in the old corral," that it is by its nature a private emotion.

There are very few examples of what I mean by the proper popular use of the film, and most of those are farces: *Duck Soup*, the early Chaplins, a few "shorts" by Laurel and Hardy. These do convey the sense that the picture has been made by its spectators and not merely shown to them, that it has sprung, as much as their sports, from *their* level. Serious films of the kind are even rarer: perhaps *Fury, The Birth of a Nation, Men and Jobs*, they could be numbered on the fingers of one hand. Because they are so rare one is ready to accept, with exaggerated gratitude, such refined, elegant, dead pieces as *Louis Pasteur*: the Galsworthy entertainments of the screen: or intelligently adapted plays like *These Three*.

"People want to be taken out of themselves," the film executive retorts under the mistaken impression that the critic is demanding a kind of Zola-esque realism—as if Webster's plays were realistic. Of course he is right. People are taken out of themselves at Wembley. But I very much doubt if Bing Crosby does so much. "They don't want to be depressed," but an excited audience is never depressed; if you excite your audience first, you can put over what you will of horror, suffering, truth. But there is one question which needs an answer. How dare we excite an audience, a producer may well ask, when Lord Tyrrell, the President of the Board of Censors, forbids us to show any controversial subject on the screen?

The cinema has always developed by means of a certain low cunning. The old-clothes merchants who came in on a good thing in the early days and ended as presidents of immense industries had plenty of cunning. It is for the artist to show his cunning now. You may say with some confidence that at the present stage of English culture, a great many serious subjects cannot be treated at all. We cannot treat human Justice truthfully as America treated it in *I am a Fugitive from the Chain Gang*. No film which held the aged provincial J.P.'s up to criticism or which described the conditions in the punishment cells at Maidstone would be allowed. Nor is it possible to treat seriously a religious or a political subject.

But this is not all to the bad. We are saved from the merely topical by our absurd censorship. We shall not have to sit through the cinematic equivalents of Mrs Mitchison's emotional novels. We are driven back to the "blood", the thriller. There never has been a school of popular English bloods. We have been damned from the start by middle-class virtues, by gentlemen cracksmen and stolen plans and Mr Wu's. We have to go farther back than this, dive below the polite level, to something nearer to the common life. And isn't it better to have as your subject "life nasty, brutish, and short" than the more pompous themes the censor denies us? He won't allow us a proletarian political drama, and I cannot help being a little relieved that we lose the lifeless malice of Pudovkin's capitalist automatons, that dreadful shadow of Victorian progress and inevitable victory. Our excitements have got to have a more universal subject, we have the chance of being better realists than the Russians, we are saved from the tract in return for what we lose.

And when we have attained to a more popular drama, even if it is in the simplest terms of blood on a garage floor ("There lay Duncan laced in his golden blood"), the scream of cars in flight, all the old excitements at their simplest and most sure-fire, then we can begin—secretly, with low cunning—to develop our poetic drama ("the power to suggest human values"). Our characters can develop from the level of *The Spanish Tragedy* towards a subtler, more thoughtful level.

Some such development we can see at work in Fritz Lang: *The Spy* was his simplest, purest thriller. It had no human values at all, only a brilliant eye for the surface of life and the power of physical excitement: in *Fury* the eye was no less sure, but the poetry had crept in. Here in the lynching was the great thriller situation superbly handled; but not a shot but owed part of its effect to the earlier sequences, the lovers sheltering under the elevated from the drenching rain, good-bye at the railway station with faces and hands pressed to wet fogging windows, the ordinary recognisable agony, life as one knows it is lived, the human, the poetic value. And how was this introduced? Not in words—that is the stage way. I can think of no better example of the use of poetic imagery than in *We from Kronstadt*. At one level this was a magnificent picture of schoolboy heroics, of last charges and fights to the death, heroic sacrifices and narrow escapes, all superbly directed. But what made the picture remarkable was the poetry, critical as poetry must always be (life as it is: life as it ought to be). We were aware all the time that *We from Kronstadt* had been written and directed by the fellow countrymen of Tchehov and Turgenev, and curiously enough among the gunshots, the flag waving, the last stands, the poetry was of the same gentle and reflective and melancholy kind as theirs.

Indeed there was a scene in this picture of humorous and pathetic irony which might have been drawn directly from one of the great classic novelists. The hall and stairs of a one-time palace on the Baltic shore are packed nearly to suffocation with soldiers and marines; they lie massed together like swine: at dawn a door opens at the stair-head and a little knot of children, lodged for safety in the palace, emerges, climbs softly down, ready to start like mice at any movement. They finger the revolvers, the rifles, the machine-guns, climb quickly away when a man moves, percolate down again among the sleepers persistently, to finger a butt, a holster, the barrel of a Lewis gun.

There were many other examples in this picture of the poetic use of imagery and incident: the gulls sweeping and coursing above the cliffs where the Red prisoners are lined up for their death by drowning, the camera moving from the heavy rocks around their necks to the movement of the light, white wings; one sooty tree drooping on the huge rocky Kronstadt walls above a bench where a sailor and a woman embrace, against the dark tide; the riding-lights of the battleships, the shape of the great guns, the singing of a band of sailors going home in the dark to their iron home. Life as it is; life as it ought to be: every poetic image chosen for its contrasting value, to represent peace and normal human values under the heroics and the wartime patriotism.

The poetic cinema, it is worth remembering, can be built up on a few very simple ideas, as simple as the ideas behind the poetic fictions of Conrad: the love of peace, of country, a feeling for fidelity: it doesn't require a great mind to conceive them, but it does require an imaginative mind to feel them with sufficient passion. Griffith was a man of this quality, though to a sophisticated audience he sometimes seems to have chosen incidents of extraordinary *naïveté* to illustrate his theme. Simple, sensuous and passionate, that definition would not serve the cinema badly: it would enable us at any rate to distinguish between the values say of *Way Down East* and *Louis Pasteur*, and beside that distinction all other discussion of subject-matter seems a little idle.

COMEDIES AND CARTOONS
By Alberto Cavalcanti

THE Lumière Brothers, cinema pioneers, discovered comedy along with news-reel and interest, and long before drama. They filmed the workers leaving the Lumière factory. They filmed the arrival of a train at La Ciotat. They filmed a boat coming into harbour. Then they filmed *L'Arroseur Arrosé*.

It was a simple story, told in a single shot of about 150 feet, playing about two minutes.

Elmer is watering his garden. Henry steps on the hose. Elmer looks down the nozzle to see where the water's gone. Henry steps off. But Elmer recovers, and turns the hose on Henry. Before he can be counted out, the bell goes.

It was followed by *The Hat Trick*. The performer stands alone against a flat. He puts on a series of hats, making faces to match. That is all.

So film comedy is as old as cinema itself. It was taken for granted from the start. It was as spontaneous as "pure" cinema—the straight recording of facts. It was not the result of a conscious effort to find a new application for the medium.

That is just what film drama was. The first film dramatists sought to turn the cinema from the simple to the grandiose. They imported actors and actresses from the Comédie Française, and put them through a series of super-dramatic gestures. They played soul-stirring dramas in front of a typical provincial stage set—rich with marble columns, ranged in false perspective tier upon tier, which waved in the wind every time the studio door was opened. One of these epics was called *The Assassination of the Duc de Guise*, but the great climax of the film was not the actual murder. It was not even a picture, but a sub-title! The villain of the piece was supposed to say the famous historic words, "Comme il était grand!" And in the shot following the caption we duly saw him, his arms outstretched in a magnificent gesture of wonder and irony, mouthing the immortal syllables.

It is impossible to go far in the discussion of the comic film without making a good many references to the art of interpretation. I hope therefore that Mr Robert Donat, who writes on Acting in this book, will forgive me some necessary invasion of his territory.

Now *The Assassination of the Duc de Guise* was the sort of film that modern audiences are sometimes called upon to laugh at. But the more intelligent actors and actresses of that time also had a sense of humour. So they tried to evolve a "cinematic" style of acting which would convey the drama without being laughable. The task was difficult. Silence compelled them to rely on movement. But then movement itself was impossible to control.

Cameras then operated at a standard speed of sixteen pictures (or "frames") a second. But the speed at which the films were projected in the theatres was by no means standard. It varied between twenty and twenty-five frames a second—always faster than the film went through the camera. The resultant speeding-up of the action often made normal movements comic, or obscure.

I remember very well on my first entry into film work being taught carefully never to allow actors to overlap actions. The simplest movements had to be split up into their component parts. An actor could not just go and sit down. He had to approach the chair, stop, and then sit down in it. In projection this looked quite natural—much more so than the normal, slurred action.

Subtle changes of expression were lost at the increased speed. The result was the development of a mask-like set of expressions for conveying the standard emotions. The mask-like effect was increased by white make-up, and by the flat quality of the orthochromatic film. The women were outstanding in this respect. Asta Nilsen in Germany, Nazimova in the U.S.A., and Eve Francis in France, were the best-known examples. The greatest exponent of this style among the men was Charles Ray, who is now almost forgotten as a film actor. He had the same round eyes, the same white face, immobile but somehow full of expression. His finest technical achievement was in *The Girl I Love*.

This limitation of movement, these mask-like expressions, were the basis of the new style of cinematic acting. In surmounting, or rather skirting, the difficulties in the way of the silent drama, the actors had in fact created a new art. True, it was a static, even a rather statuesque, affair. Stars came to attach a tremendous importance to their personal dignity.

No female star would ever run. To this day Greta Garbo resents being asked to let her face be smacked.

Movement by the actors being scrupulously avoided, pace could only be achieved by cutting rapidly from one set-up to another. Some of these set-ups were "close-ups"; these, when projected, gave an exaggerated proportion of enlargement and added to the mask-like immobility of the players. Once again the solution of a primitive technical problem led to a discovery of first importance to the cinema as a whole. Cutting was quickly recognised to be a vital element of films. It was the main source of that rhythm which gives cinema, like music, its motive force.

In early days it suffered greatly from becoming a fashionable trick. Fantastic things were done to catch the eye of the novelty-seeking intellectual. Time and again shots were cut down to the length of one frame (one-sixteenth of a second in those days). A shot of one frame is imperceptible to the normal eye. But a number of them in succession did produce an undoubted effect. It had an almost percussive quality, which actually hurt the eyes. But it was new and sensational enough to draw a good deal of admiration.

The Russians brought reason to this chaos. They understood silent cutting better than anyone. They codified it. The gave it dramatic value. This was Russia's greatest contribution to cinema technique. It is associated mainly with the names of Eisenstein and Pudovkin. But it infused the whole of the Soviet cinema, and was based on a reasoned approach to the limitations of the medium. The drama was no

Comedies and Cartoons 75

longer purposeless. The revolutionary ideal inspired the propaganda of these Russian pioneers and gave them a passionate interest in the potentialities of the cinema. The Russians have since lost their pre-eminence in cutting, mostly owing to the coming of sound. The best cutters in the world to-day are probably in America. With the further evolution of the cinema it became impossible to do effective cutting unless it were planned before the shooting. The director on the set must have the cutting in mind as he shoots.

It is easy to imagine how limited was the choice of subjects open to the scenarist of the early film drama. Subtleties of acting or complex situations were impossible. According to Samuel Goldwyn we can't, even now, make a good picture without a him and a her and a "yella coyote" to spoil the fun. Well, if we can't they certainly couldn't. Only in those days, the triangle was not just a necessary starting-point. It dominated every picture. It made impossible a real, unsentimental approach to ordinary human life. The characters had to be either princes or beggarmen, with fairy-story behaviour and associations. The big figures of the time were correspondingly unreal. These were Mary Pickford, the world's sweetheart; Douglas Fairbanks, the human hurricane; Barbara La Marr, the sinister enchantress.

Only one form of the drama used types which even remotely existed. That was the Western. Its heroes were honest, believable people: elderly, blue-eyed Bill Hart; Tom Mix, the dark and massive. Its straight-from-the-shoulder quality, its rough chivalry, its generosity of sentiment, were genuine things. They could be attributed to real people. They could be shot in real settings. They had no marble pillars to flap in the wind. And they had one tremendous advantage over the ordinary dramatic film. This was the fact that a horse is a horse at any speed. It never looks ridiculous. So they were liberated to this extent at least from the ban on movement.

Immobility and the eternal triangle together had a very important effect on the ordinary dramatic film. They made necessary the development of the individual "star", on whose personality the novelty and attractiveness of the film depended. A great deal of care had to be taken to maintain the star's prestige.

Directors, too, gained in personal importance and in responsibility towards the public. But their work did not receive the same recognition as the stars! Some of them resented this and tried to remedy it by publicising themselves. Many of them were fine technicians and great "cinéastes". But the ones who got the publicity were not always those whose aesthetic value was the highest. Too often they were more preoccupied with the development of their own personal style than with the growth of the medium itself. Even a man of the stature of Hitchcock to-day is more hampered by his personality than he will ever know.

This individualism of directors and stars helped to sterilise the dramatic film. It did not affect the contemporary comedians. From the beginning they worked in teams, of which Mack Sennett's was the type. Their films were not dependent on star appeal, because they were free to fill them with better things.

They needed to have no fear of movement. They ran and jumped, and threw things at one another with gusto. This comic effect of increased speed was a help, not a hindrance to them. Not only was it funny in itself. It enabled them to elaborate quickly situations which in normal time would be tedious. They were quick to realise this asset. They played about with speed by running the camera sometimes more quickly, usually more slowly than standard. Often they turned as slowly as eight frames a second. Even now audiences laugh when the news-reels or magazines speed-up deliberately crowd or traffic scenes.

Because they could get movement into the actual shots, comedy directors depended less on cutting for pace. A great part of the early comedies was played in long-shots, embracing the whole action on the screen at one time. Even now there is little constructive cutting in Chaplin's films, or indeed in any of the modern comedies, except for purposes of emphasis.

Because they could get more meaning into the actual shots, they also depended less on sub-titles. The deadening effect of the constant sub-titles in the more pretentious silent films was terrific.

Another limitation of silent days, the mask-like face, they turned to good effect. The grim seriousness of Charlie Chaplin or Buster Keaton, while they were doing the most fantastic things, added many times to their humour.

Freed from the eternal trio, Hero, Heroine, Villain,

they were able to create a whole series of types, infinitely various. Many of them became famous, I would almost say immortal. The cinema became an attractive medium for the best of the music-hall comedians. From being confined to a single turn of a few minutes, they found themselves able, with a team of others, to hold the screen for anything from ten minutes to an hour at a time. So at first they worked in units, turning out short, completely satisfying films.

Unfettered by the rigid dignity of the drama, they could turn themselves to any subject that offered. They had no need to escape into history, therefore their films came much closer to contemporary problems than did the dramas. They came home to ordinary men and women. Their community of purpose gave them a certain uniformity of style and atmosphere, noticeable particularly in the sets. The backgrounds of these films, like their stories, were those of everyday life. It was this almost documentary aspect of the silent comedies which gave them their appeal to all classes of the public, and their great social importance.

But once on its feet the comic film began to change in character. It threw up a number of individual comics, men like Charlie Chaplin, Buster Keaton, Harry Langdon and Harold Lloyd. Of these only Charlie Chaplin and Harold Lloyd have survived till to-day. But for the time being they ousted the comedy team. On the Continent the same thing was happening with Max Linder as the central figure.

Considering the financial hold of the Jewish race

Comedies and Cartoons

on the cinema, it was not surprising that there was a marked Jewish character in the humour of these comedies. But the German Jews, otherwise so important in the cinema of that time, produced no comedies. Pat and Patachon were not German but Danish. In any case, their work was inferior.

None of these early comedy stars were women, with the possible exception of Mabel Normand. The convention was still strong that women were not to be laughed at. They were kept as heroines; they followed in the footsteps of the actresses of the film drama. The few women who, later, attempted comedy parts followed the rather *haute école* style of the stage. Such were Zasu Pitts, Louise Fazenda, Marie Dressler and Glenda Farrell. They never approached burlesque or farce. But as the conventions of daily life altered, women were more and more used in comic parts. In the modern Marx Brothers' comedies, women are the butt. This has become a first essential of American comedy, perhaps by way of compensation for the dominance of the American woman and the adulation she demands in ordinary life. Here is film comedy in its social role again.

Some of the greatest film comedies that have ever been made were made then. They had a simplicity born of discipline and perfection of style. There was Harold Lloyd's *Safety First*, which made an epic of the ascent of a sky-scraper by a young clerk in search of a big job. Buster Keaton's *Go West* was the story of a lonely man's affection for a cow. The greatest moment of Charlie Chaplin's *The Pilgrim* was when the criminal masquerading as a parson enacts in the pulpit the story of David and Goliath, miming each part alternately.

But from their very perfection as masterpieces, these films inevitably laid stress on the talents of the individual artist. They were the beginning of the break-up of the comedy units.

The "gags", which were so spontaneous in the earlier comedies, began now to be a routine job. "Gag men" were paid huge sums to produce them as if out of a sausage machine. The "gag" became an international idea—the word passed from American into all the European languages. The principle was even extended to the drama, where gag men were employed to stick in the comic relief.

Louis Delluc, French critic of the cinema and inventor of the word "photogénie", had realised the social importance of the film comedy. He recognised in particular the genius of Chaplin, and made a special study of it. So it was in France that Chaplin first made his mark in a big way, before America thought a great deal of him. Unfortunately Chaplin came to realise that he was great. He emulated the big figures of the dramatic screen. He made full-length pictures, with himself as star, and often forgot to be funny. He was copied on all sides—especially in France. René Clair's *Italian Straw Hat* is the best-known example of the failure of the Latin mind to grasp Chaplin's secret. It was far from being the only one, and stood head and shoulders above most of the rest.

Now that Chaplin and his friends had got into long pants, there was a chance for others to get in⁺ the

ELEPHANT BOY   Directed by Robert Flaherty and Zoltan Korda
for London Film Productions, 1936-7

Flaherty is a pioneer of the documentary which looks at human life inseparably **related to its** natural environment, economical and cultural, in wild parts of the earth

REMBRANDT — Directed by Alexander Korda for London Film Productions at Denham, 1936, with Charles Laughton in the title part

A Dutch interior, its severe rectangles of floor-pattern, window-frame and side-thrown shadows imprisoning the accused girl (Elsa Lanchester)

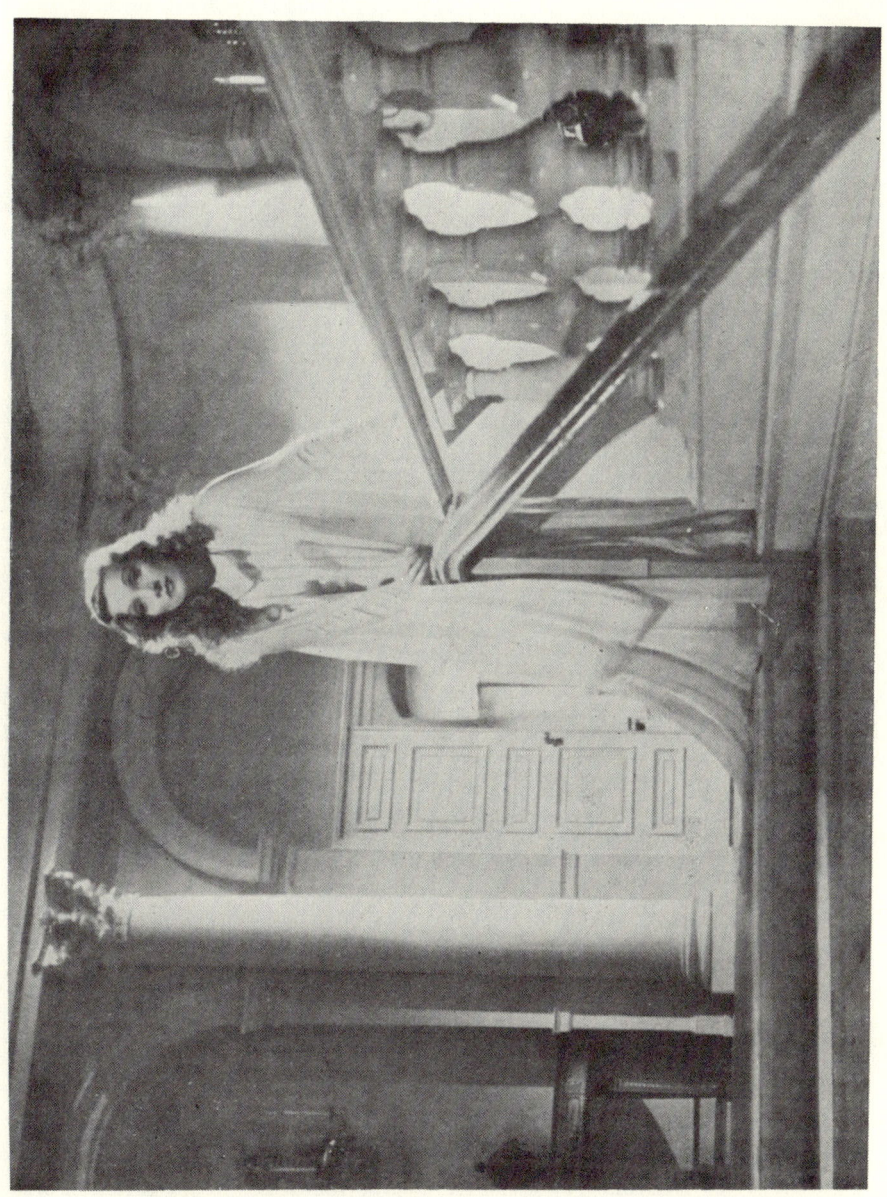

KNIGHT WITHOUT ARMOUR From James Hilton's novel. Directed by Jacques Feyder for London Film Productions at Denham, 1936-7

Feyder's treatment of Marlene Dietrich in her first British film may be compared with the more sophisticated style imposed on her at Hollywood

EDGE OF THE WORLD — Directed in Foula, Shetland Islands, by Michael Powell for Joe Rock Productions, 1936

LETZTE ROSE — German (Tobis). Directed by Karl Anton, 1935, from Flotow's opera, *Marta*

Landscape with Figures—Scottish and German

CHARACTER
ACTING

Charles Laughton as
Ginger Ted in
VESSEL OF WRATH
(1937)

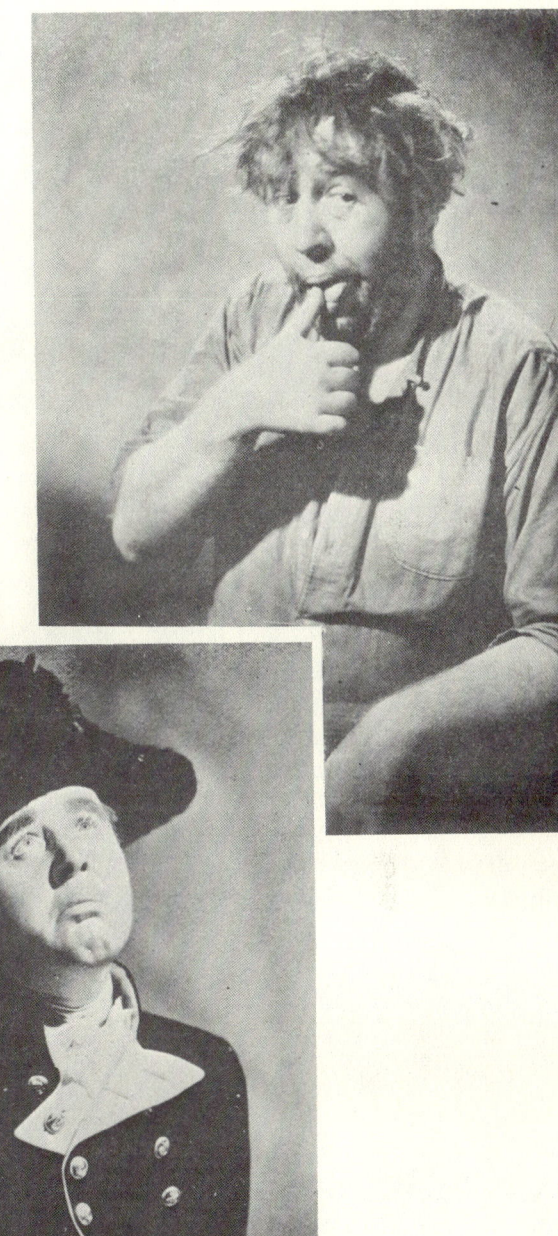

Charles Laughton as
Admiral Bligh in
MUTINY ON THE
BOUNTY   (1935)

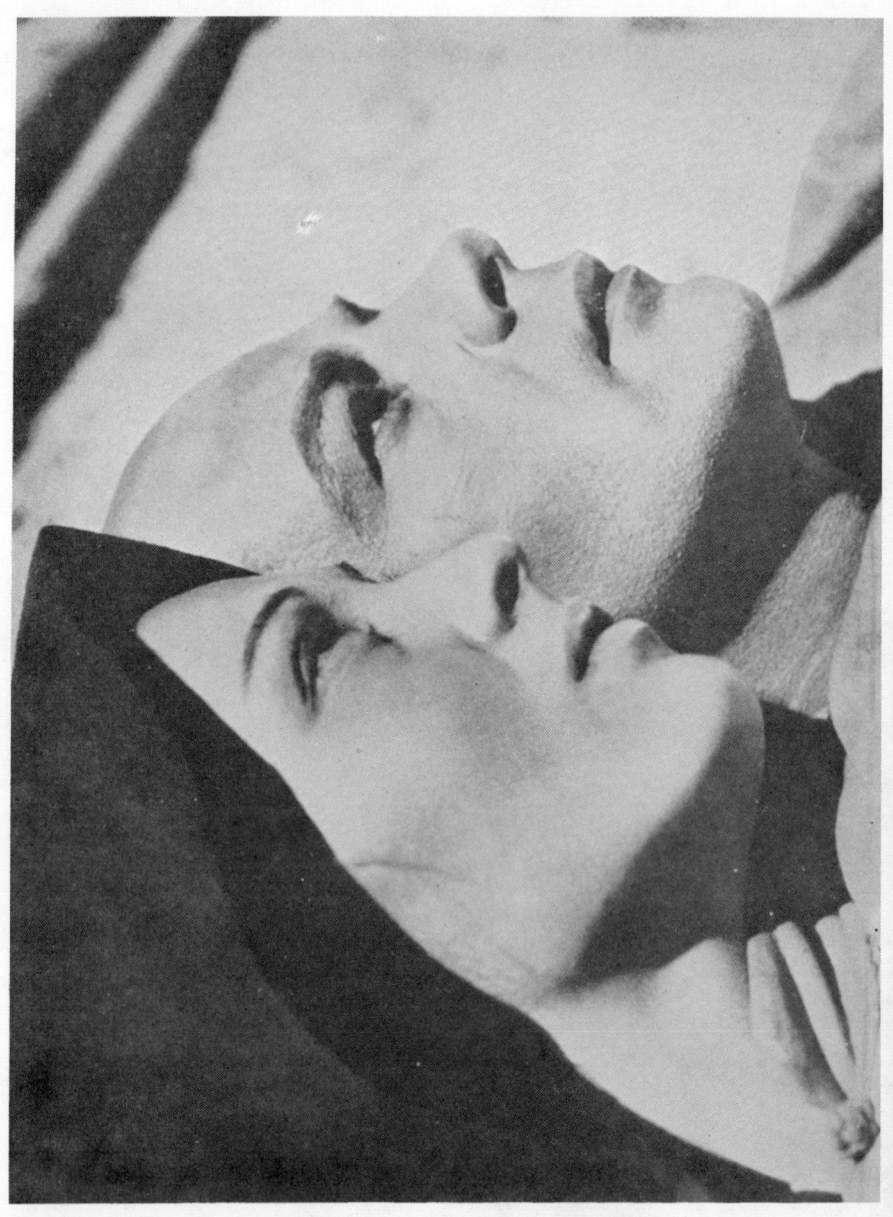

Paul Muni and Luise Rainer in *THE GOOD EARTH*

A Metro-Goldwyn-Mayer version of Pearl Buck's novel, directed by Sidney Franklin at Hollywood, 1933–6

Justification of the much-abused close-up

Greta Garbo with Robert Taylor in *CAMILLE*. Directed by George Cukor for Metro-Goldwyn-Mayer at Hollywood, 1936

Garbo's black and white costumes are a feature of this new version of Dumas' "La Dame aux Camélias", set in Paris in the 1840's

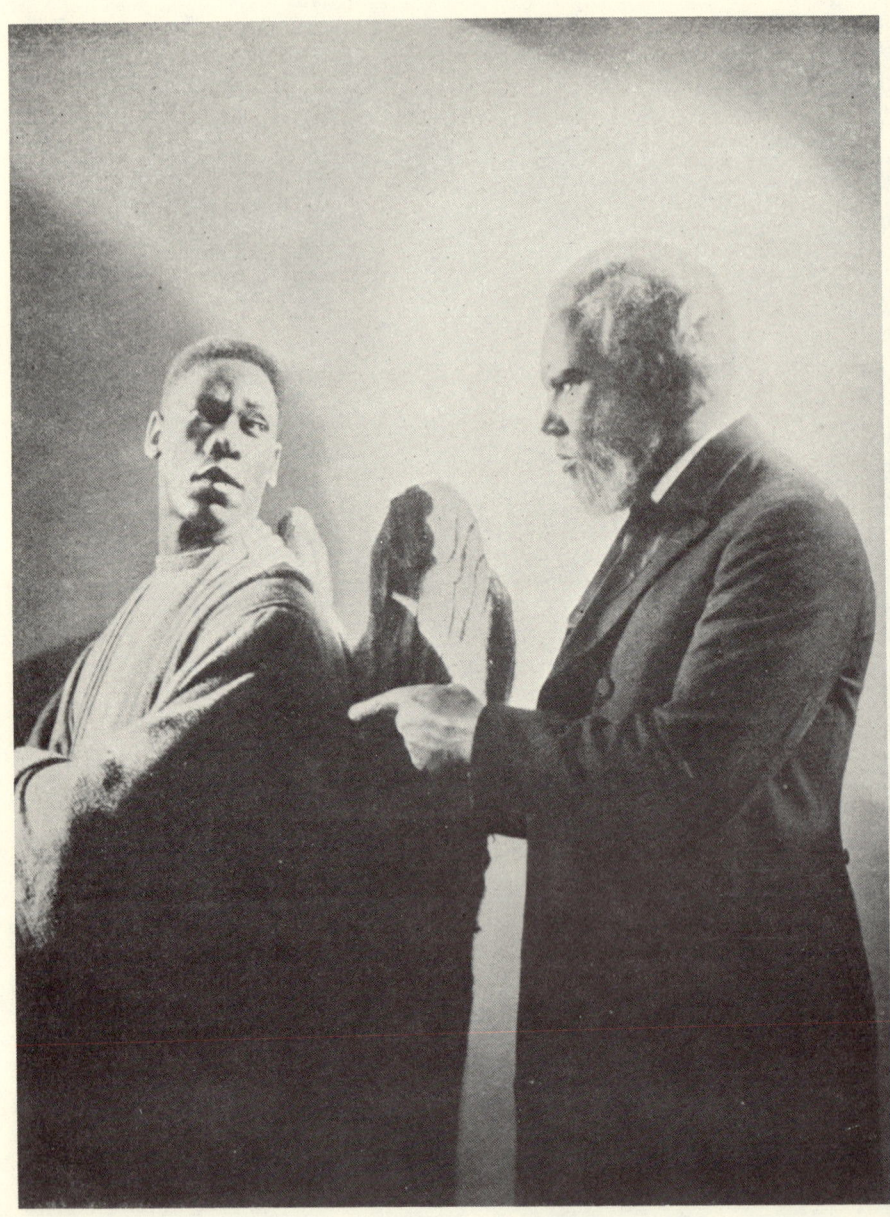

THE GREEN PASTURES

"De Lawd" and the Archangel Gabriel in version of Marc Connelly's Pulitzer Prize play, directed by Marc Connelly and William Keighley at Hollywood, 1936

Notable throughout for simple means used to convey the childlike atmosphere of Old Testament episodes as they strike the negro mind

ROMEO AND JULIET

The Montagus and Capulets on their way to church. Directed by George Cukor for Metro-Goldwyn-Mayer at Hollywood, 1936

The pride and pageantry of mediaeval Verona are taken out of the theatre into a blaze of Italian sun

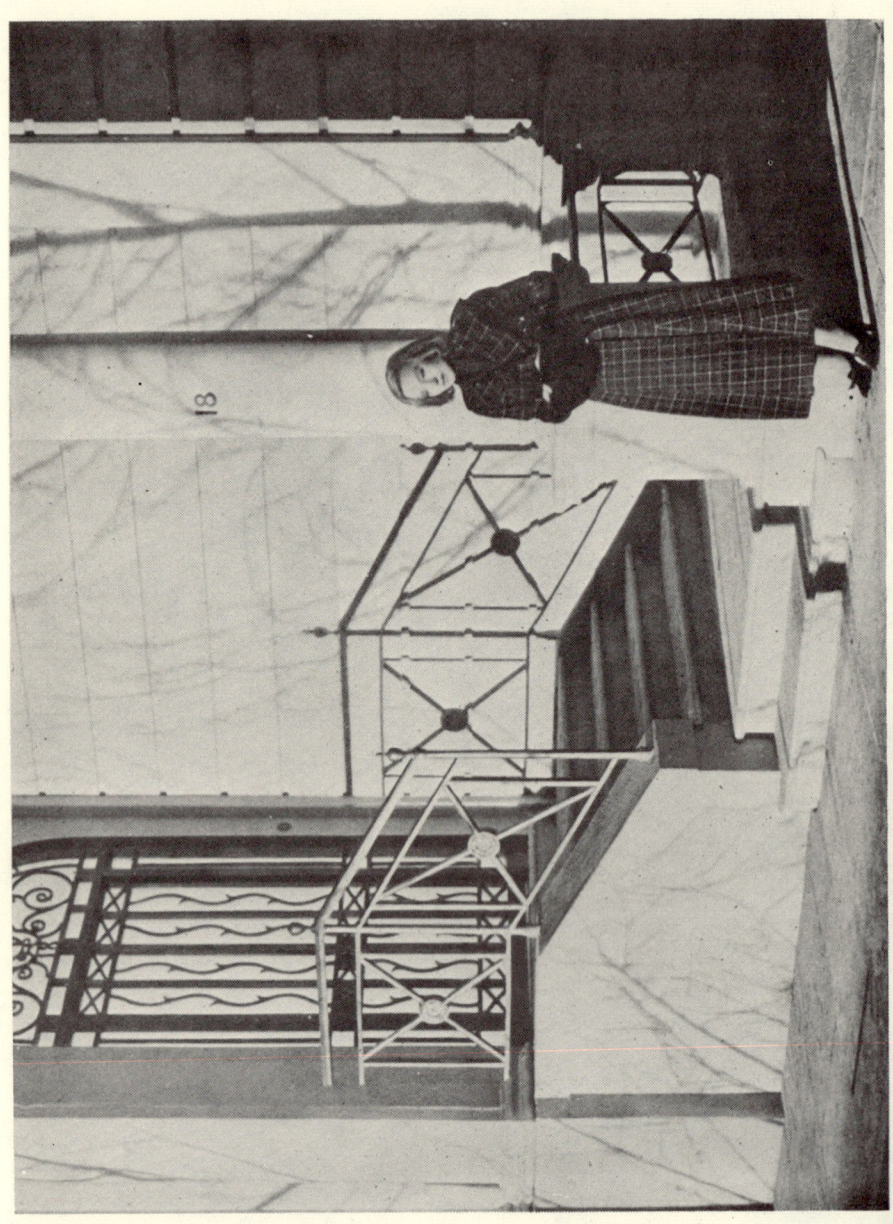

Elisabeth Bergner in
DREAMING LIPS

English version of *Der Traumende Mund*, a Max-Schach-Trafalgar production directed by Paul Czinner at Elstree, 1936

Loneliness emphasised by austere lighting and contrast of slight figure with background of tall pillar and heavy stonework. Notice echo of grille pattern in shadows of trees

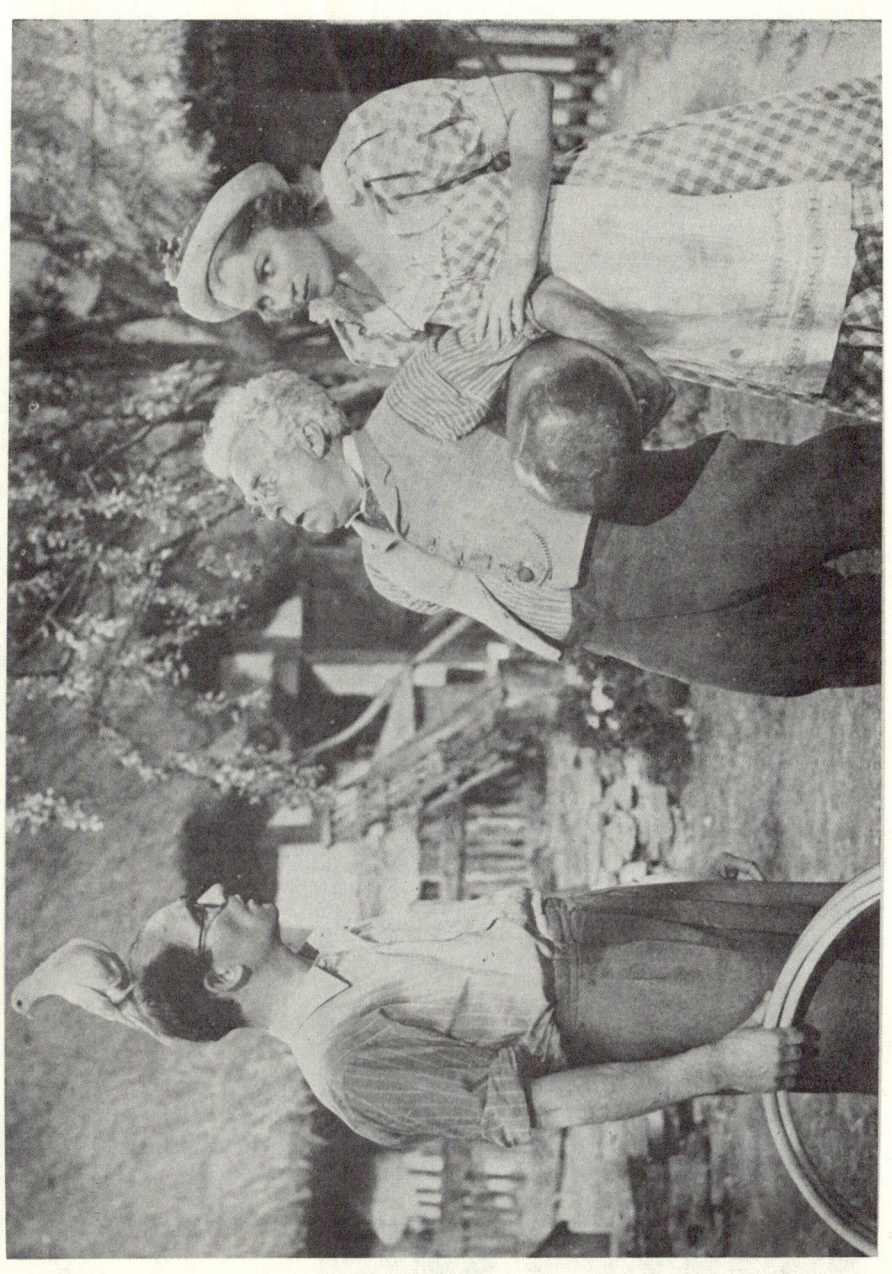

Gracie Fields in *KEEP SMILING* A Twentieth Century production directed by Monty Banks, 1938
Unexpected situation in a farmyard

THE INDIVIDUAL COMEDIAN

Charles Ray in
THE GIRL I LOVE
An early silent comedy

Charlie Chaplin in
MODERN TIMES
(United Artists, 1936)

MODERN COMEDY STYLES

LE DERNIER MILLIARDAIRE
French (Pathé-Nathan) 1934
Directed by René Clair
By courtesy of the Edinburgh Film Guild

A DAY AT THE RACES
American (Metro-Goldwyn-Mayer) 1937
The Marx Brothers: Groucho, Chico and Harpo

DICKENS ON THE SCREEN

DAVID COPPERFIELD Directed by George Cukor for
Metro-Goldwyn-Mayer, 1934

Mr Micawber, drawn by Fred Barnard for an early edition of Dickens, side by side with
W. C. Fields as Mr Micawber in the film. Freddie Bartholomew as the young David
By courtesy of the Edinburgh Film Guild

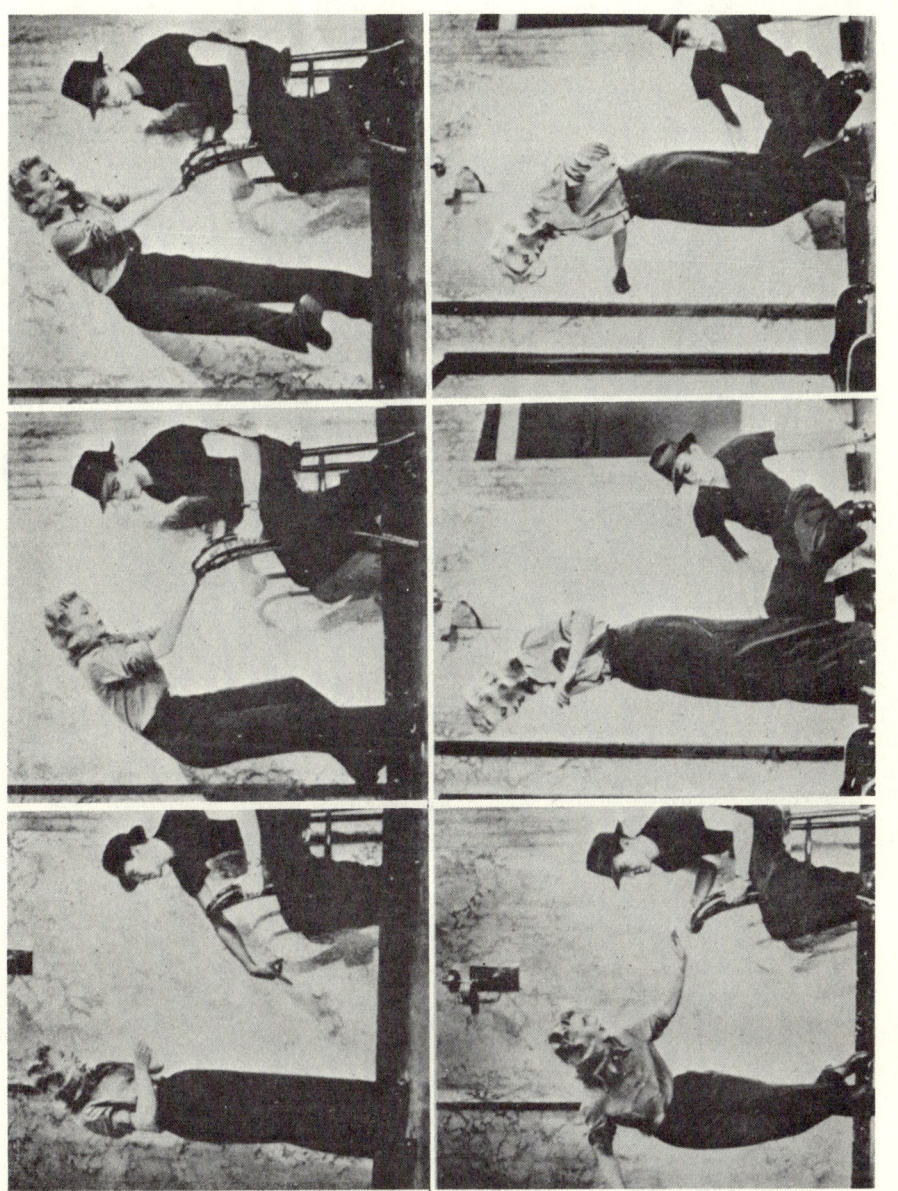

Ginger Rogers practising for *SHALL WE DANCE?* An Astaire-Rogers 1937 production. Her instructor is Hermes Pan, studio dance director for Radio Pictures

The dancing-partnership at its best provides satisfying rhythm for eye and ear, a ballet of light and shadow

STUDIO LIGHTING

ST MARTIN'S LANE Directed by Tim Whelan for Mayflower Productions, 1938

Rehearsing at Elstree. How much will the camera see?

Comedies and Cartoons

shorts. Two new groups came into the short comedy field at this moment.

The first were the cartoons—such as Bud Fisher's *Mutt and Jeff,* and Pat Sullivan's *Felix the Cat.* The cartoon did not then take on the importance it was later to achieve under sound. Its value lay in its return to simplicity and directness of attack, dictated and enhanced by its special limitations. For while the photographed comedy had to juggle with reality to make it seem fantastic, the cartoon started from a basis of fantasy, and had to build up from this a sense of reality.

The second group to produce short comedies at this period was Laurel and Hardy. In a sense they were out of date, because they harked back to the slapstick and custard-pie style of comedies. But they brought a freshness to it, and they were delightfully unpretentious. Above all, they worked as a team, and not as individual stars.

But the peculiar significance of Laurel and Hardy is that they survived the transition to sound.

This was a catastrophic event in almost all branches of the cinema. It brought with it increased cost, destroying independence and crippling experiment.

The acquisition of synchronised sound (especially speech) and natural speed wrought a great change in the drama. It was possible to bring the technique of stage acting to the screen. Nor was this slow to come. Actor after actor went over to the studios. A torrent of stagy dialogue began to pour from the loudspeakers. I remember especially *The Guardsman,* a fast-talking photoplay starring Lynn Fontane. It depended on the rhythm of speech for its effect. It was something new and had a charm of its own.

But sound brought more than dialogue. It brought the statues to life. It gave their faces expression. Action became the watchword of film drama.

Cutting lost its pride of place. Speed could be obtained by other means. The new dialogue itself restricted cutting. Actors had to be allowed to finish their (interminable) sentences. The period of the photographed play had begun. It has not ended yet.

Chaplin and Co. were terrified. For a long time Chaplin himself did not made a picture. When he made it—*City Lights*—he resorted to special devices to avoid the real use of sound. He did not know how to use it. *Modern Times* bristles with lost opportunities. And Buster Keaton was as scared as Chaplin. They were chiefly afraid that the perfection of the characters they had built up in silent films would be destroyed by the sound of their voices.

Laurel and Hardy took it calmly. They had not become so great in silent days that they needed to fear destroying the atmosphere by their voices. They modified their technique very little. They used sound with the same freshness and the same lack of pretension they had brought to silent pictures. They made it funny. They have since cut their hair and gone into long features like the others. They are now Stan Laurel and Oliver Hardy. But when sound came they were plain Laurel and Hardy, and as such they were the pioneers of sound comedy.

Soon after the arrival of sound another team made their appearance, continuing the Jewish tradition.

Comedies and Cartoons

This was the Marx Brothers. Their history is complex and unique. In the days of the silent cinema they ran a music-hall turn. The technique of their performances there was very much influenced by contemporary film comedy. They did things which, but for the cinema, no one would have dared to do. They would not have been understood by any but a movie-trained audience.

This strain of silent cinema technique they brought with them into the sound film. In this they bore a superficial resemblance to Laurel and Hardy. But at the same time they brought in a good deal of music-hall. So that although from the beginning their treatments were to a certain extent cinematic, they made several films before they thoroughly understood the nature of the medium.

The art of the Marx Brothers, and their sociological importance, are hard to define. The psychology of their work would place them in the first rank for the surrealists. The deliberate cruelty of much of their humour comes near to the spirit of revolution. It is much nearer to it than the sentimental moralising of Chaplin. Theirs is the most practical of all joking. It is in revolt against the established order.

The great strength of the early comedies, of Laurel and Hardy, of the Marx Brothers, was that they worked not as individuals but as units. British comedy has yet to grasp this secret. Nervo and Knox, Douglas Wakefield, Ernie Lotinga and many of the other great clowns of English music-hall would be valuable acquisitions for the cinema. But comedians are stuck like postage stamps on to British Films.

They are given a director and a close schedule and sent down to the set to work. No one would dream of sending them all off to a country house for a fortnight before turning a foot, so as to get acquainted with one another. Yet this is very much how the early units, like Harold Lloyd's, used to work. The whole group lived in one place. Everybody knew everybody; everybody made suggestions for gags, and the thing went with a swing. If the British companies could get some of this all-one-big-happy-family idea into their productions, they might easily make something worth while.

The Walt Disney and Dave Fleischer cartoons are fine examples of the work of a unit. Any one who still has the idea that Disney is an isolated, individual genius should forget it. He works with a unit of about 300. The other members are by no means mere copyists. They are as much creative as Disney himself. There is so much work in a cartoon that it would be absurd to attribute it all to one man. For five minutes on the screen, 7,200 pictures must be drawn. In each picture there may be any number of characters, each with their characteristic movements. One man may draw in the beginnings and ends of the movements, and others draw the intervening pictures. Each character may be allotted to a separate animator. But unless as much imagination is displayed in the animation as in the original drawings, the film will be flat and uninteresting. Actually co-operation in a unit like Disney's is much greater than that. And it is not confined to "office" hours.[1]

[1] See also Paul Nash's article, pp. 128-131.—EDITOR.

Comedies and Cartoons

In sound, the cartoon has come into its own. It has untold possibilities of accurate timing and synchronisation of sound with visual. It has perfected the use of jazz, the most vital expression of the American spirit. It has created an army of original and stylised types—Mickey Mouse, Betty Boop, Donald Duck, Pluto, Popeye the Sailor are some of them. They are reminiscent of the types that appeared in the early silent comedies and have the same value.

While colour has yet to prove its importance in the photographed film, it has found its place in cartoons. Here it no longer reminds us of seaside post-cards. It has been used in the creation of delightfully childish imagery. We all remember the pink bodies of the three little pigs, and the great moment in *Alpine Climbers* where Pluto, frozen blue, turns pink and then brown in spirals from the warmth of the rum in his tummy.

Cartoon shares the full freedom of all comedy. It is true that sound has freed the drama from some of its fetters. But Sam Goldwyn has testified that it is still weighed down beneath its eternal triangle. The monotony of modern dramatic films is an inescapable fact. They are so loyal to their stagy tradition that people would be more surprised by the appearance of a real working-class type in a dramatic picture than by a donkey in an aeroplane in a Marx Brothers' film. As the technique of the sound film steadily, if slowly, advances, we may hope to see an improvement on the choice and appreciation of material.

Comedy can deal with the bitterest realities, the

most cruel facts. It can tackle the most vital problems. Beaumarchais' *Mariage de Figaro* was revolutionary in spirit. It was the first outcry against aristocracy and caused a severe tremor in the eighteenth century. Yet it was a comedy because, as Figaro himself said, he had to laugh to keep himself from crying. Among the Japanese it is held a virtue to laugh when receiving bad news, thus avoiding an unseemly display of emotion. All over the world people use humour as a shield against grief. Only comedies can fight against injustice and at the same time elude the censor. In fun we can get nearer to human understanding, nearer to final truth than in all seriousness. Comedy ranges from extremes of cruelty to deepest kindliness. Disney cartoons may follow the ancient sages, but not too closely. In the fable the grasshopper died. Disney taught him his lesson, and let him live to act on it.

SETTINGS, COSTUMES, BACKGROUNDS
By John Betjeman

NEARLY all of us think of films in terms of personalities, plot and speed, rather than backgrounds. Now and again, when an immense amount of money has been wasted in reproducing Versailles or building Windsor Castle in real stone and covering the roof with ten acres of real moss, the film critic dismisses the laborious spectacle with the word "lavish". The public thinks: "Oh, another Cecil B. de Mille production!" and prefers to recall how lovely this or that star looked when she was kissing So-and-so. There are one or two films whose scenery may have had a certain amount of box-office value—von Sternberg, Korda, Cecil B. de Mille productions. But not even these names can bring in the people without stars. And if it comes to it, Londoners, at any rate, know that the transformation scene in the Lyceum Pantomime is likely to be more moving and more beautiful than the most dazzling pattern of limbs, feathers and smiling dentals that ever wove itself into the theme song of a. Warner Brothers' musical.

Indeed, of all the subjects connected with films in this book, that of scenery is the least considered. From the box-office point of view it is also the least important. Until it becomes important as a money-maker, I suppose the scenery of films will continue in its present state.

I imagine that the film magnate, sitting at his mahogany desk with stained-glass windows to shut out anything natural, would have a list, like that below, of the chief constituents of a film. And the order in which he puts these things is the order, to him, of their commercial value:

(1) Kisses and other displays of concupiscence;
(2) Stars;
(3) Story or type of film;
(4) Speed of action: slow for simple audiences, fast and American for sophisticated West End houses;
(5) Music;
(6) Dialogue;
(7) Dresses;
(8) Scenery.

This is not the order by which the highbrow, or even the middlebrow, judges whether he likes a film or not. But it is the order which the majority who make for the box-office value of a film has come to accept. Probably by now it would be impossible to change that order, imposed originally by minds not gifted with a love of the visual art.

The delegation of scenery to the bottom of the form is a tragedy in many ways, but it is not surprising. It is a tragedy because the scenery of a film can be so varied; the propaganda against vulgar architecture and decoration can be carried on with such intensity; the appreciation of country, and of period decoration, can be brought within every one's reach. But none of these things is done. This is not surprising. The films are in the hands of people who are purely business men. At no time have business men been noted for aesthetic sensibility. They are known to prefer a balance at the bank to a prospect of woods and fields. Their appreciation of works of art goes entirely by money value (which accounts for the existence of people called art dealers)—but this is a digression.

Many people thought that the introduction of colour photography to films would improve their decorative side. But *Becky Sharp*, careful as it was, and chaste as the colour schemes were intended to be, showed that there was really no hope in colour photography. Colour photography for the screen still uses the three-colour process; the introduction of a subtler gradations of colour—a five-colour process, say, as is used in the half-tone reproductions of old masters—would be prohibitively expensive. Not only is there this commercial objection to colour films, but however accurate a colour photograph becomes it is too like life to be like life as the human eye sees it. When you or an artist looks at, let us say, a pre-Raphaelite garden, a box-hedge in the foreground, tiger-lilies beyond, a purple-grey stone wall beyond that and an elm-tree towering above, with flecks of blue sky between the globed foliage, you do not see it all at once. Your eye is focussed on one object at a time. If on the tiger-lilies, then the tree, sky, walls and hedge become an iridescence of light of whose colours you are only sub-consciously aware. A colour photograph gives the same value to the colour of everything else in the picture as it does to the tiger-lilies. Consequently, the effect of a colour photograph is flat and disappointing. It is the job of an artist, not a machine, to give their true value, as the human eye sees .them, to the colours in a picture. Unless contrasts are employed to turn every colour photograph into a picture as the eye sees it, colour photography will continue as the *tour de force* it is at present. The variations from grey to black which we are accustomed to are easier work for the eyes and brain, and consequently quicker on the mental register, than anything else. The mental and physical effort of registering and seeing a colour film gives the audience a headache.

But the absence of colour should not be used as an excuse for having any old thing as the scenery of a film. Greys and black-and-white are no hindrance at all to the scenery of a film. The pencil artists and engravers of the past have managed to get along very nicely; so have photographers. Yet if we look at the stills outside the average cinema (unless some Russian film or a well-produced short happens to be on) we see pictures which are of no higher standard than those which confront us every morning in the penny papers. Frequently, they are lower, for they have not the quality of spontaneity and accidentally excellent composition or subject-matter which gives interest to a topical photograph.

Before going on to what might be done with scenery and background in a film, I would like to pass in rapid review the present state of films in these respects.

The décors of films can be more easily classified by dividing them into countries and companies rather than by selecting single instances which would involve interminable and tedious cataloguing. Of course, most companies have now and then made films whose décors have been well above their average productions. I am writing of the mass of films, not of exceptions. I am treating, too, feature films. In short films the possibilities of scenery, particularly in Strand Films, Walt Disney, G.P.O. Films and some of the Gaumont British Instructional, have been realised. You will notice, incidentally, that most of the best short films are British.

AMERICAN

Musicals: The décors display great ingenuity, but resemble more often than not a sort of drunkard's dream. Warner Brothers' musicals generally have a sequence of patterns shifting in time with the music. Girls' legs forming a starfish in a bathing-pool: Ruby Keeler's face set in a star repeated twenty times on different parts of a black screen. The effect is sometimes that of a surrealistic photo-montage. Certainly this sort of trick with the camera, accompanied by a haunting theme-song, impresses the mind. To the average Englishman, coming out from a lavish American musical into the quiet of an English country town, what he has seen seems to be sheer madness. Mad or not, there is no doubt that these tricks, particularly in Warner Brothers' musicals, are a real break-away from the stage conventions which dominate most musicals. They open up exciting vistas of what might be made of a musical. The Fred Astaire-Ginger Rogers partnership (Radio) has never very interesting décors. As we are supposed to watch twinkling feet, it is presumed that anything else too interesting would distract us. The result is that except as dancing there is nothing remarkable about the films of this couple. They are simply a stage show photographed. Columbia musicals (very popular about two years ago) are interesting for their music and ingenious cutting, but their scenery is far from original or even attractive.

Crime: There are often fine shots of skyscrapers, cars racing round corners, dingy rooms with bowler-hatted thugs swigging whisky and playing dice, which convey the atmosphere of a big and horrible city to perfection.

Love: There are very few tragic American films; they nearly always end happily. The settings for stories of this sort are as improbable as the stories themselves. They are expensive but hardly beautiful. They are about as convincing and pleasant to look at as the average pseudo-Tudor road-house erected in the last ten years anywhere outside London.

American film ideas of eighteenth- and early nineteenth-century architecture are equally unconvincing, but here the expert only can detect mistakes, and these bother him so much that his mind is taken off any merit the film may have. It were better that American love-stories in non-contemporary settings should pay no regard to period at all. The urbane modern love-story has a little more to be said for its settings. But here the usual fearful staginess of the dialogue, with the camera vaguely trailing round a pseudo-modern room (furnished in the Mayfair manner), is as uninspired as the adaption of stage love-stories to films always seems to be.

Settings, Costumes, Backgrounds   93

Outdoor work in American love stories is feebler still. Too often the apple-trees outside the old homestead are hung with obviously paper flowers. The inside of the homestead itself has a sort of dimity daintiness associated with vicars' daughters running a tasteful tea-shoppe. Now and then a memory of Soviet films causes the director to insert a shot of a plough team coming over the brow of a hill. The insertion of a single successful shot *ad nauseam* is popular in American outdoor work. *The Charge of the Light Brigade* repeated one good shot of cavalry charging up a valley in the middle distance so many times that a small child sitting next to me in the audience said: "I've seen that before," after its third or fourth appearance. It is odd how outdoor shots, whether they picture India or the country gentleman's English park, have a flavour of California. A country lane, often wanted in romances, seems to be devoid of hedges but to be a well-tarred stretch bordered by olive or ilex with an almost municipal quality about it.

Comedies show American films at their best. Less money seems to have been spent on sets; more brains have been used. The American humorist—many miles ahead of the English one—knows, however, that a setting must be as humorous (not necessarily lavish) as his comedy. The most subtle sets in American films are those which appear in its comedies. Charlie Chaplin exploits them admirably. Perhaps the best sets of all are those for the W. C. Fields films when that great comedian plays the part of some small town henpecked husband. An impression of what corresponds with our suburbia is admirably conveyed and never overdone. Notice electroliers, overmantels, gimcrack furniture, wallpapers and looped curtains in the next W. C. Fields comedy you see. The hand of the fashionable Hollywood interior decorator, who likes to see everything either Swedish-cum-beaux-arts-modern or what he calls "Empire," is mercifully absent.

There is no doubt that the best American film brains are used in comedy.

British

Musicals: Many successful British musicals have been of the old-time Vienna variety. On these an immense amount of money has been spent, and interiors of large overlighted Viennese ballrooms have whirled before our eyes. This style of musical was copied from the Continent, but the photography of the scenery in British examples does not display the sense of architecture and ornament noticeable in the originals. No other British musicals have had any distinction of setting whatever.

Crime: The films directed by Alfred Hitchcock have been the first to show any sense of English life in their settings. Most British crime films (and this applies to American films of British crime) regard the setting as of minor importance—rather like the background to an illustration in "The Wizard," "The Magnet," "The Hotspur" or some other twopenny boys' magazine.

Love: England's scenery for those romances which admit of outdoor work has hardly been exploited.

A few recent films contained excellent shots of fishing villages. But most films, whether in historical or contemporary settings, have a suburban notion of what England looks like. One feels that the following instructions have been given to the unit from the London studio: "Just buzz down the Great West Road, and as soon as you get to a bit where there aren't any houses, drive down a lane and start shooting. And remember to be back after lunch for the country-house scene. We've fixed up the background for that." The few fields round Denham which London Film Productions seem to think will do for any countryside (they used it for Scotland in *The Ghost Goes West*) will soon be familiar to filmgoers. They are aggressively Middlesex in their aspect.

Indeed, England's country when it appears has the atmosphere of the back-garden of a road-house. Inns themselves in English films are singularly unconvincing: heavily faked Tudor, bulging with beams and almost of the palm-lounge variety. "Say, mine host, is yon an hostelrye I see before me—let us go and scrounge therein for a pint of the goodly." Sales manager's Elizabethan, that is the sort of thing of which films, Georgian, modern or Tudor, smack.

The interior sets of English romances are almost all beneath contempt. The country house is furnished throughout in the higher suburban manner with accents and behaviour to match. Churches are fantastically inaccurate and bad. Roads are well worn and about to be built upon. I have seen a much published still of a Georgian coach trundling down a lane with a wire fence on one side. I have never seen a "period" room in an English film which comes up even to an American one.

Comedies: Slightly worse than the Love films. There is a definite style now known as "Rookery Nook." Interiors with tasteful "suites" and, of course, linenfold panelling, pouffes, and a grandfather clock: exteriors in the manner of some particularly ostentatious Building Society's advertisement, leaded panes, lamp down the drive, cardboard gables.

CONTINENTAL

German and Austrian films are particularly good at baroque interiors and mountain villages. In the latter they score because snow is so easy to photograph and does not last long enough in England to be used to advantage. French films profit, in the financial and aesthetic sense, by the cheapness of the sets. *Sous les Toits de Paris* will remain as *the* example of what can be done to get beauty out of squalor. Almost every French film of middle-class or peasant life has exquisite little touches—the twist of a lamp bracket, the hang of a muslin curtain, the pattern of wallpaper, the worn carpet, the tattered old coat hanging on the back of a door, the picture of Our Lady with light beneath. Russian films go in for scenery more than other countries. *Turk-Sib* is still the best example of how to make a thriller without using human beings as a foreground.

. . . . .

It is extraordinary how, in the last five years,

Settings, Costumes, Backgrounds 97

British and American films have been complacently static in art direction. There have been a few films whose artificial settings have been memorable. *Dante's Inferno* (with Spencer Tracy, a Fox Film), though comic enough in plot and dialogue, certainly tried to out-do John Martin and Doré; B.I.P.'s version of *The Old Curiosity Shop* contained some shots which were the best Dickensian scenes yet reproduced, particularly that of the old village church in the closing scene. This had the quality of a three-dimensional Cruikshank drawing. Mr. Micawber's street in *David Copperfield* and the exterior of Betsy Trotwood's house were as good as straight photography can make an historical film. *A Midsummer Night's Dream* contained settings which were interesting in a sort of *nouveau art*, Darmstadt manner.

National scenery has produced a few, a very few, films which have brought the country into the synthetic air of a cinema. *Man of Aran*—and, judging by stills, *Elephant Boy*: Michael Powell's films: Mr Gilkison's Cornish effort: Norman Walker's *Turn of the Tide*: about four more and that is all.

There is no doubt that British and American sets at the moment suffer from:

(1) ignorance of producers;
(2) unimaginative presentation of scenes;
(3) timidity in experiment.

A knowledgeable producer will, if he is doing a film of English country life, choose not Broadway or Chipping Camden, certainly not Denham High Street or Marlow or Henley as country life. He will go to the unexplored beauties of Northants, which rival the Cotswolds. He will frighten us with stretches of fen in Lincolnshire: make us shiver on Yorkshire moors: lose us in elm-embowered Norfolk villages: brace us with a sight of rolling downs: cool us in beech forests full of deer leaping glades: comfort us with the sight of a genuine cottage not inhabited by weekenders: let us hear the hymns shaking the lamp brackets in an oil-lit Methodist chapel: catch, for a moment, black bottle-shaped figures in hats like puddings, nodding with artificial grapes, as they walk to church of a Sunday morning.

The same knowledgeable producer showing town life—say, Paris—will not just show us the Eiffel Tower and sink back into the usual set of no particular distinction, but will go on from René Clair. If he is doing London, Westminster Abbey will not be enough, nor will St. Paul's and the Horse Guards. We must see the Kilburn High Road, and a street running like corrugated iron, bow front and beastly front door, in strips over hill-sides of New Cross. We must be dazzled with the frightfulness of the windows of a multiple store, listen for the jangle of a tram on a wet night in a shopping centre: visit a quiet plane-tree-shadowed square: see the steam from a fish-and-chip shop.

The presentation of settings is still singularly unimaginative. The Americans are ahead of any, except the French, in conveying atmosphere by detail. The impression caused by a set of an interior depends not on its elaborate walls or richness, but on its detail. A sequence of details, cut into the action of the human

Settings, Costumes, Backgrounds 99

beings, can give all the atmosphere at much less cost. In a ballroom, a dropped programme on a parquet floor: a glass half empty on a buffet table: two people's hands or fingers touching on a balustrade: a palm with a glass roof above it. In a crowded street, a newspaper trodden on to the pavement: a shop seen from the height of a human, not all at once, but as the human eye sees it: a lamp-post: a man-hole: a square of pavement: the mark of the skid of a lorry in a wet road: the tail-end of a traffic block: orange-peel in the gutter. We see by details, and that is how we remember events; detail must be used in film settings.

The timidity of experiment is the most serious fault of all. Years ago *The Cabinet of Dr Caligari* was made, a film which brought the background into the foreground, which made the scenery reflect the mental state of the particular character shown. The effect was deep and terrifying. Every one who saw that film remembers it. How many subsequent films— even films of a week ago—can one remember so vividly?

In *The Old Curiosity Shop* the art director brought to life a Cruikshank drawing. Has any one dared to bring to life the figures of Rowlandson, Leech or Tenniel, and make them move against the backgrounds for which the artists designed them?

Will there ever be a serious attempt to see, let us say, the world of Swift as Swift may have seen it in his madness and in his sanity? When that day comes, settings will assume their real position in perspective with the characters who are to-day over-dramatised, over-emphasised and given the same value as they have on the legitimate stage. When that day comes settings will be in genuine perspective, not mere decorative after-thoughts which, more often than not, had better have been left out of focus.

MUSIC ON THE SCREEN
By Maurice Jaubert

SINCE the birth of the cinema, long before it dreamed of speech, music has been intimately linked with it. At first, perhaps, music served merely to cover projection noises, for projection rooms were not so perfectly insulated as they are to-day. But it was quickly realised, too, that the projection of a film in complete silence was not easily endured by the public. Music was quite naturally called in to break this silence. It was observed, too, that there could be some connection between the image and the sound. Certain pieces of music went well with sad scenes; others with comic scenes. But over and above the power of music to accentuate the quality of this or that scene, another musical element was discovered—*rhythm*—which, united with a visual scene, prolonged and accentuated remarkably its effect upon an audience. The practice arose of duplicating a rhythm expressed in images by a corresponding rhythm of sounds; an *auditory* perception was superimposed upon a *visual* perception: synchronisation had been discovered.

Well before the birth of the talking film, musical adaptations designed to accompany the silent film had raised the very problems which occupy us to-day. And already composers were attracted by the new medium of expression offered to them.

Moreover, since the cinema lacked that quality

of literal accuracy represented by sound (human speech, real noises justified by the visual image, etc.) it avoided much more than it does to-day the *realism* now demanded of it. It was natural that music should have been required to accentuate still further this flight from the actual, which seemed for so long to be the true goal of cinematography, as well as to "explain" certain intentions of the director, who had not yet at his disposal the powerful instruments of speech and sound for elucidating the story. At the moment when the sound film was about to come into being, music constituted for the film a kind of running commentary designed sometimes to plunge the spectator into the atmosphere desired by the director, sometimes to prolong in him a rhythmic impression, sometimes to make still clearer the story that was being told to him. This conception of the rôle of music on the screen made one think of the old stage *melodrama*, which also used music to work on the spectator at suitable moments in order to intensify in him the horror or sadness which the playwright was trying to arouse.

At the birth of the sound-film, producers and directors failed to appreciate how the essence of the art of the cinema was about to be transformed. In the new possibility of music recorded once for all, they saw only a means of ensuring for their films a musical accompaniment to their taste. Henceforth this accompaniment would no longer depend on the quality of the orchestras in cinema theatres, or on the greater or lesser skill of special orchestra leaders. The first efforts in this art—new from so many points of view—bear witness to the ingenuous wonder of cinema technicians in the face of this synchronisation secured mechanically and with certainty. It was natural, since the producers had not gauged the full significance of this revolution—word and sound united with the visual image—that music should absorb the thoughts of the pioneers of talking films. The first sound films were *musical* films rather than *talking* films: *Broadway Melody*, *The Jazz Singer* . . . such are the titles which come to mind when we call up that period which is already past history.

It was quickly perceived, however, that the musical film did not offer a final solution to the problems set by the new art—that it constituted only one of the possible *forms* of this art, and perhaps the most strictly limited.

We owe to the musical film, however, some admirable achievements. In Europe the main preoccupation seemed to be to exploit this or that celebrated composition, to summon up the figure of a great musician, to make shine some great star of song. Such were the discovery of Martha Eggert (*Unfinished Symphony, Casta Diva*); the triumph of Kurt Weil with his *Dreigroschenoper*—a modernised German version of *The Beggar's Opera*; and an incursion into the realm of fantasy with films which were destined to have great influence (*The Road to Paradise, Congress Dances*).

The Americans, always daring, and inspired in part by these examples, created a kind of new cinematographic form combining the attractions of musical comedy, opera, ballet: dancing, particularly tap-dancing, taking first place. As usually happens, the first film of this sort, *Forty-Second Street*, which remains the masterpiece of its kind, bred a whole series of imitations of varying quality—*Gold Diggers of Broadway, Prologues*, etc.

Striking as musical conceptions—whatever reservations one makes with regard to the music itself—such films as these suffer nowadays from the wish of producers to "astound" the public; and one quickly wearies of these effects of grandiose settings, of these "gags" which the use of music makes possible, and which are not replaced by new ones often enough. But occasionally, even in mediocre films, the miracle happens. Avoiding the conventions of this kind of spectacle, the director finds in a song the excuse for a lyrical transposition of music into images. The most striking example of these miracles we shall find in sequences such as those of the "Forgotten Man" song in *Gold Diggers of Broadway*, or above all in those inspired by the famous *Lullaby of Broadway* (in a film otherwise very mediocre). Here there are born out of the music images which no longer need to submit themselves to that "veracity" which the non-musical film insists upon so imperiously. Freed from their rôle as copies of real objects, their expressive power flows out purely in plastic rhythms, strictly united with the music.

It is through having recognised the power, both poetic and physical, which can be drawn from this close linking of sight and hearing by *synchronisation*, that the animated cartoon has accomplished such marvellous feats. Every link with reality is broken, but behind the burlesque exterior of a cartoon it is *poetry* which the cinema encounters, thanks to daring inventions, visual and auditory. Who does not remember in a Silly Symphony the spider using her own web as a harp?

Some experimentalists—and particularly Fiesinger—have wished to push still further this emancipation of the screen. Eliminating every image which conveyed a meaning of its own, they relied on patterns, lines, dots, spots of colour which had no other object than to make apparent to the eye the patterns or rhythms of the music. But this, it seems to me, is to carry synchronisation to an extreme point where it becomes mere redundance.

We see, however, that if the musical film presents to the musician technical problems of recording, montage, etc., it does not raise any essential problem of the harmony between image and music. For here the music commands and the images obey. The musical film, therefore, represents only one particular form of sound picture—a form not yet exhausted in spite of its abuse. The general timidity of producers, directors and scenario writers has not yet allowed a full study of its possibilities. It is permissible to foresee, on the boundaries of the film proper, the development of a style which, uniting the characteristics of ballet, opera and cinema, will provide the musical-dramatic form of the future.

If we pass now to the non-musical film, whether dramatic, comic or sentimental, the music, ceasing to dominate, becomes the servant of the image. We shall see that the conceptions which governed its use in the days of the silent film, as well as the considerations here expressed on the subject of the musical film, immediately lose their validity.

For, with the introduction of word and sound, cinematographic style has undergone a profound change, a change which too few directors and scenario writers have perceived and understood. Driven by the absence of speech to a lengthy method of visual paraphrase in order to make the story clear, the silent film built up for itself, little by little, a special idiom designed chiefly to compensate for the silence of the actors. This convention became familiar to all habitués of the cinema, who believed, legitimately in those days, that it gave occasion for a special art of the screen—an art which in its finest development would be essentially allusive, and so poetic. But as soon as speech came to destroy this early convention, the cinema—although hardly any one recognised it at first—changed its character. It became, it is, and it remains *realistic*. We must understand by this that while it no longer needs the visual syntax which it had built up with so much trouble, it is now impelled to borrow even the elements of its language (images) from immediate reality. Cinematographic realism, then, must now be held to consist—as Roger Leenhardt has said in a remarkable study of cinematographic rhythm printed in the French review *Esprit*—not "in the reproduction of reality in moving images—which would have no sort of aesthetic interest—but in the succession of variously selected elements of this reality, deliberately brought together to create a new reality." And again later ". . . the essential of cinema is that its realistic raw materials should be patterned in accordance with a purpose and a rhythm."

But if now we voluntarily leave aside all that can be called the "real" music of a film (jazz in a night club, organ in a church) whose function is obvious, what is it that most of our directors demand of music?

First of all to fill up the "gaps" in the sound, because some scene is considered too silent, or because the director has been unable to find in real life a convincing natural sound—above all, if no such sound is suggested by the image. We need not stress this elementary conception.

More commonly, music is called upon to annotate the action. Is the scene tragic? A few notes of the horn or trombone will accentuate its gloom. A sentimental scene? A violin solo, it is thought, will make the young star's declaration of love more persuasive. Do the followers of this "aesthetic" perceive that they are thereby submitting to old habits bequeathed by the silent screen? In any case they fail to notice that, simply from an acoustic standpoint, the superposition of music on a voice or a sound tends to destroy the emotional value of the one and the authenticity of the other. In a film otherwise admirable, *The Lost Patrol*, the director was presumably frightened by the silence—the silence of the desert—in which his story was told (and yet how dramatically effective this silence could have been!). So he inflicted upon us, without allowing us an instant's respite, a "dramatic" score whose continuous and unnecessary presence was at every moment apt to destroy the poignant realism of the images.

If music is not called in to annotate the drama, it is required to accentuate the main incidents by making use of synchronisation, a method dear to the silent film. The closing of a door is emphasised with a chord; footsteps are accompanied with a march rhythm, etc. In *The Informer*,[1] where this technique is carried to its highest pitch of perfection, the music has actually to imitate the noise of pieces of money falling on the ground, and even, by a roguish little arpeggio, the trickling of a glass of beer down a drinker's throat. Apart from its childishness, such a procedure displays a total lack of understanding of the very essence of film music. Music is by nature continuous, organised rhythmically in time. If you compel it to follow slavishly events or gestures which are themselves discontinuous, not rhythmically ordered but the outcome simply of physiological or psychological reactions, you destroy in it the very quality by virtue of which it is music, reducing it to its primary condition of crude sound. Used for these purposes, music will never, I am convinced, prove to be a satisfactory substitute for natural sounds, justified by their authenticity.

If I reject entirely all musical annotation or synchronisation, it is because I believe, as I said above, in the essentially realistic character of the screen.

[1] It is regrettable that John Ford, maker of *The Lost Patrol* and *The Informer*, and one of the greatest directors of our time, should misunderstand in this respect the true function of music in the film.

Music on The Screen

Into the raw materials of cinema—which acquire artistic meaning only from their relations to one another—music brings an *unreal* element which is bound to break the rules of objective realism. Is there no place for it in the film?

Certainly there is. For just as the novelist sometimes interrupts the telling of a story with an expression of his feelings, argumentative or lyrical, or with the subjective reactions of his characters, so does the director sometimes move away from the strict representation of reality in order to add to his work those touches of comment or of poetry which give a film its individual quality, descriptions, movements from one point to another in space or time, recalling of earlier scenes, dreams, imaging of the thoughts of some character, etc. Here the music has something to say: its presence will warn the spectator that the style of the film is changing temporarily for dramatic reasons. All its power of suggestion will serve to intensify and prolong that impression of strangeness, of departure from photographic truth, which the director is seeking.

But the break in sensory adjustment which is provoked in the spectator by the irruption of music into the film ought to be carefully prepared. One may, in a moment of extreme dramatic tension, make use of the shock of a brutal attack (an orchestral fortissimo linked to a cry, for instance). One may also subtly mingle a musical with a non-musical sound (the noise of a train developing a rhythm which merges gradually into actual music; the shrilling of violins replacing imperceptibly the whistling of the wind, etc). There are a thousand and one possible solutions to a problem which never twice presents itself in the same way. But it is precisely the function of the film musician to feel the exact moment when the image escapes from strict realism and calls for the poetic extension of music.

Presuming that we have now approximately defined the function of music in the non-musical film, we have still to consider whether film images may not demand of music a specifically cinematographic character.

The current theories about film music, outlined above, have led specialist composers to suppose that it must be essentially dramatic and expressive. And so we have seen the birth of a kind of musico-cinematic language uniting the least respectable Wagnerian formulae with pseudo-Debussyesque sweetnesses, not to honour with mention a few more recent contributions. The result is an orgy of sentiment, thanks to which many musicians wish to prove to us that even if they are most often asked to toss off a popular couplet meant to be sung round the world, they are equally capable of expressing in eight bars, and with generous support from the brass, all the human passions.

It is on this ground and this ground only, I think, that we shall find the masters of the screen—I mean the Americans—often at fault. They seem to be satisfied with a musical style which—in itself scarcely defensible—surrounds a film with an unbearably antiquated atmosphere. How many fine films have been botched in this way by the over-emphasis and lack of taste of their musical accompaniment!

Who does not remember that in an admirable film by Frank Borzage, *Farewell to Arms*, this director was not afraid to summon the prelude from *Tristan and Iseult* to support the climax of his drama? More recently, did not *Peter Ibbetson*—which offered the musician a splendid opportunity to prove his feeling for the right relationships between imagery and music—call forth a deplorable and grandiloquent symphonic poem, whose aggressive mediocrity combined all the worst formulae of a certain type of dramatic music, inexcusable to-day even outside the film?

Let us recall musicians to a little more humility. We do not go to the cinema to hear music. We require it to deepen and prolong in us the screen's visual impressions. Its task is not to explain these impressions, but to add to them an overtone specifically different—or else film music must be content to remain perpetually redundant. Its task is not to be *expressive* by adding its sentiments to those of the characters or of the director, but to be *decorative* by uniting its own rhythmical pattern with the visual pattern woven for us on the screen.

That is why I believe it to be essential for film music to evolve a style of its own. If it merely brings lazily to the screen its traditional interest in composition or expression, then, instead of entering as a partner into the world of images, it will set up alongside a separate world of sound obeying its own laws. Even if this autonomous sound-structure reveals all the marks of genius, it will never have any point of contact with the visual world which it ought, nevertheless, to *serve*. It will live its own life, sufficient unto itself.

Let film music, then, free itself from all these subjective elements; let it also, like the image, become realistic; let it—using means strictly musical and not dramatic—support the plastic substance of the image with an *impersonal* texture of sound, accomplishing this through a command of that mysterious alchemy of relationships which belongs to the essence of the film composer's trade. Let it, finally, make physically perceptible to us the inner rhythm of the image, without struggling to provide a translation of its content, whether this be emotional, dramatic or poetic.

Freed from all its academic impedimenta (symphonic developments, orchestral "effects," etc.) music, thanks to the film, should reveal to us a new character. It has still to explore the whole territory which lies between its frontiers and those of natural sound. It should restore their dignity—as a function of some screen image — to the most outworn formulae by presenting them in a new light: three notes on the accordion, if they are what a particular image demands, will always be more stirring then the Good Friday Music from *Parsifal*. Music must never forget that in the cinema its character of *sound phenomenon* outweighs its intellectual and even its metaphysical aspects. The more it effaces itself behind the image, the more chance it has of discovering new perspectives on its own account.

Finally, let us recollect that this music, which we are assuming will arise in good time, endowed with a new style, will be *recorded*. However perfect our recording and reproduction instruments may be now, the microphone effects in the sounds a transformation of which the composer must take account. Let us not fall into the error of those who wished to see in this transformation the basis of a new technique and a new aesthetic, though the composer will certainly bear in mind that the position of the microphone may result accidentally in a reversal of sound values: a flute close to the microphone will give a more powerful tone than a trombone. And all possible investigations and experiments are legitimate in this domain. Every such practical experiment may provide the composer with valuable new resources, but it will not exempt him from the task of finding in his score, before recording begins, the solution to any problem of style which the visual content of a film may require of him.

Once recorded, the music, though it will share the imperfections of the sound-track, will stand equally to benefit from all the various manipulations which the sound-track is able to undergo. It is well known that the sound-track receives its impressions from the vibrations of light caused by the vibrating diaphragm of the microphone, itself set in motion by the sound-vibrations of the orchestra. Indeed, one can say that recording consists in the *photographing* of sound. The director, with this photograph at his command, is in a position to treat sounds just as he treats images: the technique of mixes and cuts is just the same. Indeed, the device of "dubbing," or re-recording, allows him to go further still in manipulating the sound-track. A certain sound or musical phrase, or several, can be first recorded separately and then transferred together to a single strip of film.

The example which best illustrated the possibilities of this technique is to be found in one of the first attempts at sound films: Walter Ruttman's *World Melody*. The sound-track of this film is made up entirely of fragments of sound or music, most of them extremely short, set down in sequence or made to overlap, with a most sensitive feeling for the right relationships not only between images and sounds, but also between successive sounds or phrases of music.

In this extreme example, the music is an assemblage of untreated raw material; the composer's personal contribution is negligible.[1] Here the director is dealing with music and sound in just the same way as with images: he borrows them from reality, and it is only in weaving them into a pattern that he becomes a creative artist.

We may, then, conclude that film music should never, so to speak, reveal its own musical nature. If the writing of it has pursued strictly musical ends, and if those ends have been achieved, thanks to the gifts of the composer, we shall be tempted to *listen to it*. And then it will detach itself from the image—a danger which increases in proportion to the inherent value of the music.

To-day, when the talking film, abandoning the

[1] In *World Melody* we have to do with a type of music consisting essentially of fragments of folk music—mostly not written down—borrowed from all round the world.

metaphorical and allusive style of the silent film, is beginning to substitute an elliptical narrative style, music ought to forgo—except at particular points of the drama—its own essentially lyrical quality, which is bound to bring an alien element into the film. It ought, like the script, the cutting, the décor and the shooting, to play its own particular part in making clear, logical, truthfully realistic that telling of a good story which is above all the function of a film. So much the better if, discreetly, it adds the gift of a poetry all its own.

THE COLOUR FILM
By Paul Nash

I

BY way of preface to this article I think it should be stated that the writer lays no claim to be considered an expert. His experience supplies him only with the most rudimentary knowledge of the technique involved in colour cinematography, and his sympathies are almost entirely with the black-and-white screen. But it has been thought "interesting" to invite a painter to write on the subject of Colour Films, and that invitation has been accepted and acted upon in good faith. That is to say, the whole undertaking has been, necessarily, limited; the result may well be of no value. But it is a personal record.

In approaching the subject of colour films as a whole, for the purpose of this article it seems best to divide the discussion into three parts—Colour Talkies, Colour Cartoons, and the Colour Films of Len Lye.

Colour talkies refer to the big pictures as opposed to travel and instruction films whose only voice is the commentator's. As a basis for criticism, impressions received in studying two distinctly different pictures seemed most constructive. These films are *Ramona*, made in California last year by Twentieth-Century-Fox, and the recently completed *Wings of the Morning*, made under Fox auspices by New World Pictures at Denham in this country. Both use the latest American Technicolor process.

Major Adrian Klein, who has written the standard work on colour films,[1] remarks towards the end of his excellent book that "it is certain that in the early stages of colour reproduction painters will be called in to supervise colour direction, who, by the nature of their environment and training are not equipped to understand even the elements of the theory and practice of colour photography." To this I would add, God forbid; yet I find myself in the position of one passing judgment upon the results of that theory and practice which certainly I am hardly equipped by training or environment to understand. On the other hand, for the first time, I believe, I am in the position of the spectator who confesses with such disarming frankness: "I don't know anything about Art, but I know what I like." And for the first time I begin to understand what that means; and to feel something of the comfort of its defiant impertinence. But Major Klein is right when he says that the film colourist of the future will have to possess, as part of his training, a thorough mastery of all the technical aspects involved, in order to collaborate intelligently with the specialist controlling each stage of the colour-recording and reproduction. Even then, he may lack an indispensable quality—that very seldom-considered factor, imagination; or is that taken for granted as the other part of his equipment? I doubt it. At present,

[1] *Colour Cinematography.* By Major Adrian Bernard Klein, M.B.E., A.R.P.S. (Chapman and Hall: 1936).

so far as I can discover, the use of imagination and the operation of technical processes in colour cinematography have never coincided.

To an artist, the appearance of the average colour photography picture is more or less of an abomination. It lacks everything he prizes—form, definition and subtlety. It emphasises everything he has striven to overcome—realism, banality, false values. He recognises in it potential beauty but is forced to realise that, at present, its whole apparatus is being used for stupid or venal ambitions. This is easily explained. With the arrival of the full-length colour picture, directors have mentally all gone back to the nursery. I shall never forget the scene in the hayloft during the special showing which Fox Films were kind enough to give me of *Wings of the Morning*. Every nocturnal noise calculated to alarm Annabella (and thereby give away to Fonda, also in the hay, the fact that she was a girl dressed as a boy) was recorded and then painstakingly illustrated. Squeaking; close-up of rat; rattling; full-coloured old-fashioned lantern; banging; part of interior showing door; neighing; picture of horse, twice; and, finally, a rather dim noise I hardly recognised followed at once by a most disconcerting stuffed owl—or just acting stuffed, which persisted for what seemed several minutes; the bird and I, alone in the theatre, glaring at each other. I must say it looked very much like an owl by the time they removed it. That, however, is the clue to the present conception of the colour film. It is regarded as the great opportunity to see life steadily and see it whole—i.e. in full colour.

The Colour Film 119

Anything more tedious and, generally speaking, discouraging, it is hard to conceive.

But naturalism and realism are thought to be the productive elements for entertainment value, and since the colour film costs roughly three times as much to produce as the black-and-white and grey, we have what is called *accent on Naturalism*. I regret to find that even so intelligent a person as the author of *Colour Cinematography* supports this ideal as the goal of all his fine technical skill. "The object is to give pleasure. It is said that by far the majority of the audience in the cinema consists of women. No one in their senses would say that colour does not give pleasure to the average woman, nor would they deny that it plays a very important part in their mental life. This being the case, provided that the colour reproduction is convincingly natural, practically every woman will approve of the addition of colour to the cold grey shadow at present flickering away its story upon the white screen." And again: "A travel picture of the loveliest of this world's scenery rendered only in light and shade cannot hold the attention for long. We are impressed only by elements of pictorial composition or by the skill of the photographer; but upon the introduction of colour everything is forgotten save the exquisite sensual pleasure of *recognition*; we are overcome by the magical nature of the thing this evocation of all that is most precious and evanescent in vision."

In this connection I was struck by an odd incident while watching *Ramona*. A naked baby of quite astonishing naturalness was presented in its bath or cot, I forget which. Several women, I presume overcome by the magical nature of the thing, burst into rather hysterical laughter. What surprised me more was that the same effect was produced by some realistic pancakes; even men joining in the laugh. What will happen when Steve Donoghue is seen in full colour—first in mufti at the Dorchester and finally winning the Derby on Wings of the Morning, I cannot imagine.

Yet with all the boasts and strivings of directors, cameramen and laboratory technicians, an absurd but obstinate fact remains. *Colour cinematography cannot produce natural effects.* It can produce isolated objects with an effect of verisimilitude, provided they are within focus and naturally lighted. But, as its focussing range is distinctly limited—far more so than that of the ordinary screen camera—most of its scenes are travesties, unreal compositions in which things look either too real to be credible or definitely unreal. Figures of unnatural colour force, but not quite sufficiently articulated in *drawing*, move about in landscapes where form, literally, has no definition and, in the near middle distance, gives up the pretence altogether and becomes simply blurred.

At times, ludicrous contrasts are given by shooting the stars by vivid, artificial light—for which they are "made up" in surroundings lit by the natural sun. Often this is not in the least necessary; even a veiled sunlight, I am told, is sufficient for shooting, but in the case of *Wings of the Morning* weather conditions were so bad that sun arcs had to be used frequently. This brings us up against another discouraging limitation of colour photography. *Apparently*, it can only record one temperature to any extent, and therefore no place appears cool or soft; no delicate shades enter in.

Many scenes in *Wings of the Morning* occur in Ireland where, I believe, the charm of a landscape like Killarney lies in its subtle, indeterminate colour. Also, like any lake country, its form is most interesting under changing skies. Seen at midsummer, or in steady sunlight, it has the rather vulgar "look" of a picture post-card. The result of the sequence of scenes shot to illustrate John McCormack's singing of "Killarney" was rather like upsetting the local views kiosk in the village shop; in fact, I have never seen such sunsets anywhere else.

But, again, colour cinematography does not produce even the effect of a good picture post-card. Personally, if it could, I, for one, should be satisfied. Few people realise, perhaps, the charm of certain early colour cards, clear cut and printed in clean bright, cool colours—I have a set of Toulon and one of the Desert which, pictorially, would do credit to any painter. When the great Derby scene is shown in *Wings of the Morning* there is one moment when a couple of gipsy children appear in close-up and in that one shot the camera nearly comes up to Frith, but the general view is very much below his level.

It is all a matter of the definition of form. In both films under review, *Ramona* and *Wings of the Morning*, there is a large proportion of horses. Now, horses in both films look satisfying, more satisfying and convincing than any other objects moving or static. I am still not quite sure why this is. Presumably they are shot in natural light, but still . . . Humphrey Jennings, the surrealist—who has had considerable experience of practical film colour work—explains it in this way. "On people the definition seems less good than on machines and dogs. It isn't. But one is satisfied with a sensation of dog: one is not so satisfied with a sensation of a *star*; and colour is sensation." It may be so. What cannot be disputed, I think, is that colour as used by Technicolor experts does not function as it should for their purpose. It fails to reinforce form. On the contrary it largely obliterates form. This is partly due to the ignorance of directors and cameramen. They use too much colour; they have no understanding of its proper use; they are like the children in the nursery again. They have been given a box of paints and they are having a fine time laying it on thick anywhere they can.

There is another unhappy fallacy existing in the minds of certain directors. This is the *harmony* obsession. A great deal of time seems to be spent in harmonising costumes with interiors, interiors with exteriors, and screen personalities with costumes, interiors, exteriors, and so on. The result, I regret to say, is only to reduce all to the lowest common (or vulgar) multiple in terms of colour and, in the process, to dull definition. What should be studied, of course, is the infinite variations of contrast. But not only is contrast hardly practised, it seems to be unrealised as a constructive factor in producing harmony. The fact is that the Technicolor experts have a certain amount of scientific knowledge not always

The Colour Film

comfortably digested, and applied generally only along conventional tracks. It is the same in the matter of psychology, a pet field of "knowledge", especially with women specialists.

Finally, there is the all too important question of how colour affects the *stars*. I have collected a few opinions upon this aspect and they confirm my own impression. Miss Elsie Cohen, organiser of the Academy Cinema, makes this interesting observation: "Though it does not seem to follow logical laws, I find that I am irritated by seeing a face in colour. For me, instead of lending greater depth to the face it makes it appear empty. I have the feeling that I am watching a fantasy and not a drama of life." This is a very pertinent comment. Colour photography, for the most part, because it fails to reinforce form, detracts from the structure of the face. It seems to be superimposed in such a way as to obscure the *drawing*. When a painter uses colour he builds with paint all the time, even in water colour which is translucent. The only hope for colour photography to be effective is to understate it instead of piling it on.

The requirements of Technicolor dictate the right policy in this respect where make-up is concerned. Natural beauty, we are told, will be at a premium in future. Beauty that relies on the make-up expert will be under a cloud. But the process is exacting—a close-up shows the pores of the skin. The experts have to admit that heads of hair are going to bother them. Colour does not suit blonde women, and the platinum variety, according to them, is definitely out. Black hair is difficult, browns and half-shades almost impossible. Golden hair and auburn hair seem to photograph best, which is what one might expect, though I fear it is going to add another hot colour element to an already overcharged palette.

But there is more than that to overcome. Unless colour is going to enhance the beauty and interest of the stars, it is not going to be popular with the public and certainly not with the stars. You may think it thrilling to see you pet star *as* in real life, but you may soon wish you had kept your illusion. Even seeing her or him in the flesh, carefully prepared to meet the daylight, might be less disappointing. Do you remember Miriam Hopkins in *Becky Sharp*? And how did the pale lure of Marlene Dietrich stand up to the colour test in *The Garden of Allah*—did it not almost evaporate? How many women fans are almost dreading to meet a coloured Clark Gable? In *Ramona*, Loretta Young is transfigured by a black wig and made up to look like a Red Indian on the wrong side of the blanket, so to speak. But Annabella, that delicate and enchanting heroine of so many of France's best productions, has to look first like the gipsy wife and then like the partly-gipsy daughter of an Irish peer. I could not have believed that any face so physically distinguished might be made almost commonplace, but so it is. There are occasions when her beauty penetrates the mask, but I could not help feeling that the most significant achievement of Technicolor to date was in making Annabella look *swarthy*. . . .

Unfortunately it is too easy to find faults in the production of colour cinematography and too hard to discover important virtues for a discussion of this kind to be made very interesting. Comparing the two films, as a mere spectator I had the impression that *Ramona* came nearer realising Major Klein's ambition.[1] That is to say, the colour was not too overwhelming; one took it for granted quite comfortably most of the time. But in *Wings of the Morning*, the inane pursuit of naturalism, colour for its own, or rather, for Technicolor's sake, and the naïve attempts at colour harmony, do obviously slow up the picture. Imagine travelling in a train where the engine-driver wants to pick the flowers on the railway banks or point out the naturalness of rabbits to the passengers. . . . There is no doubt in my mind that the process of colour photography is capable, perhaps even now, of something worth considering from the point of view of the art of cinematography—without developing any sort of "artistic" affair. I have recently been shown films in Cinecolor and Dufaycolor. The Cinecolor effects are by far the most natural and satisfying I have yet seen. That is because they are, in a sense, an understatement. They have gone far to solve the problem of sharp definition, both for rapidly-moving objects and for objects at varying distances from the camera. But Dufaycolor—which has been taken up by one or two American producing companies and carried further than Cinecolor towards commercial availability for film work—has considerable claims also as a medium. It is an additive process and the latest of a long

[1] "The first colour film to be received with universal acclamation will be that one in which we shall never have been conscious of colour as an achievement."
—*Colour Cinematography.*

sequence involving the most inveterate research. Its name derives from Louis Dufay, who manufactured the Dufay Diopticolor and Dioptichrome screen plates in 1908, and has since been working on a film colour matrix fine enough for cinematography. Dufaycolor and Cinecolor are British concerns, Spicers Ltd. and Ilford Ltd. having made themselves largely responsible for developing the two processes. But, whatever the process and however highly developed, the directing of the colour machine—like the directing of all machinery to-day employed in producing effects of colour form in two or three dimensions—must, sooner or later, use the artist—the "real artist" as Major Klein describes him. But not an artist without experience and understanding of film technique. He must be properly equipped and employed intelligently.

To conclude this section of the discussion I am quoting—without comment except italics—extracts from the published statements of four experts engaged in the production of *Wings of the Morning*. They appear to reveal a certain mentality, what I will call the colour-film mentality—at least one species of it. Another, of a very different sort, will be disclosed in in the second part of the review.

Mrs. Natalie Kalmus, colour director of *Wings of the Morning* :

In this picture *we are trying to preserve one level of colour throughout*. Over half the picture is being filmed out of doors, so that in these scenes the predominant colour will be the soft and restful green of the English country-

The Colour Film

side.[1] Even in the gipsy prologue to the picture, where some of the costumes are very vivid, they are offset by the masses of green. When we cut from these exterior sequences to interiors, we try to preserve the same "light level." Our sets are brown, grey and green—warm, rich shades of colour for walls, furniture, tapestries and curtains, but all soft and tending to absorb light rather than reflect it. In this way the colours of the interiors and exteriors are kept at the same level.

Ralph Brinton, art director of *Wings of the Morning*:

Colour sets the art director many problems. The worst is that characters move from set to set wearing the same costumes. Each set must be a perfect background for these costumes. *Therefore the use of the dominant colour schemes must be avoided.*

Preparation of sets takes a longer time. If you look closely at any surface—from a castle wall to a common-or-garden brick—you will find it has a series of colours in it, blending to one general tone. To reproduce such a brick, or castle wall, we must reproduce all those colours.

To secure the right shade of grey for the interior walls of Clontarf Castle, for example, we had to coat the walls first with white paint, then grey, then yellow. By that time a blue tint had appeared—so we gave a final coat of grey for luck.

Ray Rennahan, cameraman on *Wings of the Morning*:

Technicolor requires a very light make-up. An actress appearing before a colour camera could walk straight off the set into the street—and if her make-up were commented on it would probably be described as insufficient.

[1] None of the greens in the picture, English or Irish, could be described as either soft or restful.

René Hubert, costume designer for *Wings of the Morning*, takes all his range of colours from the shade of the artiste's lips, which, he says, *should be the predominant colour on the screen.* If it were not, it would mean that the colours of a costume or a set were stealing every scene from the human actors and actresses.

II

My conversion to the colour film of any description dated from the moment I beheld Walt Disney's Silly Symphony, *Flowers in Spring*. Disney is one of the few geniuses of the cinema. He stands beside Chaplin as one of the real entertainers. He, too, has made the whole world happy and better for knowing his work. Unlike Chaplin, however, his virtue does not depend upon his visible personality. It is vested in a company of people. This company works very much as the mediæval guilds worked. It is a kind of school where apprentices are at first set to study drawing

The Colour Film

and painting as in an art class. There is a good deal to learn, a very special technique to master. The preparation of a cartoon is immensely laborious. Each movement of each figure requires a drawing for itself. The average rate of articulation on the moving screen is twenty-four images per second.

I have always regarded the Walt Disney Productions as one of the marvels of our time. I once visited a cage of comic-strip artists in New York. It was a small room on the forty-fourth floor of one of the more spectacular skyscrapers, and I think it held six or eight draughtsmen. When they were excited or bored they drew on the walls. The air seemed charged with despair. The mind totters at the very thought of that human machinery which builds up line by line the arabesques of those delirious fantasies of Mickey Mouse. Even more impressive is the thought of the strange master-mind which conceived originally such impossibilities of Nature.

In the early days of the productions there was a very able lieutenant called Ub Iwerks. For some reason he separated himself, and made a sort of rivalry about a frog, but it came to nothing.

The early Disney cartoons, which I believe to be authentic Disney, are truly sensitive drawings charged with a rather pale bright colour, reminiscent of certain drawings by William Blake—the Milton series, for instance. For some time the cartoons continued on what might be called an even keel. No large displacement occurred, variety and invention kept high, and there were some surprising pictorial incidents which seemed nothing short of original. Exciting patterns made by enraged bees or indignant gnats. Lovely little arabesques of clouds and birds. Each "symphony" brought new gifts from this fertile source; not merely new flights of nonsense, but accompaniments of design which, apart from their descriptive power, were gems of pictorial fancy. From time to time there were lapses: rather obvious absurdities crudely illustrated. I credited these invariably to a different author or authors.

Actually, the development took place in this way. Disney gradually trained a large number of aides to carry out his ideas mechanically. Presently, however, the machine began to show signs of independent life, and these individual manifestations were allowed free expression within the general control. Sometimes this resulted in new and valuable contributions; now and then it tended to produce ideas of poorer quality rather crudely realised, but probably containing some element which made them popular with simple-minded audiences.

So far as colour was concerned, as I have remarked, for some time its quality did not seem to vary to a great extent. As the "machine" gained in intelligence, however, a considerable change began to take place. Roughly four hundred people work under Disney, and out of such a number new influences must arise. Unfortunately I am unable to specify at this point, so no analysis is possible. But I think it is quite clear that two distinct types of cartoon are now issued regularly from Walt Disney Productions. The first is a lapse in invention and a bore in colour. It usually concerns the interminable antics of kittens

The Colour Film 131

or rabbits. Perhaps it might be worth some psychologist's while some day to discover and describe the singular difference which exists, apparently, between the nonsense stimuli of various animals. Why has the mouse suddenly "stolen the picture" from all the animal kingdom? Why is irritability so inimitably expressed by a duck, of all creatures? Maybe it is

merely the Disney genius. In any case the cartoons of rabbits, kitten, and many of the babies, are less exciting than Mouse and Duck, and usually sentimental, particularly in colour.

The second type of cartoon has made immense strides. I am a little hazy about the order of the sequence, but I remember *The Band Concert* as something suddenly exceptional, to my eyes. The incident of the storm, from the moment the whirlwind begins, is a series of colour shocks. This was the first of many successful experiments in sound and colour pyrotechnics. Several occur during *The Polo Match*; more, I believe, during the extraordinary drama of the musical cities. The occasions of expressive colour are more than it is possible to remember. Perhaps the peak is reached in *Mickey's Garden*, a kind of surrealist extravaganza full of imagination, and heightened at every point by rich outrageous colour.

Walt Disney made his first Silly Symphony in 1933, when he adopted the three-colour process. But the problem of producing colour films from pictures where the colours are arbitrarily designed is a very different affair from actual colour photography which attempts to reproduce the natural colour of objects *in Nature*. In all cases where the camera is only required to photograph a designed picture at rest, colour reproduction is no very difficult matter. New improved processes are constantly coming forward. Apparently we are on the eve of a new development, but probably the technical experiments of Gasparcolor, the process originally contributed by Dr Bela Gaspar, the Hungarian chemist, about three years ago, carry us as far as anything yet known. The process, first worked out in Germany, was recently vested in an English company which has made some extremely lively advertising films now fairly widely distributed. Dr Gaspar's achievement was the perfecting of a new material, a film coated with three emulsion layers sensitised to three different spectral regions. By this a full three-colour continuous tone image is possible without the use of dyes or toning. Judging from the results I have seen, the Gasparcolor film is capable of really serious achievement in colour

The Colour Film

cinematography. Even so, from what I can understand, it is neither the chemist nor the mechanical inventor, but the artist who has said the last word on colour films.

III

It is a good many years ago now since I first saw the work of Len Lye at an exhibition of the Seven and Five Society at the Leicester Galleries. I was at once attracted by its unusual kind of life. It had a totally different life from any other of the exhibits. Most conspicuous of any quality was the sense of rhythm, but it had expressed itself somehow eccentrically—not in the tiresome sense, but in the way of utter independence. Len Lye is a New Zealander who came to England nine years ago. At the Brussels Exhibition in 1935 he exhibited one of his three films made for the G.P.O. film unit—*Colour Box*. It could be accommodated in no category, so one was made to fit it and it was awarded a special prize. That sort of thing is typical of this original artist.

His peculiar contribution consists in painting direct upon the celluloid film with cellulose paint. The process seems to me so simple, so interesting, that I will quote verbatim Lye's technical notes which were recently published in an article by him in *Life and Letters:*

> The colours used . . . were the colours in the Gasparcolor film stock it was printed on. These are the blue, yellow and red dyes existing in three layers on the film stock. They are subtracted and blended by printing lights. The camera used for shooting the film was an ordinary black-and-white camera without colour filters.

All pictorial matter was coloured black and white. Thus the colour palette was the ǎctual celluloid itself.

This was possible, as certain colour film systems resolve any selected colour into its blue, yellow and red constituents, which are recorded in black and white. If these black and white records of objects are thought of as densities of the blue, yellow and red dyes intended for that object, and if it is realised that it is possible to control the amount of dye by the amount of black, invested by paint or light on to the subject, then it will be seen that perfect control of colour is possible.

Len Lye conceives the colour film as a direct vehicle for colour sensation. I have studied his three G.P.O. films and I consider *Colour Box* to be a unique achievement, neat and finished. It was made by painting literally to music. The features of the musical form dictated, more or less, the pattern of the colour arabesque. The other films are both more complicated and less successful, but one—*The Rainbow*—is full of possibilities for development in its particular *genre*. Len Lye's aesthetic philosophy of colour and the film I have no space to discuss here. He believes, as I believe, that he holds in his hands a real power for legitimate popular entertainment. A new form of enjoyment quite independent of literary reference; the simple, direct visual-aural contact of sound and colour through ear and eye. Colour sensation.

What might not be done with colour films! If only the best intelligences of direction, photography and mechanics could collaborate with artists of sound and colour, that might make either an incalculable chaos, or a new world.

PART III
FILM INDUSTRY PROBLEMS

THE COURSE OF REALISM
By John Grierson

HERE is an art based on photographs, in which one factor is always, or nearly always, a thing observed. Yet a realist tradition in cinema has emerged only slowly. When Lumière turned his first historic strip of film, he did so with the fine careless rapture which attends the amateur effort to-day. The new moving camera was still, for him, a camera and an instrument to focus on the life about him. He shot his own workmen filing out of the factory and this first film was a "documentary." He went on as naturally to shoot the Lumière family, child complete. The cinema, it seemed for a moment, was about to fulfil its natural destiny of discovering mankind. It had everything for the task. It could get about, it could view reality with a new intimacy; and what more natural than that recording of the real world should become its principal inspiration?

I remember how easily we accepted this in the tender years of the century when our local lady brought to our Scottish village the sensation of the first movies; and I imagine now it was long before the big towns like Edinburgh and Glasgow knew anything about them. These, too, were documentaries, and the first film I saw was none other than Opus 2 in the history of cinema—the Lumière boy eating his apple. Infant wonder may exaggerate the recollection, but

I will swear there was in it the close-up which was to be invented so many years later by D. W. Griffith. The significant thing to me now was that our elders accepted this cinema as essentially different from the theatre. Sin still, somehow, attached to play-acting, but, in this fresh new art of observation and reality, they saw no evil. I was confirmed in cinema at six because it had nothing to do with the theatre, and I have remained so confirmed. But the cinema has not. It was not quite so innocent as our Calvinist elders supposed. Hardly were the workmen out of the factory and the apple digested than it was taking a trip to the moon and, only a year or two later, a trip in full colour to the devil. The scarlet women were in, and the high falsehood of trickwork and artifice was in, and reality and the first fine careless rapture were out.

Thinking back over the years of development, fresh air and real people do appear for periods at a time. Obviously the economics of production in the early days were more cheaply served by the natural exterior. Till we learned to create our own sunlight, the heavenly variety was cheaper; until we mastered the art of miniature and dunning and back projection, it was cheaper to take the story to a natural location than the other way round. And the effect was to give not only naturalism to the setting but naturalism to the theme. One remembers the early Danish school which exported so many films before the War; later the Swedish school with its noble exploitation in photography and drama of the Swedish light; the early English school of *Coming Thro' the Rye*, and the early American school of the *Great Train Robbery*, slapstick and the Westerns. There was fresh air in all of them, but, more importantly, there was some reflection of ordinary life in the drama. In the *Great Train Robbery* the engineers and telegraph men were contacts with the real thing, and unimportant as they now seem, it was a long time before they cropped up again. Once inside the studio the tendency of the cinema was to make the most of its powers of artifice, graduating from the painted backcloths and wobbly colonnades to the synthetic and more or less permanent near-realism of three-ply, plaster and painted glass. The supers like *Dante's Inferno*, and the highly expansive struggles for expression in a new medium which characterised the silent epics—those sweeping movements, those cosmic gestures—struck the keynote of the new art.

Cinema, I am inclined to think, has been from the first not the guttersnipe we all suppose, but something of a prig. It was not Zukor, clever little man as he may be, who first thought of attaching famous players to famous plays. The grand people of the French and British theatres had been gesturing to the studio roof for years before, and always in the grandest of causes: dealing with the destinies of Julius Caesar twice, King Lear thrice and Hamlet six times before poor Zukor had begun to think about the cinema at all. Those early days produced forty versions of Shakespeare—Dante, Napoleon and Marie Antoinette scattering—with a gusto for celebrity to which even silence proved no obstacle. So far from the latter-day Copperfields and Romeos representing a special advance of the cinema into cultural grounds, they merely show us back at the old and original stand. We may have whored in our time, but we have always been snobs at heart. Here, the higher economics. Big names and celebrated subjects brought attention, and attention brought money. They were easier to sell, for salesmen had not yet learned the art of giving cosmic importance to nonsense and nonentities. But, driven by economics into artifice, the cinema has stayed there for other equally effective reasons. It has never been quite sure of itself, never quite believed in its separate and original destiny. This, no doubt, is the price we have paid for being a new art, but the fact that we have been so largely in the hands of international traders and salesmen, may have operated too. Great qualities they have brought: fervour and excitement to the salesmanship of cinema and a certain extravagance to our spectacle. But social confidence and an easy acceptance of the right to social observation could hardly be claimed for many of those otherwise brilliant men who have built up the cinema. *Esprit* they have had, but hardly spirit. The reason may lie in the international salesman's alienation by nature from the basic life of the countries he exploits, but the factor is there, still haunting us and inhibiting us in every studio.

Be this as it may, the long neglect of the cultural world, and the absence of certain upper social strata from its nickelodeons and palaces, has confirmed in the cinema a lackeyish spirit which has put a premium on established celebrity and prevented the thought of discussing any issues close to the public life. Even now, when kings and princes sidle, like their servants, into the dress circle, and Mayfair socialites crowd the free buffets of West End premières, we film folk have not yet lost our fear of the ordinary. We would sacrifice our life for it and, so far as the British cinema is concerned, have. It is said of one of our best-known producers that before each production runs the ghost of a Mayfair audience. Great help it has been to realism. To exploit the powers of natural observation; to build a picture of reality; to bring cinema to its destiny as a social commentator, inspirator and art; to make it bite into the time and, from its independent vantage, contribute to the articulation of the time—that, one may imagine, has been difficult in the circumstances.

Here is the key to any consideration of the realist cinema. It explains why, for the most part, we have clung to artifice and the synthetic. It explains the particular and especial diffidence of our British cinema people towards the local censor and why poor dear censor Wilkinson, with his Blake's poetry and his beloved pre-Raphaelites, has, in the jungle of Wardour Street, the strength of ten. Great figure he is, for on his charming old shoulders he carries the burden of our servility and our shame. Created by the Trade as an image of gratuitous fright, it is not surprising that his slogan of "No Controversy"—which to philosophy and all the world is "No Reality"—is abjectly obeyed.

This lackeyism explains, too, why there are so many sore heads in Wardour Street to-day. For America has at least developed, and her films are rolling in, touching reality at last. The younger and braver generation of the Zanucks has begun to speak. We are mentioning unemployment, taking a stand on injustice, doing a little here and there to scourge the follies of our time. We are at last beginning to mention life as it is ordinarily lived. We are touching religion which is banned from us and mentioning blessedly the name of God. We are discussing in *March of Time* the problems and controversies of our generation. Heads, as I say, are sore. An innocent account of the League of Nations is emasculated. A film about Peace is stopped in its tracks, and only the greater spirit and sense of social responsibility of the newspapers secures its release. There is a strident note of distress in a dozen quarters because a film about nutrition merely says what every national newspaper has already printed, and political ward-heelers interfere and threaten. Worried we are, even in this day and age, and I fear will be more so as this reality grows. It will take a long time to exorcise our craven beginnings.

So, looking down the history of the actuality films, of what has seemed on the surface most natural and most real, there has been, until very recently, a lack of fibre. From the beginning we have had newsreels, but dim records they seem now of only the evanescent and the essentially unreal, reflecting hardly anything worth preserving of the times they recorded. In curiosity one might wish to see again the Queen's Jubilees and the Delhi Durbars—with coloured coats that floated in air a full yard behind the line of march —the Kaiser at manœuvres and the Czar at play.

The Course of Realism 143

Once Lenin spoke, here and there early aeroplanes made historic landings and war cameras recorded, till war cameras record again, the vast futility of the dead. Exceptional occasions, yes, and the greatest shot I ever saw came out of it with the *Blücher* heeling over and the thousand men running, sliding, jumping over the lurching side to their death—like flies. A fearful and quiet shot. Among the foundation stones, the pompous parades, the politicians on pavements, and even among the smoking ruins of mine disasters and the broken backs of distressed ships, it is difficult to think that any real picture of our troubled day has been recorded. The newsreel has gone dithering on, mistaking the phenomenon for the thing in itself, and ignoring everything that gave it the trouble of conscience and penetration and thought.

But something more intelligent has already arrived. It has crashed through from the America that succeeded the slump and learned with Roosevelt the simple braveries of the public forum. It is called *The March of Time* to-day, but to-morrow, so strong is the growth, so strong the need and so different the younger generation which handles cinema, it will be called by a dozen names—Window on the World, World Eye, Brave New World, and what not. It may or may not be significant that *March of Time* is of all adventures in cinema the most patently native and American. Certainly it does what the other news records have failed to do. It gets behind the news, observes the factors of influence and gives a perspective to events. Not the parade of armies so much as the race in armaments; not the ceremonial opening of a dam but the full story of Roosevelt's experiment in the Tennessee Valley; not the launching of the *Queen Mary* but the post-War record of British shipping. All penetrating and, because penetrating, dramatic.

There, if anywhere to-day, a chapter is being written in the realist use of the cinema. Only three years old, it has swept through the country, answering the thin glitter of the newsreels with nothing on the face of it more dramatic than the story of cancer research, the organisation of peace, the state of Britain's health, the tithe war in the English shires, the rural economy of Ireland, with here and there a bright and ironic excursion into Texas centennials and the lunatic fringes of politics. In no deep sense conscious of the higher cinematic qualities, it merely carries over from journalism into cinema, after thirty-eight years, something of that bright and easy tradition of free-born comment which the newspaper has won and the cinema has been too abject even to ask for. There are proper limits, it is true, to freedom of speech which the cinema must regard. Its power is too great for irresponsible comment, when circulations like *March of Time's* may run to nine thousand theatres across an explosive world. But it seems sensible for the moment that *March of Time* has won the field for the elementary principles of public discussion. The world, our world, appears suddenly and brightly as an oyster for the opening: for film people—how strangely—worth living in, fighting in and making drama about. More important still is the thought of a revitalised citizenship and of a democracy at long last in contact with itself.

The Course of Realism 145

In easier fields tne actuality film has found a larger career, and the easier the more brilliant. Whenever observation has been so detached from the social theme as to raise no inhibition, its place on the screen has been assured. Films disclosing scenery and the more innocuous habits of mankind have come by the thousand, beautiful in photography, idyllic in atmosphere, though never till latterly exciting in substance, each with its Farewell to So-and-So raising a pleasant ripple on the art's nostalgia. Finer still, more skilled in observation, because farther from wretched mankind, there has been the long and brilliant line of nature films. Studies of bird life, life under the sea, microscopic, slow-motioned and speeded-up adventures in plant life: how beautiful they have been, with Bruce Woolfe, Mary Field and Percy Smith staking a claim for England better than any: more continuous in their work, less dramatic at all costs than either the Americans or the Germans, more patient, analytic and in the best sense observant. Here, if anywhere, beauty has come to inhabit the edifice of truth. Nor could there be any obstacle to the highly efficient analysis in slow-motion of what happened to bullets, golfers' swings and labourers at work. In these matters of utilitarian observation cinema has built up a wide field of service, helping the research man, as it brilliantly did in the film observations on cancer research by Dr. Canti at Bart's, helping equally the industrialist and the salesman. But the devil of reality has even then not been content. Ruttman for Germany, Flaherty for America, Eisenstein and Pudovkin for Russia, Cavalcanti for France, and

F

myself, shall I say, for Britain, we have taken our cameras to the more difficult territory. We have set up our tripods among the Yahoos themselves, and schools have gathered round us. In fifteen years our realist showing, if secondary to the main growth of cinema, assumes a certain bravery.

Flaherty adoped one gambit with *Nanook of the North*. By profession an explorer with a long and deep knowledge of the Eskimos, he conceived in his simple way the notion of making a story about people he knew—not foisting, studio fashion, a preconceived story on a background for the decorative quality it added, but taking his story from within. *Nanook of the North* took the theme of hunger and the fight for food and built its drama from the actual event, and, as it turned out, from actual hunger. The blizzards were real and the gestures of human exhaustion came from the life. Many years before, Ponting had made his famous picture of the Scott expedition to the South Pole, with just such material; but here the sketch came to life and the journalistic survey turned to drama. Flaherty's theory that the camera has an affection for the spontaneous and the traditional, and all that time has worn smooth, stands the test of twenty years, and *Nanook*, of all the films that I have seen— I wish I could say the same for my own—is least dated to-day. The bubble is in it and it is, plain to see, a true bubble. This film, which had to find its finance from a fur company and was turned down by every renter on Broadway, has outlived them all.

Moana, which Flaherty made afterwards, added the same thought to Samoa. *White Shadows, Tabu,*

The Course of Realism 147

Man of Aran and *Elephant Boy* succeeded. But it was no wonder that Hollywood doubted his outlook. In *White Shadows* and *Tabu* they saw to it that a director of the other and approved species accompanied him. *White Shadows* and *Tabu* were, therefore, not quite Flaherty and were none the deeper for it. Poor Hollywood. No stars to draw the crowd, no love-story, not much to whet an appetite ballyhoo'd into a vicious selectivity—only the fight against hunger, only the bravery of the tattoo, only—in Aran—the timeless story of man against the sky. They have been all too novel for a showmanship built on garish spectacle and a red-hot presentation of the latest curves. Flaherty might well call for a new and maturer language of salesmanship which will articulate the wider and deeper ambitions of the cinema, for the old salesmanship has served him and all of us pretty badly. He might well, with such high authorities as Ned Depinet and Sam Goldwyn, demand a segregation of the audience, for this insane cluttering of all species of audience, taste and mood together, has completed the evil. The sales machine is mentally geared to take us everywhere, or not at all.

The position of the Flaherty species of realism is best evidenced in his latest film, *Elephant Boy*, a film made from Kipling's "Toomai of the Elephants" and done in conjunction with the studio-minded Korda of London Films. *Elephant Boy* begins magnificently. Toomai is set on the back of the highest elephant of all Mysore: in his youth and innocence giving a dignity to the Indian people one has never seen before on the screen. One is prepared for anything. The great herd of wild elephants is signalled. There are expectations of a jungle more exciting than the jungle of *Chang*, and of a relationship between man and nature as deep again as *Nanook*. With its synthetic spectacle of studio camp scenes and West End voices it brings the film at every turn to an artificial, different plane. It comes between the boy and the jungle, and the full perspective of reality is not realised. They say an elephant will go mad on the death of his master and that he will go more mysteriously mad *just before* the death of his master. Nothing of this. Synthesis steps in, and an actor, in a fake beard, lashes the elephant to give a more Occidental motive for madness. The jungle might have been with its thousand eyes the image of all young and ardent odysseys. Nothing of this either. The film drives on under the last of the synthesists to the mere circus excitements of an elephant hunt.

With *Elephant Boy*, realism along the Flaherty lines has struck a triple obstacle: in producer, salesman and exhibitor. The studio people insist on a species of drama more familiar and more dear to them than the fate of a native in the jungle. The limitation of their scale of values is going to be difficult to overcome, unless a producer comes along who can wed studio and natural observation in a new and vital formula. The salesmen have learned brilliantly to sell what is already important or may easily be associated with the excitements of sex and sudden death. They show no great signs of equipping themselves for the special task which the quality of Flaherty's themes demands. The exhibitors naturally must

The Course of Realism 149

prefer what has already been built into the public imagination and there is no machine in this case to do the building.

We have been luckier in the field of realism which Cavalcanti initiated with *Rien que les Heures*, Ruttman continued with *Berlin*, and some of us have developed on more deliberate sociological lines in the British documentary. The basis of this other realism is different from Flaherty's. We neither attempted so large a scale in our film making, nor did we go so far for our themes. Limiting our costs, we have not had to struggle so wearily with sales organisations; and we have, from the first, created a large part of our circulation outside the theatres altogether.

Rien que les Heures came later than *Nanook* by five years and was the first film to see a city through the turn of the clock. Paris was cross-sectioned in its contrasts—ugliness and beauty, wealth and poverty, hopes and fears. For the first time the word "symphony" was used, rather than story. Cavalcanti went on to the more ambitious *En Rade*, like Flaherty taking his "story from within" on the dockside at Marseilles, but the symphony approach had a lasting influence. Ruttman carried on the idea in a still more whirling round of day and night in *Berlin*. No film has been more influential, more imitated. Symphonies of cities have been sprouting ever since, each with its crescendo of dawn and coming-awake and workers' processions, its morning traffic and machinery, its lunch-time contrasts of rich and poor, its afternoon lull, its evening dénouement in sky-sign and night club. The model makes good, if similar, movie. It had at least the effect of turning the tide of abstraction in the German cinema and bringing it back to earth. It initiated the tradition of realism which produced such admirable films as *Mutter Krausen* and *Kameradschaft*, and it set a mark for amateurs the world over.

   The British effort, while it owes everything to the Cavalcanti initiative—latterly joining forces with Cavalcanti himself in the development of sound—has been less aesthetic and more social in its approach. The shape of *Drifters*, the first of the British documentaries, was, for all its difference of subject, closer to Eisenstein than to Cavalcanti or Ruttman. Though each chapter was a deliberate study in movement, the film took good care to lead up to and stage an event. More important still, as I have come to consider, it had a theme—the ardour and bravery of common labour—and simple themes of the same sociological bearing have served us ever since, giving each new slice of raw material a perspective and a life, leading us in each new adventure of observation to a wider and more powerful command of medium and material alike. *Drifters* seems simple and easy now, though I remember the effort it took to convince showmen of the time that an industrialised fishing fleet might be as brave to the sight as the brown sails of sentiment and that the rigours of work were worth the emphasis of detail. This, after all, was before machinery had become "beautiful" and the workaday life was fit material for the screen. Behind us were hundreds of industrial films which industrialists had sponsored in pride and film companies had made in contempt, more often than not without script

The Course of Realism

or direction, on the dismal basis of so much a foot. Work and workers were so dull by repute that, I remember bitterly, two hundred feet in the pictorials was the dead limit which showmen would offer for anything of the kind. Any director worth his salt was so busy trying to make the limelight of studio publicities that there was none so poor as to do reverence to the working theme.

This may explain why *Drifters*, simple film as it was, was so much of a *succès d'estime*, and why it so quickly became more of a myth than a film. It had the rarity value of opening, for Britain, a new vista of film reference. It may explain, too, why the workers' portraits of *Industrial Britain* were cheered in the West End. The strange fact was that the West End had never seen workmen's portraits before—certainly not on the screen. *Industrial Britain*, significantly, was hailed as a patriotic picture and is still one of the films most widely circulated for British prestige abroad. In anything we have done since, from the idyllic pictures of Scottish shepherds to the complex and more difficult cross-sections of shipyard, airlines, radio services, weather forecasts, night mails, international economics, etc., etc., we have been able to rely similarly, beyond renter and exhibitor alike, on the people, and their superior taste in realism. We have since that time put together some two hundred films of the documentary type and it is no longer so difficult to get into the theatres. The working theme and the civic reference contained in all of them are widely recognised for the aesthetic as well as for the national character they have brought to the British cinema.

But the welcome, as might be expected, is not unanimous. When the posters of the Buy British Campaign carried for the first time the figure of a working-man as a national symbol, we were astonished at the Empire Marketing Board to hear from half a hundred Blimps that we were "going Bolshevik". The thought of making work an honoured theme, and a workman, of whatever kind, an honourable figure, is still liable to the charge of subversion. The documentary group has learned freely from Russian film technique; the nature of the material has forced it to what, from an inexpert point of view, may seem violent technical developments. These factors have encouraged this reactionary criticism; but, fundamentally, the sin has been to make the cinema face life; and this must invariably be unwelcome to the complacent elements in society. Documentary, like all branches of realism, has suffered from the inhibitions of the trade, and the inhibitions have in due course been exploited by the more irresponsible representatives of the political world.

All the documentary directors have at one time or another felt the pressure of this criticism from outside. We have not only had to fight our material—new and therefore difficult as it is—but time and again there has been an attempt to apply that narrow and false yard-stick of party-political value referred to by Paul Valéry[1] which is the death of art and the death of all

---

[1] "Political conflicts distort and disturb the people's sense of distinction between matters of importance and matters of urgency. What is vital is disguised by what is merely a matter of well being; the ulterior is disguised by the imminent; the badly needed by what is readily felt. All that touches practical politics is necessarily superficial."

The Course of Realism 153

true national education. It may therefore be worth recalling that our British documentary group began not so much in affection for film as in affection for national education. If I am to be counted as the founder and leader of the movement, its origins certainly lie in sociological rather than aesthetic aims. Many of us after the War (and particularly in the United States) were impressed by the pessimism that had settled on Liberal theory. We noted the conclusion of such men as Walter Lippman, that because the citizen, under modern conditions, could not know everything about everything all the time, democratic citizenship was therefore impossible. We set to thinking how a dramatic apprehension of the modern scene might solve the problem, and we turned to the new wide-reaching instruments of radio and cinema as necessary instruments in both the practice of government and the enjoyment of citizenship. It was no wonder, looking back on it, that we found our first sponsorship outside the trade and in a Government department, for the Empire Marketing Board had, from a governmental point of view, come to realise the same issue. Set to bring the Empire alive in contemporary terms, as a commonwealth of nations and as an international combine of industrial, commercial and scientific forces, it, too, was finding a need for dramatic methods. For the imaginative mind of Sir Stephen Tallents, head of that department, it was a quick step to the documentary cinema.

Sir Stephen Tallents would refer to Henry the Navigator and the School of Navigation by which he opened up the New World, and he would point to film, radio, poster and exhibition as the sextant and compass which would manœuvre citizenship over the new distances. It may be a long time before we enjoy again the freedom of treatment that he inspired. We brought in Flaherty from America and Cavalcanti from France to strengthen our hands; the Russian films were run at the E.M.B. before they even reached the Film Society, and Cabinet ministers argued our theories. We were encouraged in every experiment which would help us to develop the new art. But the E.M.B. passed, and only the film section carried on its belief in the new instruments of civic enlightenment. The parochial voices of immediate departmental needs could at last be heard, and were. To-day the inspiration is strong at the Post Office, but much less strong where it could be nationally more useful: in Agriculture, Health, Transport and Labour. The flame lit at the Empire Marketing Board has dimmed, and the documentary film looks more and more outside the Government departments—to the vast operations of oil, gas, electricity, steel and chemicals, to the municipal and social organisations, and to the journalistic treatment of public problems on *March of Time* lines.

It may seem a pity that others will reap the full benefits of a medium which the Government service discovered but which it has not been quite inspired enough to mature. Names like Wright, Rotha, Elton, Legg, Taylor, Watt, Spice and Shaw came out of it, and they represent together an outlook which, uniquely in the world of cinema, is as deeply based in public as aesthetic effort. Personally I regret the

Government retreat, for, as I know after ten years, no service is so great or inspiring, and particularly for film makers, as a service which detaches itself from personal profit. It frees one's feet for those maturing experiments which are vital to the new art. It makes a daily bravery of what, under British commercial film conditions, is a dull little muddle of private interests and all too personal vanities. If I emphasise this British documentary overmuch it is because I know it best; and it serves as well as any school to indicate a social approach to the cinema which is springing up universally. The young men are taking command and, conscious of the problems of the day, are coming closer to the world without and to realism, resolved to give to cinema that commanding position in public description which is so well within its grasp.

The Russians, after a brilliant period in which the Revolution was starkly relived and all its triumphs registered, have found it more difficult to come to grips with Peace. The realistic powers of *Potemkin*, *End of St Petersburg*, *Ten Days that Shook the World* and *Storm over Asia* have been barely matched in *The General Line* and *A Simple Case*. Conscious of the weakness, there was for a time a tendency to slip back to the old victories, and *Storm over Mexico*, *The Deserter*, *Chapayev* and *We from Kronstadt* are all, in this sense, epics of nostalgia. Conviction has been lacking in the themes of peace. *Earth* was beautiful, but only managed to melodramatise the issue between peasant and kulak. *The Road to Life*, with its story of reformed strays, was in a Y.M.C.A. tradition of patronage. It has seemed, in the intermediate period of the last few years, that the technique of mass energies and significant symbols, suitable for the stress of revolution, only embarrass the quieter issues of a peace-time life, which is of necessity more domesticated and personal. The technique is changing in younger hands. The new films like *Men and Jobs* seem ordinary against the old fireworks and are deplored widely as representing an abject surrender to Hollywood. Possibly it was for this reason that *Men and Jobs* was turned down by the London Film Society. A larger view may suggest a larger issue.

Russia, like every other country, is coming closer to the common life and, unspectacular as its present films may seem in comparison with the old days, it is nearer the mark than most. With the United States it remains the most exciting of the film countries, capable of anything. For America has been changing front with a vengeance. It may not understand the realism of Flaherty, but another realism it has been building up, of a power and quality which must affect film production everywhere. The tradition of the epics—of *The Covered Wagon, Iron Horse, Pony Express, North of '36*, in one line, and of *The Birth of a Nation* and *Isn't Life Wonderful*, in another—has flowered again in the national renaissance which has succeeded the slump. It is difficult to know why it failed for a time. One may blame equally the complacency of the golden years which preceded 1929 and the alien invasion which succeeded the success of *Vaudeville*. There was certainly a sudden end to the epics and to those small town comedies of Cruze and Langdon which kept Hollywood so close to America, and only the desolate sophistication of Lubitsch and his American imitators succeeded.

To-day there are remarkable developments. Most significant of these is the rise of the small-part player to a degree of vitality and importance which he does not enjoy in any other country, save in Russia. Call-boys and typists, garage hands and lorrymen have been mobilised behind the star and there is a new contact with the ordinary. With every year since 1930 the films themselves have become braver and more real, as though the old men were out and the young men in. In films like *42nd Street* the element of realism has appeared as only a more detailed and observant treatment of the old romantic set-up, but there has also been an eager absorption of contemporary problems and materials in the American scene. However tenderly the more difficult problems have been handled, they have not been avoided. Prison life, the plague of gangsterism, the new police, unemployment, lynching and the secret societies, the New Deal, finance and Hollywood itself have been inspiring writer and director alike. Stories of medicine and research, aviation and labour have been added in good measure.

Breaking off to see *The Good Earth* just in from America, with its long vista'd story of Chinese peasantry, its trial by wind and drought and plague of the commonest and most persisting loyalty of mankind, its deep-laid sympathy for what is ordinary yet so spectacular because it is linked with the elements, the blank outlook of the British film seems for the moment blanker than before. We stretch back into things that were and forward into things to come; we have musicals and farces galore; but there is none of this other thing, not a whicker of it. There is Flaherty, as of old, freed from the shackles of the studio and bringing back his jungle realities, but just as surely shackled again on his return with studio sahibs and Oxford-accented head-men. There is Gracie Fields doing her Saturday night turn in a Lancashire parlour, and George Formby following, and the East End of Max Miller debunking propriety in a check suit and grey bowler. The English music hall, at least, is in the line of direct observation—even when it breaks through and takes charge of the high history of *Henry VIII*. There is the documentary, that too in the real line, but tight, tidy and removed in its own separate finances, and too wisely mistrustful of the commercial scramble to join hands with it. There is John Baxter with films that are sentimental to the point of embarrassment; but they happen to be about real people's sentimentalities.

These are all that we have to set against the American wave of realism. Such flags of vitality as are flown over the British cinemas, in spite of quotas, city millions and alien adventurers, are still, even increasingly, American flags. One reason lies with the foreigners. We have too many of them, cosmopolites of the world's cities, to whom Lancashire is only Gracie Fields's hundred-thousand a year and the men of the Clyde are not even a whisper in consciousness. How could it be otherwise? If they were artists, they might sense the *condition humaine* across whatever distance of nationality, but they are only promoters.

The Course of Realism 159

And we let it happen that promoters so distant in mind from the British scene govern the subject-matter of our films. Yet I do not blame the foreigners altogether. They are ably abetted in their unrealities by their English contracts. The West End stage, for all the presence of Bridie and O'Casey, has lost the accent of the people; and the music hall is its last oasis in an Oriental desert of picture palaces. As for the literary men, half a dozen have power together to blow the unreality to smithereens, but they are not so much in love with reality as to think the explosion worth their effort. The vanity of fantastic fees and flattering attentions is no irritant.

But even these factors are consequents rather that causes. At the back of the scene is a weakness in contemporary English life which those who, like myself, have come to it from the outside, never cease to feel. The social and aesthetic leadership, as perhaps befits an old, and in itself, brilliant tradition, has long lost that proud contact with simple labour which characterises the younger countries, and particularly America. The Labour movement, from which great aesthetic influence might have been expected, has only contrived to join forces with the old leadership. Artists who, by destiny, are the solvents of such detachment, remain, on the whole, a peculiar people in England. Following social rather than aesthetic distinctions, they reflect only a distance from the reality they should serve. The significant dramatists to-day, when they are not Americans, are, not strangely, Irishmen, Scotsmen and far Northern provincials, deriving from traditions in which contact with the ordinary life is closer and less ashamed.

Considering the forces of inferiority and snobbery which already by circumstance reside in the cinema, I should conclude that the outlook is black indeed for the English film. But I think there are two or three minor loopholes for the artists who would follow the American example. The documentary loophole is one. If the documentary directors will only realise the factors arrayed against realism in England and not stake their hand too high, they may presently bring their realism to the range of full-scale drama. Playing for the second feature position, or at most for the humble limit of, say, twenty thousand pounds, they may get through; and if they do they will work a miracle and change the entire situation. The only factors that stand to prevent them are that documentary directors, by bad social analysis, may expect too much. Or they may be taunted or flattered into the studios without securing friendly finance and find themselves bound to the old bad policies. Look then, I suggest, to the cheapies and the quickies—where the contempt of the large-scale promoter is a guarantee of freedom from his unrealities—for the more adventurous future of the British film. If these fail the only other loopholes I see are with Gracie Fields in comedy—though she is off to America—with Hitchcock in melodrama, and with patriotic epics like *The Great Barrier*.

It may or may not be part of the English nature —I carefully avoid calling it the British—that its contacts with reality should always be disguised as

The Course of Realism

contacts with something else. If so, the sooner we make our English films about Ireland, Scotland and Canada the better, for anything so alien to the English mind must inevitably classify and pass as romance. But I do not despair. All over the country critics and leaders of opinion have become conscious of the lack I have indicated and are hammering away at the forces which govern our films. The championship by members of the Moyne Committee of a cinema closer to the national life is particularly significant. With such support, and in spite of all the artifices, inhibitions, inferiorities, snobberies, censorships, alien controls and misguided party-political interventions, the British cinema may yet come, in realism, alive.

BRITISH FILMS: TO-DAY AND TO-MORROW

By Alexander Korda

THE steady progress in popularity of the cinema is one of the outstanding phenomena of modern times and one for which, by the very nature of things, there is no parallel in history. To the student of social science the fact that to-day, in this country alone, nearly nineteen million people a week visit the cinema must bring an increasing realization of the hold it has upon the public; further, it must set him thinking over its cumulative effect upon the mass-imagination. Nor can this addiction to cinema-going be dismissed, on the grounds of transitory amusement, from the reckoning of those for whom something which can almost be described as a national habit must of necessity be of significance.

Everywhere in the world to-day, where a jealous watch is kept over national ideas and aspirations, the propaganda value of the cinema is closely scrutinized and almost scientifically measured. The social problem, however, is but one facet of this multilateral thing.

In a world where the study of economics has replaced that of the more liberal arts, the present and future problems of a form of entertainment that has become an important industry, take on a significance undreamt of by its pioneers.

Unless publishers, against their better interests,

British Films To-day

have conspired to delude us, it is reasonable to suppose that the increasing number of books about the cinema is definite evidence that its problems are attracting the serious attention of the public. That this should be so is both inevitable and useful.

Anything which may serve towards a clearer understanding of the problems which beset a British or, indeed, any producer to-day, should in the long run go some way to solve those problems in so far as they are soluble. Any lead from the public, any unequivocal expression of opinion, must be invaluable to a profession that serves capricious taste. It must indeed be remembered that of the four "estates" which compose the realm of films, the producers, renters, exhibitors and the public, it is the public that has the last word. In fact, one might reasonably say that no clearer example of effective democracy has ever existed. In no other sphere has the people so great a power of veto. In a world in which artists, actors, musicians and writers abound (all by tradition and in their own reckoning arbitrators, not arbitrated upon), the voice of the people, of the man and more particularly of the woman in the street is, for all practical purposes, the voice of God; and the philosophy to be held, on pain of bankruptcy, is that of the greatest happiness of the greatest number.

While in all ages and places the artist or the impresario has had to face an economic problem, it has usually been either a personal problem or at least a comparatively limited liability. Not so with the man whom the world is to-day pleased to call the film-magnate. A generation of development that has given him almost the whole of mankind for audience has set him pondering over budgets that add up to millions. Circumstances have turned the impresario into the industrialist, and, at times, with results that are unfortunately too obvious, have tempted the would-be industrialist to become the impresario.

It is inevitable, in a world now as keenly competitive as it has ever been since the dawn of the industrial era, that the spirit of competition should be reflected in the industry of the cinema. In this struggle the test by which the producer stands or falls is the test of entertainment. In the early days when people went to the cinema because there was still a touch of novelty in it, and on through the years before the mass of audiences grew so discriminating, it was easier to persuade them to take what was offered. Those days are over. To-day the audiences shop, as the expression goes, for their entertainment. Theatres have been multiplied exceedingly; production companies also have multiplied, and we who in England have tried to build, and have succeeded in building, a national film industry have done so in competition with a rival, the greatness of whose achievement we cannot fail to admire, firmly established in our midst.

Before, however, going on to discuss some of the problems that have grown out of our struggle to build up the British film industry, and before attempting to see how we should approach the future, it might be well to deal first of all with a question, often raised in the minds of those interested in the cinema, which has some psychological bearing on the different approaches to film production in different countries.

British Films To-day

This problem has its origin in what are generally taken to be the unhappy relations between art and commerce. On looking round the film industry to-day it would be impossible to find any producer worthy of the name who could be said to be entirely devoid of artistic instincts or at least of artistic aspiration. Sometimes the industrialist is more in evidence than the impresario. On the whole, however, it is reasonable to suppose that a film producer is what he is, and not a manufacturer of armaments or textiles, by virtue of some artistic quality. This quality is, of course, with very few exceptions, never enough to satisfy that dissentient group of critics which sees the film exclusively as an art, now—alas—being put to the basest uses. It is clear that the very nature of the commercial film separates the producer in all perhaps but sympathy from this element. Their arguments are not to be despised, their intentions not to be impugned, but their advice cannot be accepted for practice.

As has already been said, the final arbiter in the world of commercial films is not some elegant and cultured Petronius, but the man in the street. If the "little man" is not on your side, howsoever exalted may be your artistic dreams, they vanish with the filing of your petition in bankruptcy.

The point at which, however, the question of art becomes important is in its relation to that side of the producer's mind which is concerned in the presentation of a story, and, to no small extent, in the choice of the story. Of course the producer is supposed—if not popularly, at least by those who have a more intimate knowledge—to sit down and analyse the story or its form of presentation entirely in terms of entertainment value. It is undeniably true that a sound producer does devote very considerable attention to this point, but it is equally undeniable that he must be influenced by his taste—his flair. It is in these moments of decision that his personal outlook will influence the film for good or bad. In the last analysis it will be these personal notes or touches which justify or condemn him as a producer, just as it is out of their cumulative effect that the national industry receives its character. Here, however, is no place to discuss the interplay of factors—some as alien, on paper, as can be imagined—which go to make up that which is rightly defined as a British film, a Dutch film, an American film and so on. Suffice it to say that here in this definite yet elusive thing we have the substance of international competition—the national industry.

That the national industry in this country has recently passed through a time of reckoning is not of itself of any fatal or final significance. Fluctuations of fortune are inevitable.

What is of the utmost importance is that we should not lose heart. On the credit side there is much to look back on of which we can be justifiably proud. In the space of a comparatively few years, and in the face of what seemed insuperable odds, not only has the British film industry grown up on ambitious lines, but it has produced a number of films that have challenged comparison with the best. In addition to this, the industry has built itself homes which, again, for equipment and technical staffs can challenge the best. We have nothing to despair of or feel ashamed about in our record. If there has been any danger it may have been one of complacency.

Yet, all has not gone as well as it should. Why? The American market has not been captured to the extent some of us had hoped. Films have been made on the hopes of the profits to be obtained in the American market. These hopes have, in certain cases, not been realized. Why? Are we to suppose a definite attitude of hostility in the United States towards our films? Nothing could be farther from the truth, for in those cases, not so infrequent as the pessimist might imagine, in which our pictures have succeeded over there, nothing could exceed the warmth and generosity of the American Press or the unstinting praise of the American people. Appreciative, however, of this as we must be, it should be said also that American criticism of British films, when made, has not always been sound.[1]

One of those American periodicals which devotes space to a review of the position of British films maintains that while our films are on the whole efficient, they are imitative. They escape from narrow nationalism but have not become truly national. By importing American stars, directors and writers, we have embarked upon a false policy of imitation. We have tended to produce pseudo-American pictures the defects of which have been all too obvious to the American people. Our only hope of salvation is to make good English films, just as the Americans make

[1] On this subject compare Mr Kann's article.—EDITOR.

good American films. We are told, too, that there is not enough of England in our plans, and America wants to see England on the screen.

It is conceivable that these criticisms have not really hit the nail on the head. No film made during the past year by a major British company comes to my mind as imitative of America. Indeed, if we went by choice of subject alone we might easily reverse the criticism. *Mutiny on the Bounty, David Copperfield, Mary of Scotland, Little Lord Fauntleroy,* and a dozen others might more than prove a case against America.

Surely the answer lies deeper. On the whole it is true that the average man and woman in every country has certain fundamental feelings in common, and it is to these feelings that the average film must appeal. When a film has reached out to appeal to the Lowest Common Multiple—or, in a more flattering phrase, to the Highest Common Factor—in human emotion, then it will succeed all over the world. It must always be remembered, too, that in doing so it need lose nothing of the highest quality in human drama. The extent to which a British film resembles a Hollywood film, or the extent to which it is national, cannot matter beside the width of its universal human appeal. In any event, if we are going to develop further it is not by following advice (though to this we may always listen) but by working out our own salvation in our own way. It may be, finally, that this will bring us to where our friend the critic would have us. One thing is certain, no living man can tell. If he could the great game would be over.

In all this business of film making, nevertheless,

one thing remains true no matter how much we analyse ourselves or take to heart the words of our critics, and it is this. Statistics are only valid up to the moment of their compilation. They hold little or no guarantee for the future.

And what of the future? In thinking of measures to be taken, and in attempting to arrive at some practical understanding of the stern realities of the situation, we cannot do better, for our guidance, than turn to the recently published Report of the Committee appointed by the Board of Trade under the chairmanship of Lord Moyne to "consider the position of British films, having in mind the approaching expiry of the Cinematograph Films Act, 1927." Here in no uncertain light, and reflected as in a mirror, we are able to catch glimpses of our own defection.

Constantly at the back of our minds, as we face the future, there must be the incontrovertible fact of what the Report describes as the dominance of the United States' film industry. It must be our aim to meet in a spirit of honourable and fair competition rivals, who, the Report says, "through their superior opportunities have in the past produced, in general, better films than those made in this country. . . . We understand that there is at present no Press or public prejudice in the United States against good British films and we think it would be very unfortunate for the industries in both countries should any such prejudice ever arise." Quite frankly the Report points to the only solution for a penetration of the American market. It must be based primarily, if not solely, on high quality in British films.

This clear call to expand our markets by the improvement of our films is accompanied by sound practical advice on how to supplement our efficiency by setting our house in order. The following passage is one to be pondered and weighed:

> We were informed that the period of production of a film in the United States is appreciably less than for a comparable film in this country, and that the subsequent stages, from completion in the actual studio to the time when the film is available for public exhibition, are much less in America than here. Slower production and tardy release of British films clearly mean higher costs and a longer period before the capital involved can be recovered and made available for new productions. It was stated to us in evidence that one major American company has admitted that 80 per cent of the cost of its pictures is amortised within ninety days after its completion, and that in the case of most other American companies not less than 50 per cent of the cost is returned in the same period.
>
> Such facts show a marked contrast to the position in this country, where several weeks or even months elapse between completion of production and the trade show, and thereafter as much as nine or ten months may pass before the film is released for general exhibition. It has been calculated that, having regard to such facts as these, a given programme in this country involves the employment of 70 to 80 per cent more capital than the same programme in the United States. It appears to us that every effort should be made by those engaged in the industry so to improve administration as to shorten radically the period elapsing between commencement of production and availability for general public exhibition.

Until such time as the film industry in this country shall expand more fully at home and abroad it is natural that the questions of protection and quota should come up again for discussion. On this score the Report is equally definite. It insists, as a practical measure, on "the absolute necessity for legislative action to maintain and establish the industry."

It would, however, be a disservice to the British industry, and quite contrary to the tenor of the Moyne Report, if we were to seek to shelter completely behind legislation and protection.

Again, there could be no more serious setback to the British film industry than a retrenching from our world ambitions. To take this retrograde step would be a disaster to the industry economically. The theory that British pictures can be made for the British market alone is unsound.

Difficult times ahead there may be, but faced with courage they may prove to be a salutary period of discipline—that period of discipline which must be imposed upon every creative force, and without which it tends to dissipate itself.

The ultimate fate of the cinema is far from being decided. Its possibilities are as yet hardly touched upon. In all this talk of industry we may easily be ignoring intrinsic elements, the dynamism of which may slowly break through to reveal more of man to man than this pioneer generation can know of. Shall it be said of us that we had not the courage to believe?

THE FUTURE OF SCREEN AND STAGE

By Basil Dean

SOME ten years ago the screen found its voice. The voice was sometimes raucous, sometimes shrill, and almost always quite unintelligible, as was to be expected of the infant of such a parentage. Just before that time unkind critics had been openly predicting the early demise of the screen as a form of popular entertainment; and they produced copious sheets of statistics, verifying beyond all doubt this failing popularity. So it may be said that the screen was saved by the force of its own lungs.

It was at about that time, during one of my frequent visits to New York, that a prominent theatrical manager—actually the model for the character of "Billings" in *The Great Ziegfeld* film—invited me to a first public showing of the original Vitaphone Short Sound Films. Stars of the Metropolitan Opera gave excerpts from some of their more famous rôles. I shall never forget the impression which these first films, crude as they were, made upon my imagination; their effect was almost as thrilling as that other blessed emotion which those of us who pass our lives in what the Americans racily describe as "the show business" always feel in a greater or less degree when the footlights go up in a theatre and the overture begins. When the performance was over my friend asked my opinion as to the effect of the innovation upon our business. I replied that I thought it would be profound: that the effect of the addition of sound to screen entertainment would be to hand the business of acting for the screen back to the legitimate actor and the writing of screen plays back to creative authorship. Nothing that has happened during the past decade has tempted me to deny that careless prophecy, so eagerly reproduced in the New York papers as an advertisement of the latest scientific marvel.

But, just as before the innovation critics had begun to wonder about the future of the screen, so to-day the voice of criticism is heard once more. It is not for nothing that serious authors such as the late John Drinkwater have said they could envisage a time some twenty-five years hence when cinema entertainment as popular entertainment for the multitude may have ceased to exist. This is an extreme view, but the reason for it is not far to seek.

Certain factors are definitely in favour of its continuance in popular favour, as, for instance, the cheap prices, the comfortable seats, and the comparative ease with which the best talent that the screen has to offer can reach even the remotest patrons. But will the people tire eventually of the entertainment in itself? Will the immense popular favour which the film at present enjoys tell against it in the long run, and the constant repetition of the same fare, due to the scarcity of original material, induce surfeit and ultimately nausea? Upon the manner in which we meet and answer these general questions depends the lasting future of the film.

A brief examination of the source of inspiration of

film entertainment and of those who take part in it may help us. Many writers and critics of the film are guilty of loose thinking in this matter; they are disposed to mistake the shadow for the substance and to advance theories and utter preferences that are really matters of technique, and consequently have little to do with the fundamental issue of life or death for the film in itself. This is no new disease for critics of art; it is well known to have existed throughout the centuries. All "entertainment" must draw its inspiration from the well-springs of human conduct. No mere abstraction of thought can possibly last long in popular favour. The outcrop of propagandist theatre that invariably follows any social revolution is just as invariably doomed to disfavour and ultimate extinction. No man will dare to say that the revolutionary methods of the modern Russian theatre have exercised in their time an influence in any way comparable with the influence of the pre-revolutionary Moscow Art Theatre. Similarly, the Russian propagandist film has lost all practical influence upon the screens of the world. It will only recover its influence just so soon as it returns to the fundamental inspiration that we must all acknowledge.

If we keep this simple fact before us, then it is quite true to say, as so many critics are apt to say with an air of discovery that does not properly belong to the remark, that the cinema should not draw its inspiration from the theatre. The truth is that both theatre and cinema should draw their inspiration from humanity. So, when critics deplore the fact that a certain well-known subject (be it either play or novel) has been acquired for the screen—a common cliché this in film journalism—they are reasoning in loose fashion. For the original creation of Character is the thing of value. If in the process of transference to the screen the author's original conception has been lost, either through lack of understanding of his original values or a too determined effort to be different at all costs, the blame should be laid at the door of the maker of the film; the author should not be blamed for a mistake he has not committed, neither should the mishap be used as evidence that original authorship cannot be successfully transferred to another medium, perfectly understood and well disciplined to the ultimate aim of the author.

It is to be hoped that the cinema will develop many new ways of using its powerful medium to achieve the maximum of effect—which is technique in other words—but for its primary inspiration it cannot go deeper than humanity itself. Philosophically considered, there can be nothing original in screen subject-matter, for we are all bounded by the limits of human personality. But there do remain original ways of presenting the same argument. Therefore those of us who say the stage and the screen are interrelated are both right and wrong; it is probably more accurate to say that they are twin impulses springing from the same source and having the same motive.

The film that says in effect: "I am something entirely original and entirely superior, and it is quite impossible to reproduce the thoughts and the emotions that I express in any other art form," betrays the cardinal error of failing to acknowledge its parentage.

Similarly, the pedestrian film that follows slavishly the play or novel, and makes no attempt to explore the possibilities of the medium in which its ideas are to be expressed, is equally at fault. Again, the development of film technique for its own sake, even to the farthest point of originality, is an arid exploration, a brainstorm in the desert of intellectuality, and doomed to extinction. Those who profess to see in film technique something deep and esoteric, far transcending the much despised human values, will doubtless advance the same crop of arguments in support of their heresy when television begins to spread its wings and to soar to the dizzy heights of popular favour that undoubtedly await it. We need not worry unduly about this, except in so far as the exuberance of these fancy writers has tended to frighten original authorship away from the screen.

So we come to this question of original authorship, which is the legitimate human expression of the source of inspiration. The screen has undoubtedly been starved of this; and unless the deep well-springs of which I have written can be tapped, its future must undoubtedly be restricted and ultimately terminated. It is precisely the same thing in the theatre; a dearth of good original dramatic writing leads speedily to decay in the theatre. Immediately there is an outcrop of fine authorship the theatre starts again into life. So it is with the film. Authors have themselves to blame for this. In the early days they were too prone to regard the screen as a source of additional revenue. They left the translation of their original creations into the new medium to second-class brains. They grumbled, and rightly so, when their characters were misunderstood and travestied on the screen. They sensed a lack of originality in films. They decided that the screen was beneath serious consideration. Here they were wrong. The original author should try to master the means of expression so that all those hangers-on attached to every big studio, second-class brains from the creative point of view, do not succeed in fogging his original conception. No artist too lazy to master the technique of his medium can expect to achieve success in it. There is urgent need of British authorship on the British screen; and by British authorship I do not mean authorship that has been semi-Americanised, nor authorship that believes there is virtue in speed for its own sake, nor one that is ashamed of its very "Britishness," so to speak.

It is by reason of this fundamental source of inspiration that there is always hope for the British Film Industry until the day of the last film that is ever made; and I say this despite the immense technical superiority of American films. This technical superiority is not entirely qualitative; a good deal of it is quantitative. Because the American industry has at its door more than sixty-five per cent of the total English-speaking market, it has been able to acquire the best writers, actors, and technicians with which to build up an immense machine of efficiency. But have we not heard of Frankenstein? Is it not just possible that in the long run the very size and efficiency of this American output might defeat its own object? Was it not Andrew Lang who drew attention to the limited number of stories or plots available for the entertainment of mankind?

The problem for the actor is not dissimilar from the author's problem. The statement that has been made that no stage actor should be employed on the screen is just as devoid of justification as many of the other critical remarks to which I have referred. Both the stage and the screen actor must acknowledge the same source of inspiration. This inspiration is the audience; in other words, humanity. Quite obviously, the physical conditions profoundly affect the actor's technique in the two media. In the theatre the actor is separated from his audience by varying distances. Spectators seated in the stalls may be distant from him only a few feet. Even in the most intimate theatres there is generally some indication of an orchestra separating him from the nearest spectators; but those in the gallery are ten and twenty times that distance away. He must make his impression equally upon all his audience. This engenders a certain breadth of treatment and a development of his voice which upon the screen would appear as gross exaggeration. The tremendous magnification due to the use of the close-up obviously develops an entirely different type of technique.

But there are certain qualities developed by the performance in public that are essential for the good performance in any medium, not excepting broadcasting. This is not to say that these same qualities cannot be developed upon the screen without recourse to stage experience. But it is rare to find the actor who is entirely devoid of stage experience quite so

Screen and Stage

resourceful in his characterisations as one who has had a certain amount of experience before a living audience. Moreover, and this is an important point, there is little doubt that stage experience does teach the actor how to project his own personality in addition to expressing the ideas of his author. Again, the resourceful actor trained in public performance undoubtedly acquires an assurance of manner that can stand him in good stead when he faces that more silent but infinitely more exacting critic, the camera.

It is not always fully appreciated that standards of acting change with each succeeding generation. The actor attunes himself to the modes of life and methods of expression that are current in his generation. Just as Burbage would probably have been considered a bad actor by the audiences who acclaimed David Garrick, so David Garrick's triumphs would have appeared unjustified to the Victorians who thronged the auditorium of the Lyceum Theatre to applaud Henry Irving. It is no reflection upon the greatest actor of his day to say that Henry Irving and his methods would be shouted off the modern stage. Much of the extravagance of the earlier schools of acting was due to the poor visibility of the candle-lit stages of the time, which provided dim illumination for the leading actors in the centre of the stage whilst consigning the smaller parts literally to the outer darkness. This is also the origin of the less intelligent modern actor's persistent search for the centre of the stage for his more important scenes.

Undoubtedly the extreme visibility of the screen has profoundly affected the technique of its acting.

Moreover, precisely the same changes in that technique are noticeable as the evolution of the new form goes on from year to year. Much of the old silent film acting of yesterday is laughable nowadays; and the best film acting of this present age will undoubtedly be scorned by generations to come. Perhaps it is a merciful thing that the physical life of celluloid is not much more than fifty years, despite all the efforts of science to achieve some degree of permanence, for memory and romantic idealisation play a great part in maintaining the reputations of the great histrionic figures of the past. If the greatest performances of some of these shadowy figures could have been made permanent in celluloid form, then, as Hamlet says, "who shall 'scape whipping?" Recently I saw some of the earlier Chaplin comedies and I found them unbelievably tiresome. Yet there is no one, having seen and loved Chaplin's earlier successes, who when asked for his opinion does not call upon the rich store of his memory and find both enjoyment for himself and praise for that great comic genius in his recollections. Acting is an ephemeral thing always; it is best not to seek to make it permanent, but to encourage memory and imagination to maintain the reputations of the great ones in our hearts.

Although it is true to say that acting is purely a thing of its day, that does not relieve present-day actors from their manifest obligation to acquire the greatest possible efficiency of technique in so far as it has been revealed to their generation. Here we come to certain practical considerations which definitely hold back British screen acting from developing as it should. The volume of film production in this country is comparatively small. Hence the actor is compelled to rely upon both stage and screen acting for his livelihood. It often happens that he is performing in both media at the same time. The results are disastrous, and form a useful argument in the mouths of those who would say not only that stage and screen acting are utterly different, but that neither derives help or inspiration from the other.

The actor who works in the theatre and in the film studio at the same time is attempting an impossible task; he arrives at the film studio early in the morning fussed and irritable, and unless he be a kind of mental chameleon he is not properly attuned to the atmosphere of the day's work. Similarly, his performance in the theatre at night is hampered by thoughts of day-to-day difficulties in the studio; in neither medium can he give of his best and in both he is physically tired. This is the reason for the slow progress of the British stage actor in the British film studio. It is also in part an explanation of his more rapid progress when he goes to Hollywood, capital city of a film colony that thinks, talks, and breathes pictures. The ideal condition for the British actor would be for him to undergo stage training for a period in his earliest years and then, should he decide that his career lies upon the screen, to devote either the whole or set periods of his time to work in the studios. I say "set periods" advisedly, because I am one of those who believe that occasional appearances before living audiences even for the screen actor are eminently desirable. They have the effect of revivifying the actor, bringing him once more, so to speak, into touch with the living pulse of his audience.

On the other hand, much of the criticism that is levelled against British screen acting is unjustified, for the basis of comparison is almost always American acting in the same medium. This is a vastly different thing, for to begin with, the actors are not speaking the same language. Many British films are intolerably slow, but this slowness is not necessarily a fault of the actor; much of it is due to bad screen writing, particularly in relation to continuity, which is often slipshod and packed with irrelevant detail. On the other hand, attempts to make the British actor speak as rapidly as his American rival have disastrous results, for this intensely virile slangy speech is not our national medium, and if it were not for our inferiority complex in this matter of film production, attempts to reproduce the American method would have been sternly repressed long ago.

Upon this question of speed for speed's sake, rather like the academic discussion that eternally flutters the dovecotes of the art critics of "art for art's sake", much might be written; but it is interesting to note that the *tempo* of American pictures is not as universally fast as it was a few years ago. In other words, the not too original discovery has been made in Hollywood that there is a correct *tempo* for each subject and that sometimes the *tempo* should be the reverse of fast.

Just as it is true to say that good acting is a thing of its own generation and of no other, so it is equally true to say that the best acting retains the national characteristics of the country to which it belongs. The so-called international acting, beloved of the film magazines, is, to use an American vulgarism, "the bunk". The almost inexhaustible supplies of dramatic talent which exist in this country are constantly called upon by Hollywood; despite the Press ballyhoo, and despite the enormous material efficiency that goes to the polishing-up of the outward appearance of the women, euphemistically described as "grooming for stardom"—although why a phrase reminiscent of the stable and the horse-coper should be selected for this process may not be immediately apparent—the amount of genuine discovery or even genuine development of British-born talent by Hollywood is virtually nil. There is to be observed in the performances of the best of British artists, after they have spent some years in the film capital, a certain blunting of their characterisations, a drying-up of the rich juices of their personalities which, despite an undoubted increase in technical efficiency, seems to rob them of genuine individuality. They have become just film actors or film stars. This is most apparent in the case of outstanding artists in British Comedy, an outwardly robust but inwardly delicate plant that does not lend itself to transplanting.

But the last word has by no means been said upon this question of the correct way to develop screen personality and screen acting. In my view these should be developed upon national lines, just as I believe that British stories should best be made into British films and not into American ones, albeit with a pro-British flavour. The film that seeks to become international must first be convincingly national.

Deep in the life of every nation lies the inexhaustible material with which that nation's films should be written and acted. With each nation's film activity strong and resurgent in its own right we can march confidently forward upon the road to the future. When that day of real advance comes, let us hope we shall have turned our backs for ever upon a condition of overgrown and domineering internationalism that sooner or later must die of its own redundancy.

HOLLYWOOD AND BRITAIN—THREE THOUSAND MILES APART
By Maurice Kann

IT is characteristic of the motion picture industry that its structure makes slight concession to geography. The details of business administration must naturally bow to national customs, but the business or the art (or both) of producing, distributing and exhibiting films follows a pattern largely similar, in warp and woof, around the civilised world.

Because of the established and irrefutable superiority of the American product, and the business technique created around that product, it is understandable how and why the Hollywood impress has made itself felt wherever the motion picture finds an outlet. For America's continued predominance various reasons have been given. One of them traces to the World War and the inevitable neglect in Europe of what otherwise might have been an orderly progress in fields of endeavour normal to nations at peace.

This explanation, beyond successful counter-argument, is, of course, correct. Britain, once the post-War reconstruction period was well under way, found the breath to touch with a rekindled life her motion picture industry. When the opportunity came, the job was proceeded with at a furious gait, and with a vigour which, while it was lacking in major accomplishment, need make no apology for speed and extravagance.

In the intervening years, what had happened? Here was Hollywood, fat and contented and basking in the sunshine of a task far from its consummation, but, in its larger aspects, done with an extreme competence. The steady stream of American motion pictures continued to make progress on its way to the screens of eighty nations. American stars, long the most acceptable to an international audience, continued to maintain their hold. With the depression forgotten quickly in the rising economic flushes of 1936 and 1937, the film industry in America strode with seven-league boots to the levels of the pre-crisis period. In the face of restrictive legislation by foreign governments, the American product, nevertheless, managed to maintain the popularity which inevitably transforms itself into terms of pounds, francs and lire. Actually a competitor worthy of the truest steel.

This, then, is the gargantuan rival England has set out to meet and to conquer if she can. And what has been done on that score? There is not time, nor is it my purpose here, to delve into the long and chequered history of the Cinematograph Films Act of 1927. Yet, the occasion is fitting to discuss it and to point out some truths inescapable about its functioning, its failure, and the consequences.

The quota law wa designed to set up a fragile industry on more steady underpinnings, on the general theory that such a procedure eventually would earn for England a place in the international celluloid orbit commensurate with her prestige as a world power. On the renter there was placed immediately a legal obligation to produce, or cause to be produced, a

Hollywood and Britain

percentage of native films, and on the exhibitor a mandate to show them to a public seeking entertainment—though not necessarily entertainment made compulsory by Act of Parliament.

Inevitably, abuses rushed their way into the British industry. It must be borne in mind that, at first, there was an industry woefully lacking in experienced production man-power. By the bounty of an indulgent but misguided Government, an inadequately equipped business suddenly found itself assured of a home market under what can be fairly viewed only as a State subsidy. Anything would do and anything did. The Board of Trade statistics reflected a steady and rising curve in the production graph, but failed to note a comparable rise in quality. The conclusion was that which might be expected. England began to do very well in the numerical column and indifferently on the merit side of the ledger.

Naturally, speculation followed. If the State, through a mounting quota impost on both maker and seller, as well as exhibitor, virtually assured a financial return, the task to be done became merely one of grinding out the film. This is no attempt on my part to charge the British production industry, *in toto*, with deliberately embarking on a wholesale and conscious endeavour to defeat the ephemeral intent of the Films Act. Rather is it an endeavour to show that, by the very complexion of the purpose planned, it became inevitable that opportunists would seek to turn a fortuitous and legalized circumstance to their financial gain. Sometimes this is called business.

Here, then, was a situation where a British enterprise, bedevilled and handicapped by a shortage of necessary experience, actually found itself forced into a most serious retrogression. These events are the background of the internal arguments and production crises imperilling the industry as I write, in the spring of 1937.

The hurt which the Films Act has inflicted upon a potentially great production industry went farther. The British film quota enforced upon the distributor was aimed chiefly at the English selling agencies of the large American distributors. It compelled them to acquire, from outside producing sources or by production financed by themselves for this purpose, a proportion of British films rising to a twenty per cent level in the closing years of the first quota Act. Evidently this law was passed to develop a home industry for Britain. Through its guarantee that quota-made films would occupy a fixed part of the limited running time in British cinemas, the booking of other films—mainly American films—was inevitably curtailed.

The attitude of American producers, under these circumstances, was one of failing completely to comprehend why they should sponsor superlative British pictures, made at a heavy investment, whose effect would be to keep their own merchandise off the screen. True, the profits from such pictures, if successful, would grace the American distributor's coffers; but the essential point was that an added cost of production would have to be met, while a comparable film already made in Hollywood found itself with no place to go in the British Isles. Further, the making of such films meant the creation or the financing of a producing organisation as an appendage to a commercial enterprise designed in the first place to engage, not in the manufacture of motion pictures, but in their sale.

For ever more and accurately viewing the Films Act as a preferential piece of legislation conceived entirely for British aggrandisement, the American agents in London originally did not see, and do not now see, why their experience and their resources should be diverted toward the creation of a competitive industry. Their decision, therefore, was to adhere to the letter of the quota law, to stay within it, of course, but only sufficiently within it to avoid legal difficulties. In terms of motion picture entertainment, this policy took form in the production or the acquisition of quota pictures, turned out as cheaply as they could be with no intent at achieving quality.

The damage thus inflicted on British production, already retarded in one direction by native inexperience, became twofold. Producers, however patriotic and zealous they may have been, were inadequate, extremely inadequate. The quota films made under compulsion by American distributors were as bad as —perhaps worse than—the works of British companies. England was getting her proportion of home-made entertainment, but no lustre was being burnished upon the lion's escutcheon. In some areas, where patriotism ran high, it was the British film which outshone the American, but comparative entertainment quality had little then to do with results.

Yet, by and large, and as testified lately by the delegation of the Cinematograph Exhibitors' Association before Lord Moyne's committee on quota renewal, it was the Hollywood attraction which the British theatre-man found most to his liking and kindest to his bank account. This was no gratuitous compliment on his part. The public was asserting its preference in terms of shillings and pence, and the exhibitor, the public's representative in these matters in a manner of speaking, was the reflection of that preference. Quite as simple as that.

The British producer's assured outlet, established on a favourite-son basis, eventually emboldened him to foray into more ambitious fields. England, by this time, had swung into a genuinely prosperous era and finance was easy to obtain. In England, as in America, there had always been a fringe of wealthy men who found the glamour of the motion picture intriguing and attractive. Wondrous tales had gone abroad of profits huge. The industry in the United States was again doing quite handsomely by itself and its financial mentors. Commercially qualified attractions were registering large intakes at the theatres. America was successful and, by simulating her methods, a parallel could be drawn in England. Thus the line of reasoning went, and thus events thereafter shaped themselves.

The fluidity of the British money market, the willingness of banks, insurance companies and private groups to speculate in the films, unleashed a golden flood of funds. Again, studying from the book of American experience, but lacking the rich background of the successful makers of motion pictures in that country, England now launched a production programme based on the expectation of substantial returns from the coveted transatlantic market.

In this regard, *The Private Life of Henry VIII* earned for itself a two-way reputation. The success of this meritorious film in America served to stress the impression, never widespread there, that England had learned how to make motion pictures good enough to command attention from the American public. Rumour flourishes in the film world, and to every tale of what *Henry VIII* was doing in America the British industry lent a willing ear. By the same token, the harm done was incalculable. No one bothered to spare time for an intensive study of the possibilities of British product in America. No one paused to debate whether *The Private Life of Henry VIII* had been a phenomenon that might have caught on in the United States for any number of varied reasons. The assumption became automatic that England finally had found a formula for easy success through all the days to come. An entire national enterprise, it appeared, had fastened its present and its future on the success of one motion picture.

The authentic observation might be made that not a single British motion picture since then has approximated the achievement of *Henry VIII*, and that might well mark the end of it. But the tracings of the pattern would be incomplete. Grave consequences followed. Producers in London, unpardonably neglecting to submit the foreign field they most desired to the slightest of analyses, primed their guns and turned them toward America. Fantastic tales of American market possibilities earmarked their plans, their schemes. They produced their programmes at a cost which nothing short of American profits could meet, only to find their product failing to secure these profits. Many of the expensive films undertaken along these lines reflected a loss, not because they did not do well in England, but because they were too extravagantly turned out to pay their way in the home market alone. The current difficulties in certain sections of the British industry find their answer here.

In her hectic desire to establish the physical machinery for film-making, England has been proceeding at a headlong pace, too, in the construction of studios. They were needed, of course. Every producer has the right to ask for efficient tools. Since last summer, when I was shown all round the Gaumont British studio at Shepherd's Bush, I have often reflected over the difficulties which must have beset that organisation's producers and directors in their daily work. Cramped in floor space, lacking the height—seventy-five feet or more—found in modern studios, and not always able to provide for the filming of scenes in that orderly progression which is made possible by going straight from one set to another, the Shepherd's Bush stages struck me as more of a handicap than a help.

At Denham, Alexander Korda, experienced in Hollywood, showed his appreciation of the importance of a craftsman's tools by the development of his magnificent plant. It is spacious, furnished with a complete

Hollywood and Britain 193

array of modern production devices, and the equal, certainly, of anything in Hollywood.

Pinewood—to which Gaumont production activities are now transferred—was last July a beehive of construction activity, planned on an impressively broad scale. Yet it should be noted that this development at Iver drew on the blueprints of the Radio Pictures studio at Hollywood. The British industry, thereby, loses no standing. It is entirely natural to look to successful physical arrangements elsewhere as a model for the housing of future British production. But there is something further to be said. Modern studios, properly equipped, are an integral part of the business of making motion pictures, but obviously the British industry cannot expect to found a lasting reputation simply on a construction job well done.

For a long time at Hollywood, by comparison with the more prepossessing lots of Warner Brothers and 20th Century Fox, the Metro-Goldwyn plant was a shambles. It is only during the last year, since prosperity began to return, that Metro has embarked on a rehabilitation programme. New modern stages are now going up and there is thought to spare for architectural planning. The obvious point here is that star power and executive ability are the resources which count in choosing stories, peopling them with players whose names sell tickets, and assuring them skilful dramatic treatment. Metro, far more than any other company, has proved that what matters in making successful films is who makes them, not where they are made.

Gauguin painted his finest canvases in a South Sea

island hut; Poe wrote his classics in a hovel. Granted basic mechanical necessaries, superior motion pictures can be produced anywhere.

However, in spite of all mistakes and troubles, past and possibly still to come, no fear about the emergence of a strong and healthy British production industry is justified. Hollywood has known a phase of mushroom growth; England must muddle through her own phase, learn her lesson and comport herself in the light of what such an expensive lesson should teach. To prophesy how much time must pass before this happens would be an elusive undertaking.

Further, everything depends on how the British industry approaches its problems. British stars and British stories can, and do, find a substantial outlet in the United Kingdom and throughout the Empire. They do not find a far-flung reception in America. England can turn her energies toward the furtherance of a production industry resting upon and glorifying her own traditions. If she so determines, her market will be confined to spheres of British influence and America must be forgotten. If it is an international goal on which Denham, Pinewood and Elstree have set their hopes, success on a large scale is quite outside the realm of possibility without a fuller appreciation of what will and will not be acceptable to the American public. Yet that would be only the start of the struggle, for appreciation, though going far to make the problem more understandable, would not itself furnish a solution.

From time to time over the years the star system in America has been a target of attack. The time was when one large American company publicly announced its studio concentration on directors and producers; the stars were to be used where they fitted the vehicle, not the vehicles twisted to fit the stars. The outcome was wellnigh disastrous. The American public, moronic or not, according to the point of view, has its favourites. It demands them, it supports them, and it gets them. No Hollywood producer to-day will argue against the importance of names. He is not interested in questioning the public's judgment, nor does he care about diagnosing motives. He views it as his responsibility, within the tenets of good taste and of worthwhile endeavour, to supply a saleable commodity to a public eager to purchase it. The worthwhile endeavour actually and usually is striven for, where it does not conflict with the drawing-power of the star. Indeed, the most commercially minded producer in Hollywood will forgo much on behalf of star power, and does. The Utopian combination, obviously, becomes a strong vehicle plus a money-making player. Then the attraction becomes what is known to the American trade as a "wow".

And so it is the unvarnished truth to-day that personalities are riding high in their heavens. England understands this, fortunately. Her understanding is shown in the marauding campaign directed at the Hollywood studios in the last three years. Salaries beyond the Hollywood level, which is ridiculously high, have been dangled temptingly before the eyes of available talent. *De luxe* travelling accommodations from Hollywood to New York, and from New York to London, at the expense of the British studios, have been furnished. The instances are many where London has outstepped Hollywood offers by fully one hundred per cent. And, in some instances, it has worked.

The intent, of course, has been to people major British offerings with personalities powerful enough to crack the American market. Not altogether a successful foray. In accordance with the fundamentals of any properly functioning business, Hollywood, its eye less on London than on competitive studios within its own boundaries, keeps its talent safely tucked away on contract. Under the American system of selling in blocks, each major producer contracts his output for a complete entertainment season. He will undertake to deliver a stipulated number of films with an announced star. For that star to be submitted to competitive bidding would not and could not do. His services must be pledged by contract, or the producer could not keep his own promises.

It follows automatically that box-office timber is not waiting around for jobs. It follows, too, that all the essential talent is pledged by contract to one studio or another, and the conclusion is that England must be content with what she can find or with what Hollywood wants her to have. Aside from Marlene Dietrich, not a single outstanding personality has forsaken Hollywood for London, and there are some engaged in American exhibition who no longer view Miss Dietrich as significant to their theatres. While this circumstance has tended to make more arduous England's struggle for a place in the sun, her prospects have suffered recently a further set-back through

Hollywood and Britain 197

the influx into London of a lengthy array of American has-beens, male and female, who have been signed shortsightedly for British films when they could no longer get work in Hollywood.

Understandable perhaps as a temporary measure until producing in Britain finds firmer ground, this sort of policy has no lasting value. Recognising that for success in the international market—which means selling to America—personalities are essential, Great Britain will have to find another answer. That answer is the development of her own stars. Not merely stars acceptable to the British public, but stars of proven drawing-power in the United States. How to achieve this becomes the next consideration.

It will not be easy. It will be anything but that. It will mean patience, hard work and a full determination to invest heavily. It will mean experimenting constantly with new faces, surrounding them with the most expert production ingredients, and finding stories with a flavour of appeal to American audiences. From its beginnings Hollywood has been experimenting at a huge cost to foster new favourites, alternately with success and failure. The process means a balancing of production judgment against public reaction, and the outcome, perforce, is entirely in the lap of the gods. For no one can accurately lay down a list of definite essentials. Stories play their part, and often it can be a most vital part. Yet, not always does this hold.

In the routine Hollywood manner, a male star must have looks, personal appeal, and, on occasion, an ability to perform. The formula for a female star runs pretty much along the same lines. Then along come the exceptions to disprove the rule; there was Marie Dressler, for instance, who reached her cinematic fame in the winter of her career. There are now Alison Skipworth and May Robson, sterling actresses fitting into the Dressler mould. Their studios have done all but move the heavens in their attempts to cloak one or the other, or both, with the mantle of the departed Dressler. It has not worked. It has failed, not because the producers have not tried, but because the public, always the final court of appeal, has determined otherwise.

Hollywood has tapped the world talent markets for additions to its imposing array of merit. In this respect, its principal production figures have been astute and are likely to continue to be so. But, essentially, Hollywood has fortified itself by making itself largely self-contained. This has been brought about by hurling parsimony to the four winds. England, to succeed, must prepare to follow suit or abandon any idea of making her mark in world production.

British stars—or call them, rather, international stars —can be developed. But it should be clearly realised from the start that the fruits of this work of development must be competently protected. Hollywood has its tentacles reaching out in all directions. No country or clime is immune from its princely offers. Britain's stars to come will be subject to its competition, and over that competition Britain must be prepared to battle. This will mean greater and greater investment, perhaps eventually uneconomic, but unavoidable.

Any survey of the road to be travelled must take into

Hollywood and Britain 199

account other factors, among them one at least which the British producer has overlooked. He who would be successful in an industry characterised by stern and frequently ruthless competition must learn that industry. The English maker of films has paid little attention to the market he most ardently desires. For him to ship to America productions which are mediocre or worse is a foolhardly procedure. The American theatre-man is burdened with more indifferent entertainment than he now knows what to do with. If he is honest with himself and with his business, he understands that he might justifiably expect any one major producer to deliver him from six to eight outstanding pictures each season. With what may seem to be a pittance, when it is remembered he may have bought from forty-eight to sixty films to get these six or eight, he is, nevertheless, eminently satisfied.

If the producer encounters a streak of luck and delivers a greater number, the advantage then becomes the theatre's. This occasionally happens, but no one familiar with the high and low curves of the American industry depends upon it. Yet under the booking contract, the lesser attractions either must be played or paid for, and usually they are played. The available screen time of the average American exhibitor, as a consequence, leaves little room for films not purchased in advance. Were the time available, it is perfectly obvious that little would be gained by making it available to average or inferior product from a source foreign to Hollywood.

The American exhibitor, on an average, will invariably select American product, though not for reasons of patriotism. Not at all. He will make the choice because, inferior as it may be, the Hollywood attraction will at its worst include cast names of more commercial value to him than are available in routine pictures from England. Moreover, it is usually a better-made film technically, and its players speak an English which American audiences will understand. In short, if he must have indifferent celluloid fare, he will select indifferent American fare. Certainly, the supply is more than sufficient.

It is not solely talent shortage which hampers British films in America. The difficulty arises also from a difference in approach, in temperament, in mood. The Londoner finds the Yorkshireman difficult to understand, if he does not find him quaint. The Kansan does not always comprehend New York wisecracks in a Hollywood-made film, which is frequently unfortunate for the film. How this same Kansan reacts to Cockney, or to English humour of the too strictly insular type, the reader may conclude for himself. Further, a common complaint about British films is lack of pace, which does indeed afflict many of them. Actually, this slackness is not always present, and to the more discerning American filmgoer this is quickly apparent. But films are not made for the intelligent few. To succeed they have to be of mass appeal, and to the masses they must therefore be acceptable.

About the average Hollywood output there is an unmistakable breeziness and speed, both part of the American mentality. They are as much an indispensable part of the attraction as the settings or the players who perform in them. American audiences, quite naturally, prefer a reflection of the things they know about and, indeed, indulge in themselves. To give them something too distinctly and too distinctively English or Gallic or Teutonic is to provide something which may interest them, but only superficially.

In view of these facts, it behoves the British producer to pay stricter attention to the selection of his material. His properties should be thinned out and mulled over with an eye on his foreign markets. It took the American export manager years to convey to the Hollywood producer the peculiarities, as well as the requirements, of his foreign markets. To-day Hollywood embarks upon its activities fortified with detailed information about the overseas territories to which it appeals.

The Forty Days of Musa Dagh was never produced, because of the sensibilities of the Turkish Government on the Armenian question. *Paths of Glory*, a scathing denunciation of French military high-handedness during the World War, was scrapped because the Quai d'Orsay expressed its displeasure. Words, phrases and occasional idiomatic expressions acceptable in America, but bearing other shades of meaning in England and Australia, are known to Hollywood and paraphrased with both eyes on Britain and Empire markets. Additional scenes are often specially photographed for inclusion in prints or copies headed for England. These are practical methods by which America bends a wise knee to the requirements of that foreign business without which it cannot endure.

Except in a general and vague fashion, the British industry is not cognisant of these commercial sleights-of-hand. It is not aware of them because no effort has been made to learn seriously and sincerely wherein Americans are peculiar about their motion pictures. The task of conceiving a worthwhile product is itself one yet to be widely learned in England. To attempt it without a thorough grasp of the standards which must be met is not only foolhardy, but futile.

British producers, if they so elect, can continue to remain aloof on their island, turning out films and hoping for the best. That best will run to the form of the years which have come and gone; but England will remain a second-rate power in the international making of motion pictures.

PART IV

FILMS AND THE PUBLIC

WHY I GO TO THE CINEMA
By Elizabeth Bowen

I GO to the cinema for any number of different reasons—these I ought to sort out and range in order of their importance. At random, here are a few of them: I go to be distracted (or "taken out of myself"); I go when I don't want to think; I go when I do want to think and need stimulus; I go to see pretty people; I go when I want to see life ginned up, charged with unlikely energy; I go to laugh; I go to be harrowed; I go when a day has been such a mess of detail that I am glad to see even the most arbitrary, the most preposterous, pattern emerge; I go because I like bright light, abrupt shadow, speed; I go to see America, France, Russia; I go because I like wisecracks and slick behaviour; I go because the screen is an oblong opening into the world of fantasy for me; I go because I like story, with its suspense; I go because I like sitting in a packed crowd in the dark, among hundreds riveted on the same thing; I go to have my most general feelings played on.

These reasons, put down roughly, seem to fall under five headings: wish to escape, lassitude, sense of lack in my nature or my surroundings, loneliness (however passing) and natural frivolity. As a writer, I am probably subject during working hours to a slightly unnatural imaginative strain, which leaves me flat and depleted by the end of a day. But though the strain may be a little special in nature, I do not take it to be in any way greater than the strain, the sense of depletion, suffered by other people in most departments of life now. When I take a day off and become a person of leisure, I embark on a quite new method of exhausting myself; I amuse myself through a day, but how arduous that is: by the end of the day I am generally down on the transaction—unless I have been in the country.

I take it that for the professional leisured person things, in the long run, work out the same way. Writers, and other inventive workers, are wrong, I think, in claiming a special privilege, or in representing themselves as unfairly taxed by life: what is taken out of them in some ways is saved them in others; they work, for the most part, in solitude; they are not worn by friction with other people (unless they choose to seek this in their spare time); they have not to keep coming to terms with other people in order to get what they have to do done. They escape monotony; they are sustained in working by a kind of excitement; they are shut off from a good many demands. Their work *is* exhausting, and by human standards unnatural, but it cannot be more exhausting than routine work in office, shop or factory, teaching, running a family, hanging on to existence if one is in the submerged class, or amusing oneself. I make this point in order to be quite clear that my reasons for cinemagoing are not unique or special: they would not be worth discussing if they were.

I am not at all certain, either, that the practice of one art gives one a point of vantage in discussing another. Where the cinema is concerned, I am a fan, not a critic. I have been asked to write on "Why I Go to the Cinema" because I do write, and should therefore do so with ease; I have not been asked to write, and am not writing, *as* a writer. It is not as a writer that I go to the cinema; like every one else, I slough off my preoccupations there. The film I go to see is the product of a kind of art, just as a bottle of wine is the product of a kind of art. I judge the film as I judge the bottle of wine, in its relation to myself, by what it does to me. I sum up the pleasure it gives. This pleasure is, to an extent, an affair of my own palate, or temperament, but all palates and temperaments have something in common; hence general "taste", an accepted, objective standard in judgment of films or wine. Films, like wines, are differently good in their different classes; some of us prefer to seek one kind, some another, but always there is the same end—absolute pleasure—in view.

Cinemas draw all sorts. In factory towns they are packed with factory workers, in university cities with dons, at the seaside with trippers (who take on a strong though temporary character), in the West End with more or less moneyed people with time to kill, in country towns and villages with small tradespeople and with workers scrubbed and hard from the fields. Taste, with these different audiences, differs widely, but the degree of pleasure sought is the same. A film either hits or misses. So affectable are we that to sit through a film that is not pleasing the house, however much it may happen to please one personally, causes restless discomfort that detracts from one's pleasure.

(Avoid, for instance, seeing the Marx Brothers in Cork city.) This works both ways: the success of a film with its house communicates a tingling physical pleasure—joining and heightening one's private exhilaration—a pleasure only the most weathered misanthrope could withstand—and your misanthrope is rarely a cinema-goer. There is no mistaking that tension all round in the dark, that almost agonised tension of a pleased house—the electric hush, the rapt immobility. The triumphantly funny film, hitting its mark, makes even laughter break off again and again, and the truly tragic suspends the snuffle.

The happily constituted cinema-goer learns to see and savour a positive merit in films that may do nothing to him personally, films whose subjects, stars or settings may to him, even, be antipathetic. To reject as any kind of experience a film that is acting powerfully on people round seems to me to argue poverty in the nature. What falls short as aesthetic experience may do as human experience: the film rings no bell in oneself, but one hears a bell ring elsewhere. This has a sort of value, like being in company with a very popular person one does not oneself dislike but who does not attract one. Popularity ought to confer a sort of hall-mark, not have to be taken up as a challenge. I speak of the happily constituted cinema-goer—I mean, perhaps, the happily constituted, and therefore very rare, person. The generality of us, who hate jokes we cannot see and mysteries we are out of, may still hope to become sophisticates in at least this one pleasure by bringing with us, when we go to a cinema, something more active, more resourceful than

LA KERMESSE HÉROÏQUE French (Films-Sonores Tobis) 1936
Directed by Jacques Feyder

Richness of period detail (the Netherlands under Spanish rule in the sixteenth
century) used together with faces and gestures to establish prevailing mood

SOUS LES TOITS DE PARIS   French (Tobis). Directed by René Clair, 1929

"*Will remain as the example of how to get beauty out of squalor*"

Marie Bell in
UN CARNET DE BAL
Directed by Julien Duvivier for Vogue Films, 1937
Memories from the programme of her first ball

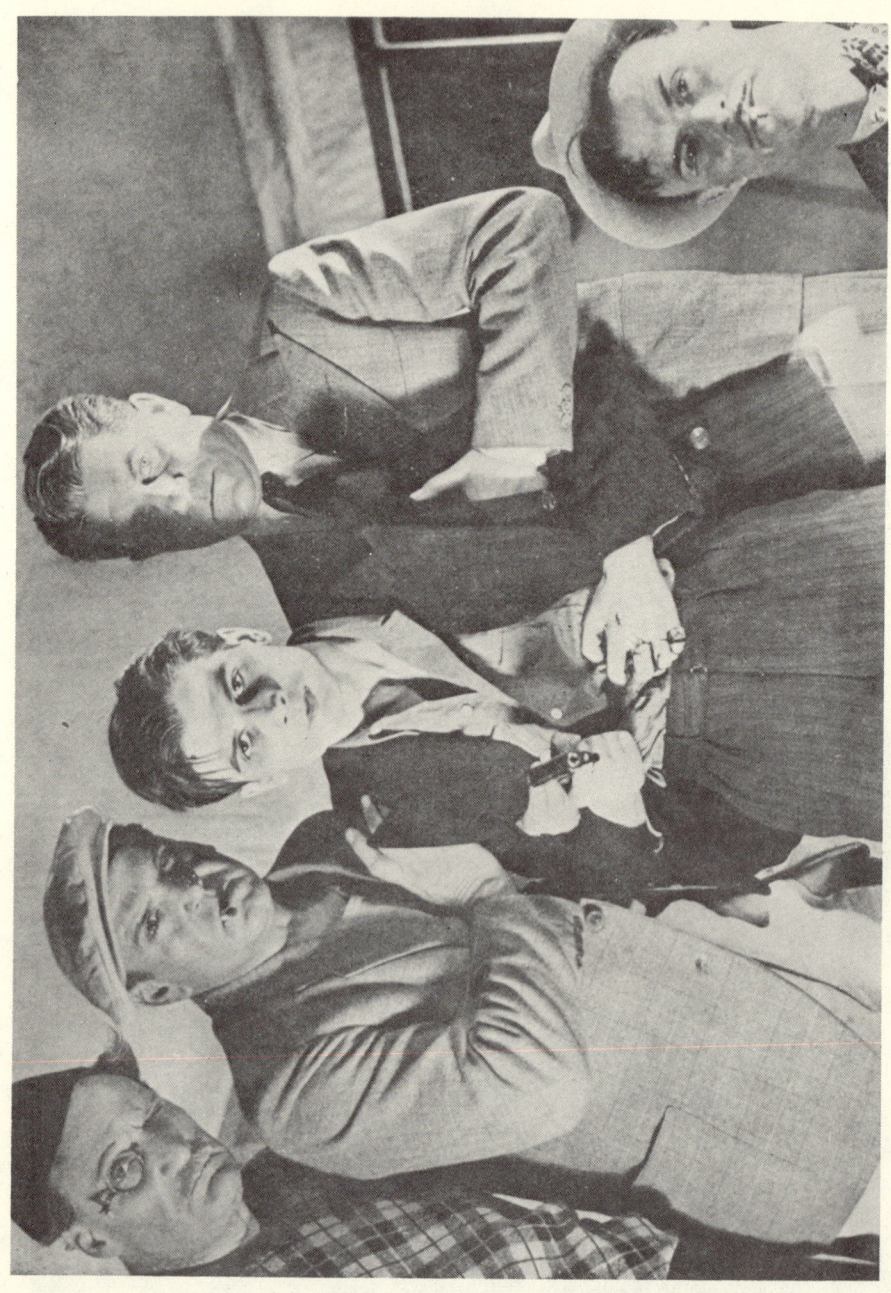

PÉPÉ LE MOKO — French (Paris Film). Directed by Julien Duvivier, 1936
Toughness in close-up—French style

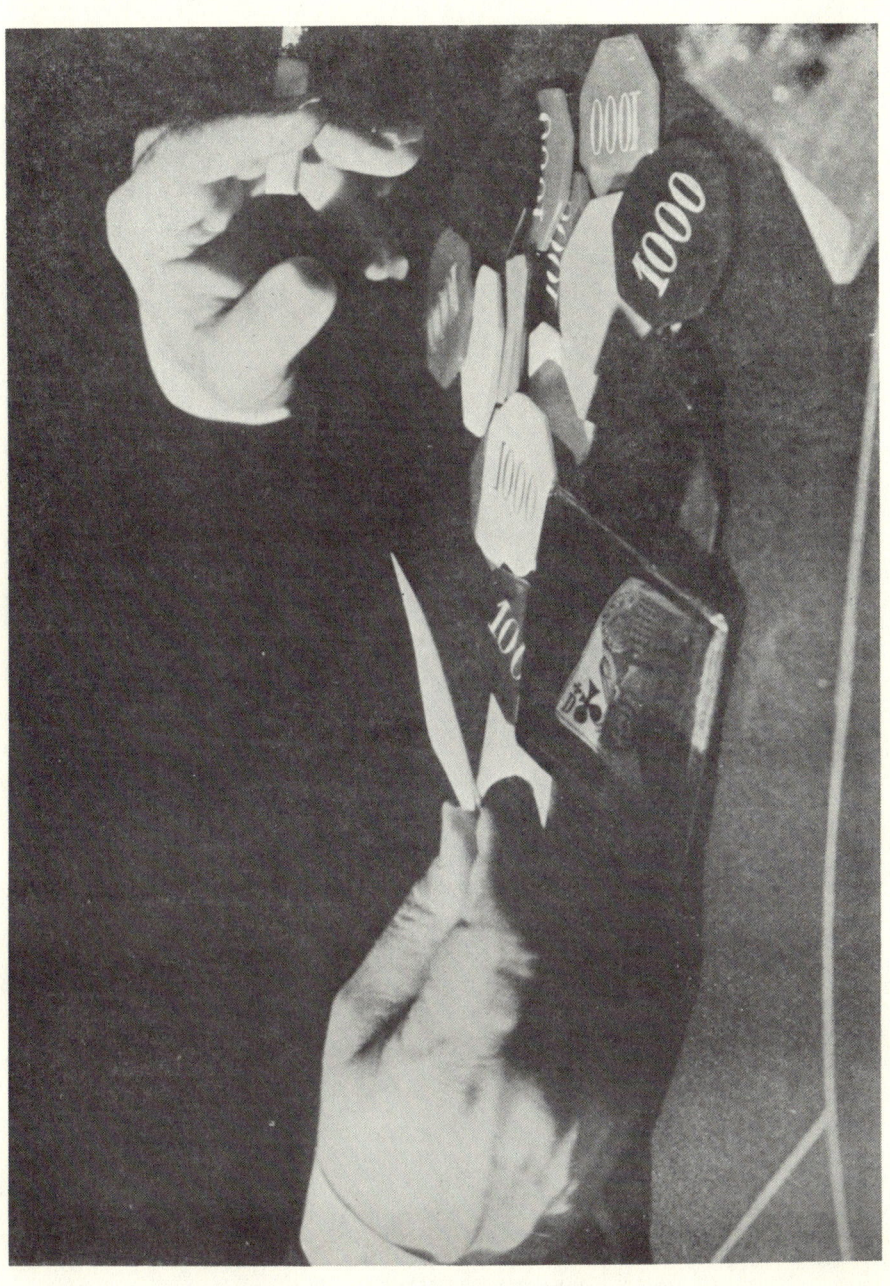

THE CHEAT
(Le Roman d'un Tricheur)

Written and produced by Sacha Guitry, 1937
Guitry's hands. Character from details in close-up

CLOSE-UPS—RUSSIAN STYLE

WE FROM KRONSTADT   Directed by E. Dzigan, 1936
THE CIRCUS   Directed by Alexandrov, 1936

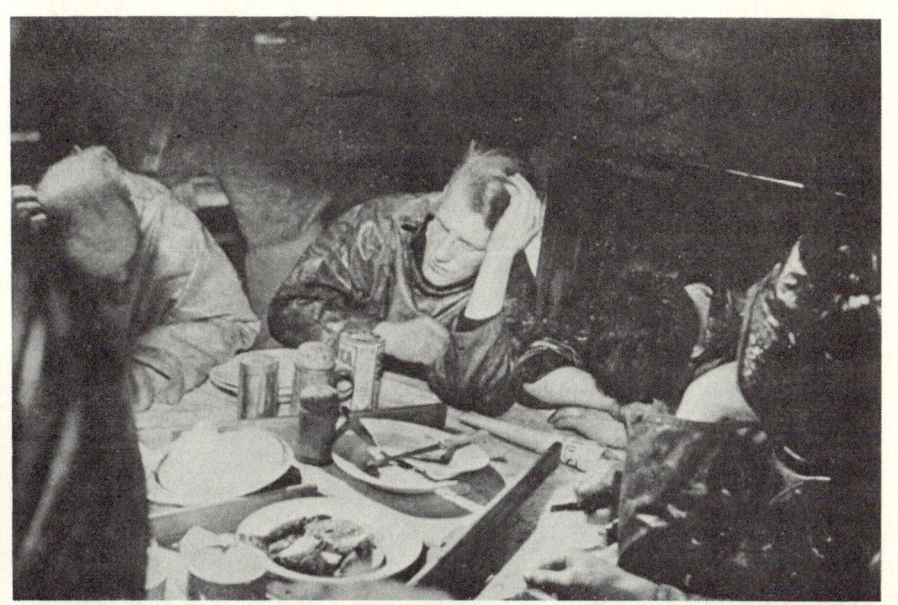

DOCUMENTARIES: BRITISH AND GERMAN
NORTH SEA (1938)   Made by Cavalcanti and Watt.   (G.P.O. Film Unit)
OLYMPIA (Olympic Games, Berlin, 1936)   Made by Leni Riefenstahl.   (Olympia-Tobis)

BRITISH STUDIOS

London Film Productions, Denham, Middlesex

Pinewood Studios, Iver Heath, Bucks

THE THIRTY-NINE STEPS
Hitchcock directing Madeleine Carroll and Robert Donat—handcuffed together—in the moorland scene mentioned in his article

Gaumont-British, 1935

ORDEAL BY CAMERA

An American court scene from
THE WITNESS CHAIR

Directed by George Nicholls Jr. for
Radio Pictures, 1935

"That terrifying taskmaster, the camera lens, with a 'mike' on a boom hovering overhead"

"TIME MARCHES ON"

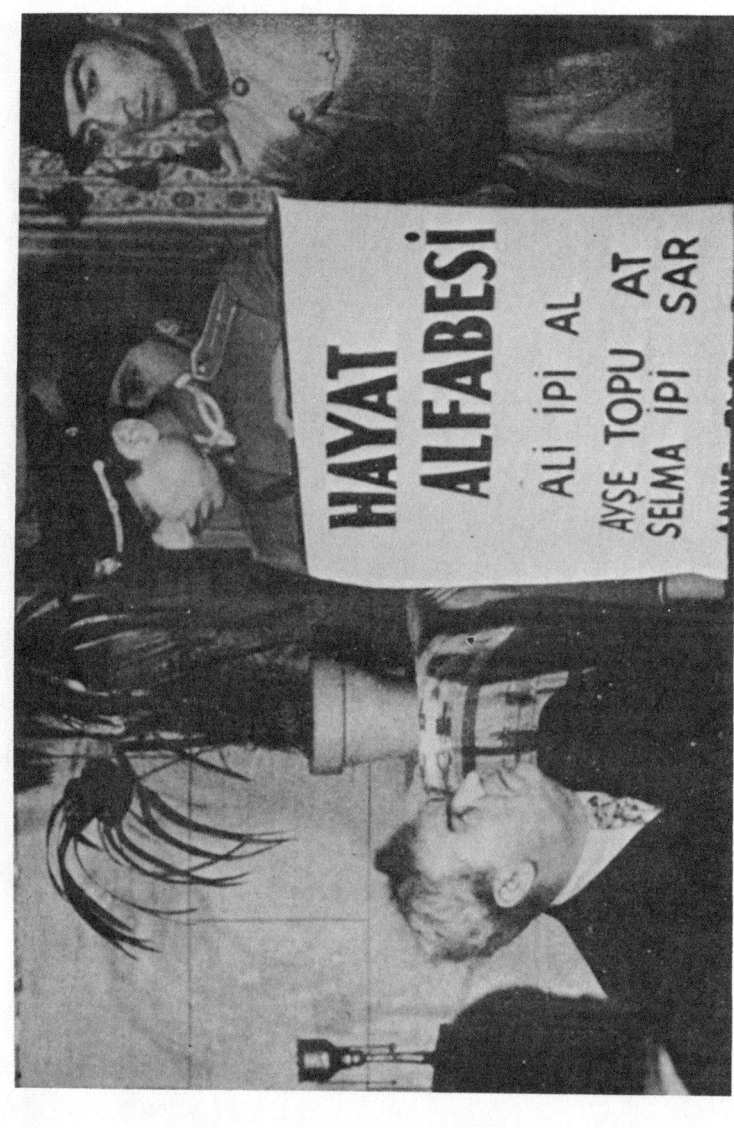

FATHER OF ALL TURKS A March of Time documentary, 1937
Kemal Atatürk sends soldiers round the cafés to examine Turkish citizens in the new Arabic alphabet

POETRY OF FACT

SONG OF CEYLON Produced by John Grierson. Directed by Basil Wright for Ceylon Tea Propaganda Board, 1934

The pattern of this film, embracing images, natural sounds, music and commentary, was designed to contrast the traditional life of Ceylon with the invasions of Western commerce

THE NATURAL
HISTORY FILM

*By courtesy
of
Gaumont-
British
Instructional*

ROCK POOLS
(1936)

TAWNY OWL
(1936)

By courtesy of Paul Rotha

THE CABINET OF DR CALIGARI
German (Decla-Bioskop) 1919.
Directed by Robert Wiene

EXPRESSIONISM

Distorted scenery used to suggest a madman's mind. In foreground, Werner Krauss as Dr Caligari

SILHOUETTE FILMS BY LOTTE REINIGER

THE ADVENTURES OF PRINCE ACHMET (1926)

THE LITTLE CHIMNEY SWEEP (1935)

FILMING THE FUTURE

THINGS TO COME Directed for London Film Productions by William Cameron Menzies, 1935
Passworthy (Edward Chapman) and Oswald Cabal (Raymond Massey) discuss the firing of the Space Gun, A.D. 2054

tolerance. This is worth while: it doubles our chance of that fun for which we paid at the box-office. To my mind, any truly popular film is worth seeing—granted one happens to have the time and money to spare. I say, *truly* popular film, the film that after release has triumphantly stayed the course; not the *should-be* popular film, the film stuck with big names or inflated beforehand by misleading publicity. If nothing else, the popular film I don't like adds to my knowledge of what I don't like and don't want. One's own apathies are complex and interesting.

Films have—it is a truism of the trade—a predetermined destination. Every film made makes a bid for the favour of certain localities whose taste has been gauged in advance, correctly or not. Local appeal, at its strongest, is strongly delimited. If one is to go to a film for its popularity-interest, one should go to it in its own country—its areas may be social, not geographic, though largely they *are* geographic, for climate and occupation do condition an audience. For instance, my great respect for Miss Gracie Fields does not alter the fact that I would not willingly see, for its own sake, at my nearest London cinema, a film in which she appeared. But I should feel I had missed something if I missed seeing a Gracie Fields film in the Gracie Fields country. There she operates in full force, and I cannot fail to react—to the audience, if not to her. I see a great girl in play. The comedian's hold on his or her own public is hard to analyse: in some cases (such as Miss Fields') it has a strong moral element. Or it may have a healthily anti-moral element. The determining factor must, I think, be social:

hard-living people like to have some one to admire; they like what is like themselves. The sophisticated are attracted, titillated, by what is foreign, outrageous, by what they may half deplore.

But it would be misleading, as well as precious, to overstress this rest-of-the-audience factor in my reaction to films. I do really only like what *I* like, I go to please myself, and when I sit opposite a film the audience is *me*. My faculties are riveted, my pleasure can only be a little damped down or my disappointment added to by the people cheek by jowl with me in the dark. I expect a good deal, when I go to the cinema: my expectations absorb me from the moment I enter. I am giving myself a treat—or being given a treat. I have little spare time or money, the cinema is my anodyne, not my subject, and my objective interest in its emotional mechanics is not really very great. Nine times out of ten, it is alert, exacting expectations of pleasure that carry me to the cinema. The tenth time I may go from abstract curiosity, or at random—as when I have hours to pass in a strange town where it is raining or there are no buildings to see. This tenth time I will discount; it is seldom serious—though it does sometimes turn out to have started up a new fancy, or left a residue of interest behind.

I expect, then, to enjoy myself. This end I do all I can to further by taking as good a seat as my purse, that day, will allow—a seat giving room for my knees, in which I need not tip my head back or keep craning my neck round, and from which I have an undistorted view of the screen. (In the up-to-date cinema this last, of course, is all right in all seats.) Cramp or any other physical irritation militates quite unfairly against the best film: if a film is worth seeing at all they seem to me worth avoiding. Sometimes I can't avoid them: if a film is booming I'm lucky to get in at all, and have to sit where I can. But there is a good deal in waiting till the first rush is over, then seeing the film in comfort: a film, I try to remind myself, doesn't lose quality in the course of its run, and the urge to see it at once may be sheer vulgar topicality. Anyhow, I seek comfort—and how important smoking is. I start slightly against the best film in a foreign cinema where I am unable to smoke. Very great films (generally Russian) and moments in any good film do suspend my desire to smoke: this is the supreme test.

I have—like, I suppose every other cinema-goer—a physical affection for certain cinemas. In London the Empire is my favourite; when I settle down in there I feel I am back in the old home, and am predisposed to happiness. May it never come down. I suppose I could rationalise my feeling for the Empire by saying I like Metro-Goldwyn-Mayer films—but though I have enjoyed these all over Europe, the last drop of pleasure is added by being at the Empire. However, one must take films not only as but where one finds them. In the provinces, I have often had to desert my favourite cinema in order to see a promising film elsewhere: this gave the evening, though the film might prove excellent, an undertone of nostalgia: "I wish this were at the Such-and-such." The sentiment was absurd, and is only mentioned because I think it is general. Pleasure is at its best when it has in it some familiar element. And the pleasure-seeker has a difficult temperament; he is often as captious as a spoilt beauty, as whimsical as a child, and given to fretting against conditions not in his power to change. This may be because, in most cases, he goes to his pleasure tired. He does not know what he wants, but he knows when he does not get it. It is for him—myself—that the cinema caters; and how much the cinema has to overcome!

I hope never to go to the cinema in an entirely unpropitious mood. If I do, and am not amused, that is my fault, also my loss. As a rule, I go empty but hopeful, like some one bringing a mug to a tap that may not turn on. The approach tunes me up for pleasure. The enchantment that hung over those pre-War façades of childhood—gorgeously white stucco façades, with caryatids and garlands—has not dissolved, though the façades have been changed. How they used to beam down the street. Now concrete succeeds stucco and chromium gilt; foyers once crimson and richly stuffy are air-conditioned and dove-grey. But, like a chocolate-box lid, the entrance is still voluptuously promising: sensation of some sort seems to be guaranteed. How happily I tread the pneumatic carpet, traverse anterooms with their exciting muted vibration, and walk down the spotlit aisle with its eager tilt to the screen. I climb over those knees to the sticky velvet seat, and fumble my cigarettes out—as I used not to do.

I am not only home again, but am, if my choice is lucky, in ideal society. I am one of the millions who follow Names from cinema to cinema. The star system may be all wrong—it has implications I hardly know of in the titanic world of Hollywood, also it is, clearly, a hold-up to proper art—but I cannot help break it down. I go to see So-and-so. I cannot fitly quarrel with this magnification of personalities, while I find I can do with almost unlimited doses of anybody exciting, anybody with beauty (in my terms), verve, wit, style, *toupet* and, of course, glamour. What do I mean by glamour? A sort of sensuous gloss: I know it to be synthetic, but it affects me strongly. It is a trick knowingly practised on my most fuzzy desires; it steals a march on me on my silliest side. But all the same, in being subject to glamour I experience a sort of elevation. It brings, if not into life at least parallel to it, a sort of fairy-tale element. It is a sort of trumpet call, mobilising the sleepy fancy. If a film is to get across, glamour somewhere, in some form— moral, if you like, for it can be moral—cannot be done without. The Russians break with the bourgeois-romantic conception of personality; they have scrapped sex-appeal as an annexe of singularising, anti-social love. But they still treat with glamour; they have transferred it to mass movement, to a heroicised pro-human emotion. I seek it, in any form.

To get back to my star: I enjoy, sitting opposite him or her, the delights of intimacy without the onus, high points of possession without the strain. This could be called inoperative love. Relationships in real life are made arduous by their reciprocities; one can too seldom simply sit back. The necessity to please, to shine, to make the most of the moment, over-shadows too many meetings. And apart from this— how seldom in real life (or so-called real life) does acquaintanceship, much less intimacy, with dazzling, exceptional beings come one's way. How very gladly, therefore, do I fill the gaps in my circle of ideal society with these black-and-white personalities, to whom absence of colour has added all the subtleties of tone. Directly I take my place I am on terms with these Olympians; I am close to them with nothing at all at stake. Rapture lets me suppose that for me alone they display the range of their temperaments, their hesitations, their serious depths. I find them not only dazzling but sympathetic. They live for my eye. Yes, and I not only perceive them but *am* them; their hopes and fears are my own; their triumphs exalt me. I am proud for them and in them. Not only do I enjoy them; I enjoy in them a vicarious life.

Nevertheless, I like my stars well supported. If a single other character in the film beside them be unconvincing or tin-shape, the important illusion weakens; something begins to break down. I like to see my star played up to and played around by a caste that is living, differentiated and definite. The film must have background, depth, its own kind of validity. Hollywood, lately, has met this demand: small parts are being better and better played. Casts are smallish, characters clear-cut, action articulates. (Look at *It Happened One Night*, *She Married Her Boss*, *My Man Godfrey*.) There is family-feeling inside a good film—so that the world it creates is valid, water-tight, *probable*.

What a gulf yawns between improbability—which is desolating—and fantasy—which is dream-probability, likeliness on an august, mad plane. Comedy films show this fantasy element more strongly than tragedies, which attempt to approach life and fail too often through weakness and misrepresentation: comedies are thus, as a rule, better. A really good comic (a Laurel and Hardy, for instance) is never simply improbable: it suspends judgment on the workaday plane. Comedy-drama needs some verisimilitude.

When I say verisimilitude, I do not mean that I want the film to be exactly *like* life: I should seldom go to the cinema if it were. The effective film (other, of course, than the film that is purely documentary) must have at least a touch of the preposterous. But its distance from life, or from probability, should stay the same throughout: it must keep inside its pitch. The film that keeps in its pitch makes, and imposes, a temporary reality of its own.

Any cinema-goer, however anxious for peace and for his own pleasure, may detect in a film a *gaffe* that he cannot pass. I quarrel most, naturally, with misrepresentations of anything that I happen to know about. For instance, I have, being Irish, seen few films about Ireland, or set in Ireland, that did not insult and bore me. (*The Informer* was one remarkable exception.) But I could sit through a (no doubt) equally misrepresenting film about Scotland, which I do not know, without turning a hair. I know only a very small part of America—and that superficially —so that American films can take almost any licence with me. In fact, years of cinema-going probably did condition my first view of America: I felt as though I were stepping into the screen. Dreamlike familiarity in the streets and landscapes not only endeared the country but verified the cinema. But I cannot know how greatly Hollywood's representations, however idyllic, of New England small towns may offend New Englanders, or how cardboardy, to the Southerner, may seem the screen face of the Old Colonial Home. I cannot challenge falseness in setting, detail or manners past the point where my experience stops. As a woman, I am annoyed by improbability in clothes: English films offend rather badly in this way. Dressy at all costs, the English heroines hike, run down spies or reclaim lovers from storm-girt islands in their Kensington High Street Sunday bests. An equal unlikeliness blights the English film interior: I revolt from ancestral homes that are always Gothic, from Louis Seize bedrooms in poverty-stricken manors, from back-street dwellings furnished by Mr Drage. The frumpy and unsatirical flatness of the average English stage-set is almost always transferred by the English film to the screen. The French make *genre* films in which every vase, tassel and door-handle thickens the atmosphere, makes for verisimilitude and adds more to the story: why cannot we do the same?

Why are there so few English *genre* films? All over this country, indoors and out, a photographable drama of national temperament is going on, and every object has character. By-passes, trees on skylines, small country town streets with big buses pushing along them, village Sundays, gasometers showing behind seaside towns, half-built new estates, Midland canals, the lounges of private hotels, stucco houses with verandas, rectory tea-tables, the suburban shopping rush, garden fêtes and the abstract perspectives of flyblown, semi-submerged London are all waiting the camera and are very dramatic. English interiors are highly characterised; English social routine is romantically diverse. As it is, the same few shots—which might, from their symbolic conventionality, have been made to be exported to Hollywood—drearily reappear, to give English films their locality: Westminster Bridge, crazy gables stuck with oak beams, corners of (apparently) Oxford colleges masquerading as Great Homes, clotted orchards (that might be faked with a few rolls of crêpe paper), the spire of always the same church, and those desolating, unconvincing, always-the-same rooms. There are exceptions to this—Anthony Asquith shows feeling for landscape, and Hitchcock gets humour into interiors—but not nearly enough exceptions. Generally speaking, English films lack humour in the perceptive, sympathetic and wide sense. They lack sensibility; they do not know how to use objects. Are we blind to our country? Too many English films are, humanly speaking, dead. Character in them is tin-shape and two-dimensional. The whole effect is laborious, genteel, un-adult and fussy. Comedies, technically "clean," are unbearably vulgar; there is no fun, only knockabout and facetiousness. It is true that we are beginners, that we have admittedly much to learn, still, in the way of technique. But we fail in more than technique; we fail, flatly and fatally, in conception.

At present it appears, discouragingly enough, that to make outstanding films one must either be sophisticated, like some Americans; disabused and witty, like the French; vividly neurotic, like the Germans; or noble, like the Russians. One must know how to use convention, and when to break with it. One must either, like the Russians, take the heroic view, or else be iconoclastic, racy, though still know what to honour. One must have an eye for what is essential, telling, in action, scene or face. One must know how to hitch one's particular invention on to the general dream. Human fantasies are general; the film, to live, must discover, feed and command these.

I am discussing, throughout, the "story" (or "entertainment") film. That is the film I go to see; I go to the cinema for amusement only; my feeling for it may be exceptionally frivolous. I more than admire, I am often absorbed by, good "interest", or documentary films that may occur in a programme, but, as these are not the films I seek, I do not feel that I am qualified to discuss them. I go for what is untrue, to be excited by what is fantastic, to see what has never happened happen. I go for the fairy story. I state—I do not see why this should rank as a confession—that I would rather see a film in which a (probably doped) lion brings a tense plot to a close by eating a millionaire than the most excellent film about lions in their wild state, roving about and not furthering any plot. If I am to see a documentary film, I prefer what I can only describe with Lower-form vagueness as "films about foreign countries"—preferably, European countries. I like to get some idea how foreigners spend their day—and the incidental beauty of "interest" films is often very great, their rhythm admirable. But I have very little curiosity, and an inordinate wish to be entertained. If many more cinema-goers were as lazy-minded and fantasy-loving as I am what a pity it would be—but I take it that I am in a minority. I hope that the cinema may develop along all lines, while still giving me many more of the films I like—grown-up comedies, taut thrillers, finished period pieces and dashing Westerns. I want no more American tragedies, Russian comedies or crepitating Teutonic analysis. I should like still more dramatic use of landscape and architecture. I like almost any French film—perhaps I have been lucky. I have rather dreaded beforehand, as one dreads drastic experience, any Russian film I have seen; have later wished, while it lasted, to protract every moment, and finally found it, when it was over, more powerful than a memory—besides everything else, there had been so much more fun than one foresaw.

I am shy of the serious aspect of my subject, and don't want to finish on an unnaturally high note. It is, of course, clear to me that a film, like any other attempt on art, or work of art—all being tentative—can have in it germs of perfection. Its pretension to an aesthetic need be no less serious than that of a poem, picture or piece of music. Its medium, which is unique to it, is important: fluid pattern, variation of light, speed. In time, the cinema has come last of all the arts; its appeal to the racial child in us is so immediate that it should have come first. Pictures came first in time, and bore a great weight of meaning: "the pictures" date right back in their command of emotion: they are inherently primitive. A film can put the experience of a race or a person on an almost dreadfully simplified epic plane.

We have promise of great art here, but so far few great artists. Films have not caught up with the possibilities of the cinema: we are lucky when we get films that keep these in sight. Mechanics, the immense technical knowledge needed, have kept the art, as an art, unnaturally esoteric; its technical progress (more and more discoveries: sound, now colour) moves counter to its spiritual progress. An issue keeps on being obscured, a problem added to. Yet we have here, almost within our grasp, a means to the most direct communication possible between man and man. What might be a giant instrument is still a giant toy.

How much I like films I like—but I could like my films better. I like being distracted, flattered, tickled, even rather upset—but I should not mind something more; I should like something serious. I should like to be changed by more films, as art can change one: I should like something to happen when I go to the cinema.

WALK UP! WALK UP!—*PLEASE*
By Sidney L. Bernstein

EVERY week some eighteen million and a half people in Great Britain go to the pictures. Greek drama, Roman circus, mediaeval joust or fair, Victorian penny-readings and socials were never so regularly provided or so generally patronised. The cinema, indeed, is a modern portent.

According to individual interpretations of the social pattern, it is a punishment which fits the crime, a cure for the disease, or a reward for the labour of the day: and the cinema, measured by various ideological standards, is the opiate of the people, taking the place of religion and confusing the political issue; the means of artistic expression of a technical age; or the most democratic contribution ever made to the entertainment of the masses.

The cinema is certainly an efficient provider of ready-made day-dreams: it is an escape and a relaxation from workaday conditions. Because of this, the influence which it has on the receptive mind is continually affecting public opinion, manners, customs and fashions. This influence is sometimes good and sometimes bad, and the film industry must accept some responsibility for directing the trend of public opinion.

It is unfortunately easy for the director of a film to handle his material in such a way as to present a picture which has all the appearance of truth, but which, in fact, is travesty. Seeing is so rarely disbelieving; and the adept cutting of a film, the subtle juxtaposition of shots, can convey, more cunningly than words or statistics similarly mishandled, a totally false impression.

The dangers of this facile misrepresentation of fact have recently been illustrated by the effects of some documentary films and news-reels. Film-editors, purporting to convey no more than a record of contemporary occurrences, have implicitly expressed a point of view in their documents.

The first function of the cinema should be not propaganda but entertainment (allowing to the word "entertainment" the most catholic significance, to include the provision of aesthetic enjoyment for such as are capable of it!).

Whilst the cinema has an influence on the social structure, at the same time, like the newspaper, it must reflect (that is, follow as much as mould) public opinion.

Throughout Great Britain, during the course of a year, there are about five hundred feature films issued. The picture-goer chooses his film entertainment from an average of ten films a week. Efficiency of transport enables him to go farther afield than ever before, and the wide publicity given to films and film matters in the Press and in books helps him to shop for his entertainment. Even if he has acquired a *habit* of going to the pictures, he has a fairly wide choice of entertainment available to him any week.

Now since the pictures are patronised by so large

a section of the public and are essentially designed for the majority, it is obvious that a film, to be successful at the box-office, must be sympathetic to contemporary opinions and taste.

The fact that there is no general outcry against the standard of entertainment which is offered at the cinema is not a sure indication that the majority of films are up to the level of public taste. A more accurate deduction can be drawn from the fact that, of the five hundred films issued in any one year, only six or so are record-breakers at the box-office, whilst another twelve, perhaps, produce excellent receipts and another twenty good receipts.

To analyse public tastes in films by any other standard than that of the "box-office reflex" is difficult, because the faculty of articulate criticism is not generally developed. The cinema manager, however, is in a better position to know the wants of his patrons than the film producer, because he is in closer touch with them and day by day he observes their reaction to the current programme.

In the suburbs and provinces it is Monday's audiences that make or break a film: by Monday evening film-going families have made up their minds whether or not the week's programme merits a visit, and on Tuesday the offices and the warehouses have already first-hand information.

Attempts which I have made to analyse the general taste, through personal contacts with a large number of representative picture-goers, through the examination of box-office figures and through a film questionnaire which I issue periodically, indicate that the level of taste is by no means low and that the picture-goer has a considerable degree of discrimination.

It is apparent, for example, that the public can distinguish between sentiment and sentimentality, and between sincerity and window-dressing, approving the one and rejecting the other.

Increasing appreciation is being given to direction. The best example of this awareness is the case of Frank Capra, who has a world-wide following. To-day Capra's name on a cinema poster is in type almost as big as that of the star.

Of course, the most important factor determining a film's success is still its "star value." Naturally enough, the stars with the greatest followings have the largest body of antagonists: Garbo, Mae West, Shirley Temple, Clark Gable, Charles Chaplin are individually as heartily detested by one section of picture-goers as they are adored by the other.

Among cinema audiences the film-fan is increasing in number. He is the graduate, as it were, of the picture-going school. His critical faculty is developing, he can distinguish between good and bad photography and knows something of the technique of film-making. Sometimes he can even differentiate between the good and bad acting of his favourite stars. He is acquiring some degree of articulateness in the correspondence columns of his fan magazines and is eager for pertinent information.

The film-fan is not to be confused with the hero-worshipper, who is completely "gaga" in his appreciation and who is heavily represented in the cinema audience. His interest is not critical. His approach to the film is one of identification. For him the hero is the answer to his own day-dreams and the picture a world which causes the realities around him to dissolve for a while. The films are his release from the frustrations of a dull day.

Public taste is largely determined by local conditions: the industries and political complexion of a district, its age, sex and wealth composition—the local culture, as it were—have all a strong influence on reactions to the cinema. The problem of the artistic development of the film from the important angle of the public which it has to reach can be solved only by reference to general conditions of culture. How relevant they are can be deduced from a comparison of likes and dislikes (measured by box-office receipts) in, say, an industrial area and a black-coat suburb. Films such as *Scarface*, *I am a Fugitive from a Chain Gang*, *Fury* and similar social documents have proved enormously popular in depressed, "proletarian" districts, and less successful with "bourgeoisie" On the other hand, the dormitories of London express a strong preference for romantic entertainment.

Acceptance of the postulate that taste is influenced by local conditions involves the consideration of another question. The majority of films released in this country are produced in America, which is both the largest supplier and the largest consumer of film entertainment. The question is how far the product of any alien culture can satisfy the native demand. (It must be remembered that the product does not reach a highly sophisticated or aesthetically cosmopolitan audience. The great majority of Englishmen—

or Frenchmen, or Dutchmen, or Fiji Islanders—are dyed-in-the-wool local patriots, unlearned in any tradition but their own, insular in their institutions and associations, neither readily amenable to foreign influence nor widely sympathetic to other ways of living.)

Continental films with foreign dialogue, however outstanding they may be and though adequately subtitled, are not a success with English audiences outside the West End of London. It seems that the majority of regular picture-goers are not prepared to make any *effort* to be entertained; their appreciation of a film must not be qualified by the need to exercise intelligence.

A film is always more successful in the country of its origin than a foreign film of equal merit. Even a good Hollywood production is not so popular in this country as a good British film. There are many reasons for this. The national culture plays its part; patriotism is a factor; and the English people—particularly outside London—like to hear the English accent on the screen for the simple reason that they find it easier to follow.

There exists a substantial demand in this country for British films about English life, but only provided that they reach the acknowledged standard of competence which characterises the Hollywood product. The public has too often complained that so many British pictures are imitations of Hollywood's most commonplace efforts—cheap musicals without even the liveliness of their American prototypes, or penny-dreadfuls without Hollywood's technical efficiency.

Yet we have more unexploited "native" screen material than America. (Hyde Park, the Caledonian Market, the Port of London—chosen at random—might supply admirable backgrounds for films of English life.) The Hollywood studios have given notable leads in this direction; they have produced some excellent documents of American life.

In one department of production—the documentary film—Britain is leading: but unfortunately the majority of picture-goers pay to see the feature film only and not the newsreel or documentary (although the popularity of the realist film is growing).

The films of John Grierson and his G.P.O. Film Unit, the *Secrets of Nature* series and the admirable work of Julian Huxley are fine pieces of cinema and have done great credit to their producers and to the British film industry. British newsreels, too, compare very favourably with American: on the whole they are more lively, more informative, more topical and better edited.

However much scope there is for the future development of films in general, and however great the advances which could be made in the satisfaction of cultural demands, figures suggest that the public is in a large measure getting what it wants. But in the boom days of an entertainment such as the cinema, this suggestion must not be taken smugly. Because films have become popular, it is likely that still another two million tickets could be sold weekly.

Eighteen and a half million people a week get three and a half hours of film entertainment at prices ranging from 3*d*. to eight and sixpence. The average price of admission is one shilling; and there are approximately 4,350 cinemas in Great Britain, with an average seating capacity of about nine hundred each. Cinema-owning companies are paying their way, and the major American producing companies are financially in a healthy state. The elementary economics of the situation indicate that—in the short run, at least—there is an adequate balance between supply and demand.

There are two vital problems for the film industry. The first is how to cater for the minority, whose critical faculty is highly developed and whose demands are not met by the ordinary run of pictures. The second is how to attract the absentee who, for one reason or another, stays away from the cinema and has no interest in its progress.

As far as the needs of the minority are concerned, the problem of the supply and distribution of suitable films is economic. The question for the producer is whether he can afford (assuming he is able) to make films which, he believes, will have a limited appeal. The initial outlay of capital on the production of a film is great, and it can only be recovered if the finished product reaches a wide market. The film producer is not in the fortunate position of the producer of a play or the publisher of a book, whose first expenses are lighter and whose costing factors of production can be more easily adjusted to suit the probable demands of the markets.

A strong case can be made against the vested interests of the cinema, and the economic conditions which make the production and selling of film entertainment as much a business proposition as the production and selling of any other consumers' commodity. It is significant that the film has made great progress where costs of production need not be recovered by direct receipts (e.g., in commercially sponsored documentary films). In Russia, too, where the film is produced under a different economic system and to a different end, results have been challenging.

It is an old problem whether aesthetic and commercial values can be reconciled; and it is arguable that the film can never achieve the status of an art until it is freed from profit-making. (With reference to the Russian production of films, it is an equally debatable point whether art and entertainment can be reconciled with politics and propaganda.)

For the exhibitor, the question is whether he can take the risk of alienating his "regulars" in order to satisfy the requirements of the few. The demand of the minority has been met, in large cities, by the provision of specialised cinemas and by the establishment of the film societies. Under present conditions there is a diminishing supply of films for this particular purpose.

To attract the absentee is another thing. There is a section of the public which is definitely antipathetic to the cinema, some from a sort of spiritual opposition to any form of merriment or enjoyment, some from an out-of-date subscription to notions that the cinema is an unhealthy influence. The former are not likely to be seduced from their dour convictions by any efforts of the propagandist. The latter section is obstinate. At one time there was perhaps reason for their criticism; but to-day it is generally admitted that the cinema plays little or no part in corrupting impressionable minds.

The numerically largest section of absentees is not so much antipathetic to the cinema as apathetic. To attract them the cinema manager can rely only upon an extension of those methods by which he has built up and maintained his regular audience. In this connection the cinema meets powerful competition from other forms of entertainment, and it is not the merit of the programme alone which draws custom to the picture theatre. The goodwill element is important.

As a social institution, the local cinema represents to a section of the population the peak of glamour. Warmth and colour are to be had there; there are pleasurable distractions; there are comfort, richness, variety. The cinema is so often the poor man's sole contact with luxury, the only place where he is made to feel a sense of self-importance. With his ninepence in his hand he is able to command something approximating to the attention and service which is part of the pattern of the rich man's everyday life. The West End picture-goer and the film critic should bear in mind that his own appreciation of the cinema is not typical or general. Not only the film programme, but the deep carpets, the bright lights, the attention "fit for a king", are the weekly delights of the majority of picture-goers.

A sense of showmanship, too, is indispensable to the cinema manager, and there is still a place for the

Walk Up! Walk Up!—*Please* 231

direct descendant of the circus "barker" with his top-hat, drum and compelling voice. It is an unfortunate fact that, with the increase of large-scale cinema operation, there is a corresponding decrease in the number of managers with a personality of their own. The show suffers and the loss is the picturegoer's as much as any one's.

What method the cinema can employ to influence public taste for the better is best indicated by a reference to other factors which affect opinion.

It is certain that literature, journalism, the drama, painting and so on, all at one time or another have coloured general sentiments. It is accepted that, by an increased technical efficiency in the use of any means of communication or expression, it is possible to raise the general level of sophistication and to improve general critical standards in so far as they relate to executant proficiency.

Further, at one time and another, public opinion has been influenced by the trend of artistic expression. The film is no exception to the general rule. During the last twenty years the film has achieved a tremendous improvement in methods of production, and naturally parallel with this progress there has been a development in the critical faculties of audiences.

But whether it is possible, by consistently producing the better rather than the worse, permanently to influence taste is a question which does not admit of too ready an answer. An historical survey of taste presents the most astonishing paradoxes.

The cinema manager's altruism, or his personal

wish to widen the scope for artistry in the film, has not been encouraged by the vehement invective and obstruction to which he has frequently been subjected. The "puritans" have found in the cinema a victim for the outpourings of their most active venom. The original stimulus for the attack was probably the fact that the cinema can take the ordinary human being out of himself, can satisfy his normal desire for excitement, adventure, laughter, tears. The arch-apostles of no-joy have been seriously affronted by the achievements of the film, and they have devoted much of their ingenuity to devising new accusations against the film industry.

The demand for further censorship, the opposition to the Sunday opening of cinemas, the suggestions in magistrates' courts that films have increased the number of juvenile delinquents, are continual reminders of an obstructionist attitude which may be sincere but which is not helpful.

Despite these attacks and despite the fact that ordinary standards of commercial morality appear to demand nothing more than honest trading, there are many film producers and exhibitors who have a sense of duty and an urgent desire to improve the standards of entertainment. This can be achieved only with co-operation from outside bodies—from educational and social workers and from the general public. The problem is to encourage the public to understand and appreciate the better rather than the worse.

Perhaps the film trade has not a continuous tradition of serving the best interests of cultural progress.

Beachcomber's "Sol Hogwasch" has his actual archetype, whose treatment of history and of social fact has been based on a generous conception of what-might-have-been rather than what is.

Cinema advertising, too, has on occasion conveyed more enthusiasm than verity. Superlatives have featured too prominently in the showman's vocabulary. It is not surprising that the austere disciple of the arts has looked askance at such lack of reticence and has doubted the aesthetic validity of a means of expression guilty of such lapses.

But it is to be remembered that the cinema, if it is an art, is a popular art. Its progress is essentially a reflection of the progress of general artistic awareness. How is the cinema most satisfactorily to lead public taste, and what opportunities are there for the collaboration of film producer, exhibitor and public?

It seems to me that the most promising approach is to the young, the new generation of picture-goers. The drama is taught in the schools; an attempt is made to encourage the appreciation of literature; instruction in music and painting is given. (My remarks apply only to the universal acceptance of the principle of instruction in the arts and not to the pedagogic methods employed.) Very little, however, has been done to encourage a critical appreciation of the cinema.

In the U.S.A. the Museum of Modern Art Film Library has recognised the need for the creation of a school of the cinema. Copies of films—from the early efforts to the latest productions of world studios—

are being acquired. Programmes are circulated to schools, universities, technical and cultural associations, to illustrate the trend of cinema development; literature on the history of the cinema and the appreciation of its method has been made available. At some universities specific courses of instruction in the cinema are provided.

There is scope for a similar organisation in this country.

Approach to the young can also be made by means of special children's shows. Five hundred cinemas in this country are now running regular weekly shows for children, in response to a definite demand. Unfortunately, the general level of programmes is not high. In many cases these special shows present edited versions of the current week's programmes. In other cases programmes are chosen—rightly and properly—to satisfy the juvenile taste for blood and thunder, and consist of "Westerns," serial pictures and cartoons. Only rarely is any attempt made to influence or lead the taste of the children. I would not change the general character of these programmes, remembering the boredom of "improving" books in my own youth. But there is no reason why an exciting film should not be made as well as, and I hope better than, some of the treatments of classics we so frequently see, which are offered as evidence of the progress of the cinema.

Experiments are being made by enlightened educational authorities. Naturally, however, these efforts have been mainly educational and have been inspired not so much by a desire to improve the critical faculties as to supplement the teaching of subjects such as geography and botany.

Difficulties of supply, the financial failure of special children's shows, and lack of co-operation from outside, have hindered the extension of the idea within the film trade.

I recently made the suggestion, at a conference on films for children convened by the British Film Institute, that a non-profit-making company should be formed for the acquisition of copies of good films for circulation to theatres showing special children's programmes. Such a company, given sufficient financial support and adequate co-operation, could re-edit and cut films of merit (unsuitable for exhibition because of certain incidental developments of plot or unessential scenes) so as to make the best of the film product available for children.

Eventually the organisation might be sufficiently influential and well-endowed to commission the production of special films for children as a publisher commissions a book.

The juvenile mind is impressionable, amenable to suggestion. The adult mind is not so plastic: a method of approach is more difficult to find.

Every intelligent theatre-owner wants films of a better quality. He knows that, if he does not get them, his public will desert him. In 1927 the cinemas were not in a happy state: competition from the wireless and from other forms of entertainment threatened their popularity, and meanwhile the quality of the films was not improving. Then the talkies arrived. The talking film was something as a novelty; but with the rapid improvement of its technique it became an entirely new form of entertainment, as different from its precursor, the silent film, as the *Queen Mary* from the *Mayflower*.

Although the talkies are still improving, the producer of films is without guidance if the public does not voice its requirements. A falling-off in box-office receipts would indicate that something was amiss, but it would not demonstrate in what particular film entertainment was lacking. If methods of film production allowed the artist a free hand there would be scope for experiment. But the plain fact is that many interests are involved in the making of a film, and that, on the technical side, too great a division of labour is needed for the film to be the product of a single genius. The field for experiment is limited by the need for a sound financial policy. A too adventurous policy would result—and has resulted—in bankruptcy.

Films such as *Man of Aran* and *Moana* are examples of a bold, experimental policy of production. Other experimental pictures which have been a comparative success at the box-office are *The Informer, The Story of Louis Pasteur, Fury, Mädchen in Uniform, Mr Deeds Goes to Town, The Private Life of Henry VIII*. The production and release of films such as these have done a great deal to influence general taste for the better.

But it is not possible to lay down hard and fast rules for the development of the cinema as an art-form or a social institution. There are important conditioning factors which can only be briefly indicated here. In my opinion present trends of political and social thought are going to have a decisive influence on all cultural forms. Perhaps the greatest service that can be rendered is the attempt to maintain that freedom of expression which threatens to disappear from the social structure.

The future of the cinema, from this view-point, like the future of all institutions, is in the lap of so great a company of gods.

THE CRITIC IN FILM HISTORY
By Alistair Cooke

A CRITIC is more things than a pawn in the hands of time. But I don't think it has been remarked on often enough that a film critic to-day is what he is through the force of film history, as much as through sucking his thumb when he was a child. This essay considers only this aspect of him and his work: the effect of the early cultural status of films; the public conditions of his work; his private scruples; the practical difficulties of criticising a form so young and so wide in its appeal. By "a critic" I mean not a writer on the theory of film, but a practising reviewer.

A film critic to-day appears to be historically in the position of Aristotle in the three-hundreds B.C. The material to criticise is small and like and there is no tradition to his profession which might confuse his observation. It seems that the film critic is, therefore, in a happy position to repeat Aristotle's performance and to startle the world with good obvious remarks. In the beginning he was. Thirty years ago it was possible for an early critic to define the movies with no more misgivings than Aristotle defined tragedy: as "electricity in its application to the arts." You can be as lucid as that only when there is no risk of being thought naïve. Aristotle could look on tragedy with the bright curiosity of a child working its toy railway.

The Critic in Film History

He could say that tragedy seemed to work best when the "reversal" and the "recognition" came together, and he could say it as pat as that because they were both novelties in those days, even to the learned. In the early days of cinema, of all the critical apparatus that the movies challenged, the sense of wonder was the first. At a time when the flickering image of a train, watched in a Paris basement, was enough to send a hundred intelligent men bolting in fright for the door, critics had clearly not yet acquired a reflex to ridicule or to protect their cultural heritage.

But once the sheer fun and novelty of the thing were over, most people did not fall to speculating on the future of the movies as an art; on the contrary they were soon overcome by an uprush of belated shame. At the start the movies had been sold expensively to people who could afford the luxury in their own homes. As with television to-day, rich people excitedly invited intelligent friends to see an entertainment that none of them would go round the corner to see in a public music-hall. Once a large audience had paid to watch a private owner's performance, the movies were culturally doomed. It got known that they were being operated by ex-hardware dealers and drug-store clerks, and that soon they would be on view for a nickel in the fun-fairs and flea circuses. Thus dedicated to a large and on the whole illiterate audience, the movie men set about providing appropriate fare. The producers knew the sort of audience they had to cater for and they worked logically and exactly to use a type of entertainment which would play on simple sensation and not disturb the audience with literary irrelevances like imagination, verisimilitude, subtle characterisation. At a crucial moment in film history, when it seemed that every resource of the new invention had been exhausted and not even the brilliant, baffling magic of French trick films could keep the public interested, at this moment somebody thought that the visual thrills, which has been itemised in a short, varied programme, could be tied together as a story. *The Great Train Robbery* is a simple thing to look back on, but it was the first feeler into a new world of experience which we now call the movies. After *The Great Train Robbery* the perfect type of movie story was quickly evolved, namely the Western. None of the early producers dreamed that this kind of entertainment would ever compete with the holy illusion of the theatre. They knew they had bought up a crude magic as artless and raffish as the increasingly large audiences that enjoyed it. If magazine and newspaper editors had ever thought of the possibility of film criticism, they could now confidently dismiss the idea. The movies were already, and it seemed finally, taped and labelled.

For a decade many serious men were busy experimenting with this new toy, yet hardly one of them could save the face of a potential audience of millions. Griffith might explain that he got the idea of the "flash-back" and much of his lighting from Dickens, but most people would be content to believe he got them from a mawkish imagination (which might be, of course, in that instance, the same thing). Elie Fauré might write some very fanciful and shrewd speculations about the nature of "cine-plastics", but he was writing for his friends. To Alexander Bakshy, looking ahead, the movies might mean a prospect of "choreography in place of movements which imitated actual life", but to the vast audience that had seen them the movies meant custard pies and John Bunny; the only *deus ex machina* they ever knew was the sheriff.

So through a trick of snobbery the simple Aristotelian lost his chance. There *may* have been some god-like looker-on who, twenty years ago, committed to a private diary "some problems aroused by seeing *Ben Hur*", but they have almost certainly been lost like Aristotle's notes on Homer. It is hard to think, anyway, where he could have usefully published them. The producers from the first looked on the movies as an industry and editors did the same. No practical comparison with the status of a theatre critic could be made, for at that stage the movies were so grossly inferior to the theatre in naturalism, verisimilitude, and in general seriousness that it would have seemed an insult to newspaper or magazine readers to offer them disinterested movie criticism. It would have been like appointing mannequins in the Stone Age. But editors were glad to print the producer's own account of his wares, since they were paid for like any other advertisement. This studio publicity, as it would now be called, filled space and brought in revenue, and in provincial newspapers all over the world it is still, to most editors, the only acceptable movie criticism.

Artists and potential critics were forced to form secret societies where the thought of the general

I

indifference to the movies as a new art stimulated correspondingly exaggerated enthusiasms. It was a pity that so many writers whose odd theories might have been tried and found wanting in a studio did not then need to undergo such practical proof. They could bear their martyrdom proudly and at their leisure elaborate the movies into an art more complex than they ever were, or perhaps ever will become. Sometime in the early 1920's there fell into the lap of these strenuous thinkers the very explicit writing of the Russian directors. When serious men write at length about a trivial art, the reaction of the readers is to take the art as seriously as its commentators. Thus the martyred school of critics made the mistake to which the intelligentsia is always susceptible, the mistake of assuming that the most articulate artists are the best ones. Luckily few of these writers, now bound in honour to every foot of Russian celluloid, had the talent or money to make films as pretentious as their writing, except in one country.

It is not remarkable that in America, where the movies were clearly going to live or perish as popular entertainment or nothing, the movies and the intelligentsia never got together, or at least not till very late. But it was also not remarkable that in France they did, since it is true, I believe, that the French have always retained more respect than most nations for the critic as a participator in the act of creation. Once the French started to theorise about the movies, and to see them with their inner eye as a ripening and complex art, it was to them an inevitable step to set about communicating this vision. The critics and experimentalists started their own studios and together produced the only organised *avant-garde* school of film producers. Though a lot of their work now seems pretentious and overwrought they did not first think of it as the hobby of a coterie, though the later emergence of the movies as the overwhelming popular art of this century has made it seem so. The performance of these films was, and for that matter still is, restricted practically to secret societies. When the films were shipped for foreign showing it was also necessary to export the jargon to understand them, and inevitably the foreign reception of these films was less honest than the French impulse that went to make them. There was recruited an earnest army of art film societies which picked up the jargon, and as with most jargon assumed the new words referred to new and enlightened processes outside the ordinary commercial ways of making films.

This was the first-class dead-end in the history of film criticism. It was a ritualistic jargon and so autonomous that ordinary intelligence seemed out of place. If the critics were agreed that Flugenspiel excelled in "post-reflex dynamic montage", well, it looked as if Flugenspiel would have to be left there. The jargon was already too advanced to be related intelligently to the critical language of painting, say. The period in which this criticism flourished is dead but the jargon is still being stealthily junked on an unsuspecting world.

It may be a long time before all critics are free from its influence, for it prompts reactions, objections, attitudes in many writers who would be the last to think themselves its victims. When a film-goer reads much of this criticism, his reaction is to wonder whether he saw the same film. He wonders whether he even knows how to look at the movies at all, and has an uncomfortable feeling that it must be a very private act, like the confessional or freemasonry. Nobody has more clearly stated this dilemma than Otis Ferguson. He says:

> The appreciation of pictures is much like all other forms; but there is the sad fact of its having thus far got so little intelligent consideration that intelligence, when it appears, tends to become the high priest guarding marvels. Every one goes to the movies, to laugh or delight his heart; they are a part of common experience—and very common at that, usually. Now and then one is good, but in thinking of it we do not think of art. It's just a movie; we only went for the fun. So when some one comes along and says down his nose, Art in the cinema is largely in the hands of artists in cinematograph experimentation, we think, Mm, fancy such a thing, I wonder what *that* is like. When some one, almost holding his breath, says, Well, there is surely no better *montage* (or *regisseur*) than this *montage* (or *regisseur*), we are apt to be discouraged: Oh, damn, I missed it again, all I saw was a story with people and action. And when some one says of *Three Songs About Lenin*, This is pure cinema, implying that you couldn't say more for it, we think, Well, well, can't miss that surely.
>
> The pay-off is that *regisseurs* are in ordinary life directors, that *montage* is simply the day-in-day-out (in Hollywood) business of cutting: all you need, except for the higher technical reaches, is a pair of shears and a good sense of timing. As for pure cinema, we would not praise a novel (in which field by this time you must, to be

intelligent, be intelligible, or perish) by saying merely that it was pure *roman*. . . . *Three Songs About Lenin* may have been attacked with a new attack, may be an awesome experiment. My point is that it is not a good picture, and my quarrel with movie criticism is simply that if it was, those who thought so have not done one thing to show why, in so many simple words.[1]

Time and human impatience will kill this jargon or train it into something practical and handy; increasing Government control of the film industry, for instance, would either kill off good experimentalists or bring them and the commercial studios closer together. But the critic who is outside paid commitments has still and continually to tell himself that the language he uses to describe the effect of films should be understandable by the audience he writes for. This is no special condition of film criticism, it is the ordinary good faith of journalism. But it is certainly harder to maintain when you are writing about a medium that is still inventing its language as it goes.

This is only one difficulty of film criticism, but the way a critic resolves it, the way he finds himself writing, depends on a greater, indeed on the central, critical principle: namely, the right to free and disinterested comment. Honest opinion is by no means the rare pearl that many highbrow periodicals suppose, but the free expression of it in a sick society (or to talk critically, let's say a changing society) is blocked by forces that are normally outside the practice of criticism but which to-day everywhere

[1] From "Artists Among the Flickers," *The New Republic*, December 5, 1934.

generate or stall its energies. These are, in any country, the degree of autocracy; the dependence of a newspaper on its advertising; and also in England the paralysing nicety of the libel laws. Most critics writing to-day in whatever language have to keep one eye on the advertising columns. All editors know this and many regret it, and only a magazine like *Variety*, which is the shop-window for movie advertising, can afford to disregard a studio threat of withdrawal. *Variety* must know that it is the studio, not *Variety*, which will lose in the long run from withdrawing its advertising, so it has often happened that a two-page spread announcing the movie of the century would be healthily and uniquely sterilised over the page by Miss Ager's dry-point irony. But *Variety* is a blessed anomaly in trade journalism and not its arch-type. In other trade journals, and to a lesser degree in newspapers and magazines that advertise motion pictures, the critic cannot retch over the hand that feeds him. It is not surprising, therefore, that independent criticism exists chiefly in the serious weekly periodicals and in literary monthlies and quarterlies. (The independence of cinema periodicals is more suspect because it is an independence committed to certain slogans and *a priori* ideas.)

Before the critic can try to clarify his social function he must first know his market. For no criticism, however mild in general tone, can possibly be free and independent if it is to compromise with practical and ulterior motives. This is a pitiful situation but it is the one we live in, and any theoretical discussion of critical method and function is a mere pawing of the stratosphere until these virulent social checks have been acknowledged. So far I have been representing society and advertising managers as sending the critic reeling to his corner every time he makes a show of fight. And so they do. But if this essay is to continue we must imagine him to be ideally backed. And then see what functional difficulties he will have anyway, what dark passages lie between his work and his conscience. Even though we put him cleanly on his feet with a pencil in his right hand and a glove on his left, it is as well we should see that he is not much more than toddling, for he has had little more than ten years to gauge the audience he is writing for. It is only during the last decade that editors began to see that practically everybody went to the movies and that it was physically possible, granted an iron constitution, to see about 650 feature films a year; most editors saw it would be a service to have some one pick out the kinds of movies and say roughly what they had to offer. So the film critic became a fact, a sort of cross-breed between a dramatic critic and a motor correspondent.

It always seems intellectual to talk about the function of those sorts of practical criticism which allow little time for spiritual meditation and the issues, or at least the objects, of which seem so transitory. But every critic, however cheerful and reassuring he may appear, is constantly compelled to take stock of his job and to try to see what he thinks he is doing. This is no place to sketch the infinite number of critical theories that bear on the way a critic treats his material and his audience. This theoretical confusion is always exaggerated because it is assumed that a critic bears on his back and in his memory the accumulated load of theory from Longinus to Granville Hicks. But at any given period in history the critical issue is always clear-cut to the interested people: with Castelvetro it is the unities, with the Elizabethans it is the offence and defence of rhyme, with the gay 'nineties it is "Is literature moral or isn't it?" Film criticism may be expected from its working conditions alone, and from the popularity of its material, to be well behind current critical theory. Perhaps to-day, of the several simple attitudes which the film critic is most likely to take over, there are two which are pertinent to, and certainly most common in, practical film criticism. They are popular simplifications of two opposing post-War credos: the position of Mr Mencken and the most famous position of Mr Eliot.

In literary criticism to-day the issue—between enchanting the reader and simply explaining to him—seems to have been decided in favour of Mr Eliot's doctrine, if not his practice. It is the credo that: 'in matters of great importance a critic must not coerce and he must not make judgments of worse or better. He must simply elucidate; the reader will form the correct judgment for himself . . . the free intelligence is that which is wholly devoted to inquiry." This is a noble doctrine but it is often forgotten that criticism even at its best is written by human beings. Mr Eliot may write this historical pronouncement in all sincerity in his early thirties, but a few years later Mr Eliot has eased up sufficiently to be making all sorts of spry comparisons and judgments "of worse or better", coercing us into overwhelming admiration for Charles Whibley, saying in two consecutive sentences that: "Dickens's best novel is probably *Bleak House*, that is Mr Chesterton's opinion and there is no better critic of Dickens than Mr Chesterton. Collins' best novel is *The Woman in White*." Which is more like hi-jacking than coercion. I don't know whether this is a failing in criticism, the warm desire to persuade people into an opinion, but it seems that later in life a healthy impulse rescued Mr Eliot from his earlier Papal Bull.

Yet of the two attitudes this is probably a safer, and harder, way to follow—the growing human by degrees. For the alternative is to come right out at about the age of twenty and chant Mr Mencken's no-nonsense assurance that no judgments can be permanently valid, so why not go ahead and express yourself. This unfairly telescopes the critical doctrine he popularised just when film criticism was beginning to stammer, and his full passage is worth quoting:

> . . . the delusion that criticism may be definitive—that appeals to the emotions, which shift and change with every wind, may be appraised and sorted out by appeals to the mind, which is theoretically unchangeable. Certainly every reflective student of any of the fine arts should know that this is not so. There is no such thing as literary immortality. We remember Homer, but we forget the poets that the Greeks, too, forgot. You may be sure that there were Shakespeares in Carthage, and more of them at the court of Amenophis IV, but their very names are lost. . . .

Criticism is thus anything but scientific, for it cannot reach judgments that are surely and permanently valid. The most it can do, at its best, is to pronounce verdicts that are valid here and now, in the light of living knowledge and prejudice. As the background shifts the verdict changes. The best critic is not that fool who tries to resist the process—by setting up artificial standards, by prattling of laws and principles that do not exist, by going into the dead past for criteria of the present—but that more prudent fellow who submits himself frankly to the flow of his time, and rejoices in its aliveness. Charles Augustin Sainte-Beuve was a good critic, for he saw everything as a Frenchman of the Second Empire, and if his judgments must be revised to-day it still remains true that they were honest and intelligent when he formulated them.[1]

This, it is true, would be the most natural way of writing if it were not true that the human mind, like its body, runs to fatty degeneration and senile emphasis. And anybody starting out in this belief may go on for several years by sheer vivacity expounding vital opinion, but in no time the "personal" touch will have become a pulse of prejudice and the gift of observation will have grown all too humanly selective. Certainly it is honest to say that you do not expect to be right for all time, but that doesn't prevent your being wrong even for your own time. There are at least two ways of submitting yourself "frankly to the flow of your time". There is the way Sainte-Beuve had by health rather than choice: the way of submitting your intelligence without

[1] From *Prejudices: Fifth Series.* "The Critic and His Job." By H. L. Mencken. (London: Jonathan Cape; New York: Alfred Knopf).

inhibition to the forces of your time, which are creating, you have no doubt, a good and interesting world you will never know. And there is the other way, of submitting yourself completely to the flow, not of your time, but of your generation so that you are borne along with it and can flow with no other. It is doubtful whether Sainte-Beuve thought of himself as what now we know him to be—a man seeing everything "as a Frenchman of the Second Empire". He gives himself to his time but he is hardly aware of himself as holding a watching brief for his place and time; he is steeling no age against posterity, least of all the Second Empire.

These two attitudes may have seemed an odd choice, yet I think they are the alternatives that a film critic is most likely to face, because they represent the two strongest competing impulses from which a critic, when called upon, will try to rationalise his social position. That of Mr Eliot is one of withdrawal from the material you are criticising. That of Mr Mencken is complete surrender in the hope you will reflect some of its contemporary *tempo* and flavour. Film critics especially must soon come to terms with these rival impulses, for the work they criticise does not come to them primarily as a concept; it comes directly as a sensation. No art, entertainment, or whatnot, is more direct than the film. It may be that whatever reserve a critic wishes to keep for himself, he involuntarily yields more of it than he knows. For the movies do not represent emotion, they communicate it almost irresistibly by magnifying and quickening the way emotion comes to us in real life, that is, through optics and dynamics. We cannot say at the moment where film criticism ends and literary or political criticism begins because ideas come at us in the movies with all the beautiful confusion of life itself—we may be moved one moment by a line of dialogue, at the next by the look of the veins on somebody's hands, by the sound of a train's siren fading as the countryside fades. Whether we like it or not, we are *in* a movie all the time, we're not seeing, as we do in the theatre, a level picture grouped at a given distance. We are on trains and falling down cliffs, we are watching with a quick turn of the head a whip hurtling towards a man's ankle, we are staring face downward in a pool, we are at one second watching from the gallery, at the next we are in the stalls, the wings, or the flies. It is we that lean back in chairs and see sympathetic faces come to *us* for pity's sake, and a dreaded door opens suddenly in *our* face. But then, by the snipping of a pair of shears, we are outside looking imperturbably on at a conversation between two people up there, a conversation that is private from every other person in the plot. We are at once audience, confidant, and victim. If a critic is an assessor of something that is presented to him, then we shall have no film critics until the psychologists and the eye specialists get together and tell us when and how and why we react to such things as double-exposure, to a magnified tear, to dissolves, wipes, movement across the screen and movement into your face; for these are the mechanised units with which the movies attack your nervous system and leave you battered and bedraggled and a willing sucker for a piece that as a literary product, or an example of the best that is known and thought, is pathetic besides the play at the local repertory theatre which leaves you, behind a yawning hand, laughing softly at its naïve conventions, at the archness of its movement, at the engrossed *naïveté* of its motives.

To practise film criticism honestly but without pain, it is necessary to grasp this dilemma, that we do not yet know the social or artistic power of the movies. We talk about them culturally, while all the time their action is less like painting and more like music or a hypodermic needle. So it is harder in the movies than in any other art to distinguish intensity from quality of emotion. All critics, to whatever intellectual or artistic principles they are committed, feel this difficulty, that the better a film is directed, the more certain will the spectator be absorbed in what is happening on the screen. And there is no means of getting a context clearer, or thinking twice about it, for you can't go back, as you can with literature, or painting, or music, and ponder the thing over. But, however much this absorption gets in the way of acute or disciplined criticism, there's no use writing about it as a nuisance. It may not help us to say what movie criticism should be, but it does help us to see what the movies are. And if we get a clear notion of the nature of the cinema, we are nearer to knowing what are the requirements and limits of cinema criticism.

The notion is not far to seek. When a newspaper critic protests that *Zéro de Conduite* is a coterie or "specialist" film; when a highbrow critic is put out by the "popularity" of Frank Capra just when he was about to become a highbrow favourite—they are both girding at something which is the essence of the cinema, at its innate and impenitent democracy. Twenty years ago movie experimentalists could legitimately believe that whatever was good in the movies would be pearls before swine. But since the movies have developed as industry and as popular entertainment, it happens all the time that certified pearls seem to contain ingredients essential to the nourishment of swine. I have preferred the historical or materialist explanation ("since they have developed as industry and as popular entertainment") because I believe it is still too early to diagnose "the nature of film" and to say, therefore, that this development was a natural and inevitable growth. Whichever it may turn out to be, there is no doubt that, whereas critics of music and art and politics can feel themselves to be sitting outside the turmoil, outside the emotion that created the thing they are criticising, a film critic is willy-nilly one of the mob. It is this identity of the spectator with the performer in an emotion which is often simple but always intense which makes us think constantly of the movies as a probable folk art. The evidence of the annual box-office toll is enough to show that the movies are already the greatest folk entertainment in history. From this realisation it is but a step to the sentimental and confused assumption that therefore like will find like, water will reach its level, the only sincere interpretation is a sob or a smile, and the critic is an impertinence.

It is a mistake to say that because the movies are

at their best in dealing with strong popular emotions, they should not be discussed in intellectual terms. This is a common and I believe a fatal error, propagated especially by people who want to release the study of English literature from its academic prison and who talk, with the best intentions, about bringing literature into the sun and air. In practice this means reading a ballad aloud and saying, "There, what could be simpler. No need of footnotes to that, surely." Which may be true enough if you happen to be an Englishman, or, better, a Border Scot. The teachers of Balinese dancing might suppose it would be needless to explain their children's dancing, and indeed they will considerately make no effort to do so, until the bewildered foreigner confesses he has no idea what sort of emotion is being represented and he finds it impossible to know whether the basic gestures are of the knee, hip, pelvis, or finger-joint.

Perhaps the closest analogy, in miniature, and one that may point to the fate of folk art in a world with our means of physical and mental communication, is the case of what is now called "swing" music. For an ideal discussion, it has this advantage: the impulse that creates it is even farther away than the movies from the intellectual level on which it gets criticised; it spans almost the human opposites from Sir Richard Paget's "instinctive cries" to the meditations of philosophy. American negroes, and Americans generally, notice that foreign fans, French and English especially, grow extremely solemn about the relative merits of a solo by Barney Bigard and another by Hodges. American fans may choose to be solemn, but to other

Americans, and to negroes especially, the solo is a simple pleasure. To the Englishman who is not a fan it is something vile. I once heard a darkie postman walking along with his mail-bag whistling the trumpet solo in Redman's *Saratoga Swing*. He seemed a tender and naïve man, but he had no difficulty at all with the tricky accenting, and he would probably have been appalled by a musical Englishman who thought the piece horrible to hear. The Englishman might be equally tender and naïve, but not in the same way, and we are made to wonder if there is a simple idiom in music which is universally acceptable as something gay, or funny, or sad. A minor chord may soothe a Persian, but to a Western European it announces an omen. So while the negroes play their swing and twinkle to the smallest nuances of tenderness, ribaldry, and noise, the moment the white, or at least the European, starts to like it, he is on the way to discussing the music in intellectual terms. He has to discuss busking not as a humorous expression but as a musical device. He falls to noting the similarity of harmonic texture between Delius' *Walk to the Paradise Garden* and Ellington's *Rude Interlude*. (Ellington himself was told about this and said he must take a look some time at this Delius guy, which he probably never has.) I suppose a foreign understanding of a folk art could not be alone a profound familiarity with technical detail, nor a simple swoon of delight. It would be both.

The fact that the *St. Louis Blues*, originating in New Orleans, can in twenty years be heard in every capital of the world, does not prove the "universality" of jazz.

The Critic in Film History

It proves, if anything, that we have better communications, by air, radio, film, than we used to. Many negro writers have been unduly proud of this circulation value. But whatever the *St. Louis Blues* means to a negro, it happens to offer to non-musical whites and westerners an easily accepted formula of self-pity which is not primarily its appeal to the people who wrote it. This is a large sentence and it may be wondered what *is* its appeal to those people. Well, maybe there are more appeals than one. Gaiety may be one element, but marijuana's another. Yet, not to trim the argument too cynically, there is a quality which is a special endowment of negroes, or perhaps it's only the technical exuberance that expresses it. I don't know how you pin down this quality in words, but I think one negro has diffused it over a memorable paragraph. Louis Armstrong, or the negro friend who helped him write his book,[1] describes the first time he left New Orleans on a river-boat as the member of a band. He says:

> We shoved away early in the morning, so we could make Baton Rouge, our first stop, by night-down. It was a run of about eighty miles, upstream. A few passengers were on board, as it was to be a day trip, although the *Dixie Belle* was not meant to be a boat for regular passenger travel but only for big excursion parties, so she was not fitted out with many staterooms.
>
> It was a warm spring day and the river was high with water, but not flooding. The musicians did not have much to do except laze around on the decks and watch the shores, or now and then throw a little dice or something.

[1] *Swing That Music.* By Louis Armstrong (Longmans, Green: London and New York. 1937).

258   Footnotes to The Film

After a while, when we had had our last look at New Orleans, I found myself a nice corner up on the top deck right under the pilot house and settled down with my trumpet and a polishing rag. I had bought myself a fine new instrument just before starting out, but even that wasn't shiny enough for *this* trip. No, suh! So I took the rag and shined her a little and then I put her to my mouth and tried out a few blasts. She sounded strong and sweet, with a good pure tone. I swung a little tune and saw we were going to get along fine together. So then I rubbed her up some more, taking my time, until I was satisfied. Over on the left shore a great cypress swamp was passing slowly by—there must have been hundreds of miles of it—stretching away off to the west—dark and hung all over with Spanish moss. I felt very happy where I was. The sun was just warm enough, the chunking of the paddle-wheels was now pleasant to hear and everything was peaceful. Pretty soon I spread the rag on the deck beside me and lay my new trumpet on it and began to think of how lucky I really was. There I was, still only nineteen years old, a member of a fine band, and starting out on my first big adventure. And I had my new trumpet to take with me. I reached over and let my hand lay on it, and felt very comfortable, and then before long I dozed off and slept most of the rest of that first day.

Some of the charm of this is the genuine and unselfconscious personal relationships with his trumpet and the music it will play, and also his dependence on them. For when he is depressed or overworked, swing music delights the heart of the darkie, whatever it may do to whites. When delight is as spontaneous as swing, it seems a pity to start defining it. Yet, however delightful the emotion that Louis Armstrong's prose expresses, it is also a fact that it is a piece of remarkably good prose. Heaven knows what would happen to Armstrong's prose or his music if he were told he is the Izaak Walton of jazz, but if a literary critic feels inclined to say it, it is his job to do so. This is the active mischief of a critic of folk art: by making the art known to itself he is quickening the process of its decay, he is helping artists who act on a hunch to sit down and work out their "artistic purpose". As long as the critics can be kept away from the directors, unless a new kind of critic is born, the director who has some understanding for communal emotion may work unspoiled. But now that Mr. Capra's early comedies, put out as cheerful entertainment, are being recognised as "classics," Mr. Capra himself is beginning to feel the responsibility and is embarking on the heavy literary seas of *Lost Horizons*.

This last example assumes that the movies *are* a folk art, whereas it has been the point of the long and, I hope, helpful analogy to suggest that a folk art of any value is nowadays hard to achieve. It's easy to talk about the movies as the twentieth-century ballad. But however folksy the ballad was in the fourteenth century, compared with the total audience for a film, it was a minority product. "Sir Patrick Spens" may represent certain simple universal emotions, but it is a nice point to know if they are what made the ballad popular. The localisms are equally endearing to a Scot and once these are not understood it's not easy to make much of it. "Clerk Saunders" in French or Chinese would confront those nations with some curious conceptions.

The movies, if it is indeed their fate to be a great folk art, are faced with a task unique in history. They will have to discover for the first time the universal impulses which can be represented for the equal delight of the Eskimos, the Americans, the French, the Japanese, the Arabs, the Zulus, and the English. This seems a ludicrous ambition, but oddly enough it has happened. It has happened with Chaplin and it has happened with at least one film of Frank Capra. One would have thought the Riskin conception of the wise under-dog, the shrewd hick, in *Mr. Deeds Goes To Town* was very western and extremely American in its easy fusion of irony and sentimentality. But the Poles loved it, the English voted it the best comedy in years, the Near East was charmed. If a critic is going to write relevantly, he will have to know a great deal about ordinary men and women, even if he knows little about anthropology. It may not be his ambition to spot winners. But if they become winners, and he had never thought it, it's likely he overlooked their essential qualities.

The film critic who will diagnose the universals of a film is not yet alive. And at the moment it seems dangerous high-falutin' to say that this emotion or that is universal—until the Japanese verdict is to hand. The film critic seems at his worst when he is aware of literary or theatre comparisons of style, when he is making his own (superior) cultural position clear, when he is apostrophising the illiteracy that went to the making of a film. To date he seems to be at his best when he is telling himself what he likes about a movie. This is, I expect, an early stage in the critical history of the arts, but it is an honest and an exhilarating one.

I have been hoping all this time that the movies don't pretend to be anything more than baked beans, but I've been writing of them at least in the hope that they might become art. And it is time to end as we began, with the reminder that to the people who make them they may be incidentally all sorts of fun, but they are first of all an industry.

To the industry, then, what help can this critic be, who when he is most honest, I have said, is so busy communing with himself and wondering why this turn of a wheel gave him a shock, why that long shot and the men pulling down a flag made him cry? The industry may say that the critic, however useful he may be to a man who wants a tip for his shilling, can be no use to it. And they who say so may be right. But that is only because critics to-day are not specifically film critics, they are literary critics and tipsters and professional decoys all in one. Up to now, I doubt if a film or a film-cycle has ever been started through the advice of a professional critic. For the very good reason, as the producers, directors and film-editors know, that critics are notoriously vague about the vital processes of film construction, about the actual moments in a film that give it speed, fluency, or what else. I don't mean critics have not spent many harmless hours speculating *in general* about the emotional effects of rapid or slow cutting, or about the use of dissolves and so on. But a man may write good philosophy without knowing when to take his meals. And most of the speculation of the best film critics takes for granted processes of film-making which are basic: I mean, story-construction, the effective relationship of director and cameraman, and continuity—especially continuity. This has been bluntly stated and needs sharpening.

Most critics would probably resent any suggestion that they should be directly helping to make good films. But few critics will deny they mean to give pleasure by their writing and they would be flattered if that pleasure seemed relevant to the film under discussion. But however endearing their writing turns out to be, as invective, mockery, social observation, it is not often that a man who had worked on the production would feel the critic knew where the film went wrong or right. The producers can say this much for their indifference to the professional critics, that they know a critic will almost invariably fail to recognise the weaknesses which were the nightmare of the crew when the film was in production. Sometimes, this may mean nothing at all. More often it creates in the film-makers the sort of confident distrust of the critics that a sonneteer would feel of a reviewer who was not aware that a sonnet turns at the eighth line. So the producer is not very distraught over the very personal reactions of Mr. Fink who writes for the "New World" and the "New Era." If, while the producer was making a film, he was in doubt about the way it should end, he would give his bank balance to have the uncanny sense of "idea" possessed by the late Irving Thalberg; instead of the finicky, not to say neurotic, presence of the critic, he would prefer the more genial and practical presence of Mr. Schenck, who knows by the unfailing gluck of a lump in his throat whether a film "goes" or not.

In this impasse, there appear to be certain qualifications for the good critic which are not often united in the same man: namely, a freedom from inhibition, so that he does not have to invent motive; a real nervous knowledge of the mechanics of film, so that he feels where the engine is "missing"; a practical and healthy emotional balance, so that he can look on at simple feelings without being forced into literary giggles or precious dissociations. These seem rare ideals, but there have been critics who possessed them. Yet in the end there's no sense in arranging what the perfect critic shall be and then looking around for a human being to fit. The fact is, there have been, and will go on being, many sorts of good critic. In the present state of British and American film criticism there are a score of critics who are thoughtful, clever, ingenious. But it is hardest of all to be apt. It may be we are already too sophisticated, too literary to criticise with a clean and alert intelligence a game with the folk simplicity and strength of the movies. For time and again in English criticism one reads a clever remark and feels what a good remark it would be if only it were true.

CENSORSHIP AND FILM SOCIETIES

By Forsyth Hardy

ONCE again there is a state of acute conflict between the Film Censor and those who seek freedom of expression for the cinema. Previous memorable conflicts have been over the early Soviet films, from some of which the ban has only recently been lifted; over *The Night Patrol*, the anti-white-slave traffic film so vigorously defended by Bernard Shaw; and over *Outward Bound*, the American film version of Sutton Vane's after-life play. The same tendency to prevent the discussion on the screen of public affairs and issues affecting the lives of men and women is apparent again to-day. Most notorious of recent cases was the holding up of *The Peace of Britain* until a flood of Press comment forced the Censor to release this short peace film.

If this and other actions had not appeared to be part of a definite policy, concern would not have been so widespread or so great. But any faint doubts that these may have been chance deviations from a more liberal attitude were dismissed when Lord Tyrrell, the Film Censor, addressing film exhibitors in June, 1936, suggested that cinema needs continued repression of controversy in order to stave off disaster. "So far", he congratulated himself, this country had had no film dealing with "current, burning political questions", but now the "thin end of the wedge" was being inserted, and who knew to what lengths it might go "unless some check" were put on soon? After that there could be no doubting the tendency and emphasis of film censorship in Britain. The edict had gone forth: No controversy.

Every one of liberal spirit instinctively objects to this situation. By tradition and temperament we are impatient of censorship and the limitation by one of the freedom of all which it implies. Freedom for much which is worthless or even harmful, I suggest, is preferable to restriction which might exclude at its first approach something valuable to politics, art or morals. Had censorship been given its head, as Bernard Shaw has reminded us, much of the art and many of the ideas that influence the world would have been denied to us. Some of the greatest films yet produced have been kept from the people of this country through the operations of the Censor. It is intolerable to any one of liberal outlook that censorship should impede the freedom of the screen for the normal purposes of public address. The platform and the pulpit, books and plays, can be used with comparative freedom by any one with something new and vital to say about religion, politics or the relations between men and women; but censorship would deny this right to the screen. Cinema has peculiar advantages, in range and graphic appeal, over other mediums of expression and persuasion; but those who would use it freely are tongue-tied. This restriction of the free and healthy use of the cinema and the consequent encouragement of "the enervating romanticism of the average film" has been properly described as "a pathetic breach of public responsibility" (*World Film News*, September 1936).

"We cannot allow ourselves to be ruled by a gang of mystery men," said H. G. Wells when *The Peace of Britain* was held up. Who are the mystery men, and how did they come to have such power? The British Board of Film Censors is an unofficial body, appointed by the film trade and paid out of fees received for censoring films. It was set up in 1912—at a time when the cinema was suspect of being exploited for pornographic purposes—as a voluntary censorship to examine films before they reached the screen and thus ensure a measure of protection for the trade. What official status the Board has, came through alliance with the local government constitution. By the Cinematograph Act of 1909, inflammable films may be shown only in premises licensed by a County Council or other competent authority. By a gradual process, most of the authorities throughout the country made it a condition of licence-holding that no film could be shown in the licensee's cinema—without their express consent—unless it had been passed for general exhibition by the Board. This condition was contested but eventually upheld in the Courts. Thus an Act whose primary object was to ensure that cinemas should be safe, sanitary and well-conducted became a medium of censorship. Though still without official or legal status, the Board of Censors has gained authority over the screen.

The local authorities, it should be added, did not altogether abrogate their powers, and they still retain responsibility for the films shown in their areas.

Their opportunity to exercise their legal right, however, was recently indirectly limited when the Kinematograph Renters' Society required its members to enter individually into an agreement with the Board to rent only those films which had received a Censor's certificate. This step, apparently taken out of fear that repeated passing by local authorities of rejected films might attract Government attention and bring about censorship revision, has further strengthened the position of the Board by handicapping the circulation of uncertificated films.

Having gained unofficial but effective power over the screen by this quaint and devious route, what is the Board of Censors doing with it? According to a pamphlet, "Censorship in Great Britain", issued by the Board, it is guided by "the broad principle that nothing will be passed which is calculated to demoralise the public. . . . Consideration has to be given to the impression made on an average audience which includes a not inconsiderable proportion of people of immature judgment." The mental pace, it appears, is to be set by the half-witted. But the Board, as I have pointed out, was not originally established in the interests of the public. It was not set up for "the ultimate purpose of defending public morals, but for the purpose of defending private commerce."

The Board has, of course, gone far beyond this latter purpose. Further indication of its guiding principles is contained in the familiar lists of prohibited categories mentioned in the annual reports. This censorship by category is a vicious system. To recall only one example of its unreasonable application. When Miss Baxter, a London social worker, made *The Night Patrol*, a film dealing in part with the white-slave traffic, it was refused a certificate in view of the Censor's standing rule that there must be no reference to the white-slave traffic on the screen. This decision drew from Bernard Shaw the pointed comment: "When I find an official who is entrusted with the arbitrary control of the picture theatres allowing unlimited liberty to pornography and absolutely refusing to allow honest and decent social welfare films to be exhibited . . . then I appeal to public opinion to sweep that official and his powers and his department into the dustbin."

The Censor apparently does not consider the meaning and purpose of a film in coming to a decision. He works by rule of category alone. But if films are to be banned because they deal vitally with politics, religion, crime and sex, cinema expression in this country will be reduced to the level of puerile prattling. The Censor's categories, in the light of changing social conditions and the new and purposeful applications of the film, have become untenable, especially in view of the wide interpretation which has been put on them. One of the prohibited categories, for example, is "Themes likely to wound the just susceptibilities of Friendly Nations." This was given as the reason for banning a film pleading for the release of Thaelmann from a Nazi prison where he had been held for three years without a trial. A similar reason was given for the deletion, from a *March of Time* item dealing with the Abyssinian War, of a reference to the precautionary massing of a large part of the British Fleet at Alexandria—a matter of common knowledge at the time. Here the Board, under cover of its categories, was invading the realm not of opinion but of fact.

So far only the Board's attitude to completed films has been discussed. For some years, however, the Censor has exercised a measure of direct control over production by offering to give an opinion on any film script submitted to him. From the practical point of view, such an arrangement has certain advantages: the alteration of a completed film can be an awkward and expensive matter. Further, it is conceivable that, in some hands, this policy might keep much that is silly and shoddy from the screen, though there is little evidence of it being used for that purpose so far. But if this is to be a means of enforcing a uniform standard on film production by a Board which confines itself "to the question of what is or is not permissible as reasonable entertainment by the average members of the public who frequent the modern cinema," then it is merely a sinister tightening of the Board's stranglehold on the screen as a free medium of expression. How can the British cinema ever grow up if every script is to be adapted to meet the mental outlook of those of immature judgment? If the producer happens to be a pioneer with something new and vital to say, and his script is in potentiality a film which will shock people out of complacency, then the door to the cinema will be locked and barred against him from the beginning.

It is admittedly difficult to point to many concrete

cases of film projects of this kind being submitted to the Censor and rejected. One which received some publicity, however, was the proposal to make a British film about Judge Jeffreys, which was abandoned when the Censor stated that no reflection upon the administration of British justice at any period could be admitted, that no phrase so lurid as "The Bloody Assize" could be used, and that various incidents in Jeffreys' career would have to be omitted. But open protests from the trade at the decisions of the Censor Board are comparatively rare, for the reason already suggested: that the trade does not wish to do or say anything which might lead to the abolition of the present form of censorship set up by itself and the substitution of a body under direct Government control. There are, however, hints of dissatisfaction behind the scenes. "At the request to bring complaint and grievance into the open," comments *World Film News* (August 1936), "deep calls hush to deep, the stories temporarily cease to circulate and an uncomfortable silence prevails until the menace of publicity is past. In plain words, Wardour Street is scared stiff of the Censor."

It is remarkable that an industry so vocal over other issues affecting its welfare should be so silent over the vital matter of censorship. True, the Association of Cine-Technicians, following Lord Tyrrell's "no controversy" speech, passed a resolution maintaining that "the elimination from cinematograph subject material of any controversial question deprives the cinema of the possibility of playing any useful part in the life of the nation, and will have the effect of holding it permanently at the 'nickelodeon' level from which the skill of generations of technicians has raised it to the heights of an art unlimited in potentiality." The technicians however, have made the only reported protest. We are left uncertain as to the attitude of the producers.

Is the obvious timidity in the treatment of the real interests and dramas of British life the result of lack of courage and enterprise, or of fear for the Censor? It is not a question which can be decided without more evidence. Perhaps an indication of whether or not it is the Censor who is keeping British films at their present unrealistic level might be given if one of the producers adopted a suggestion made by J. B. Priestley (*The Star*: July 3, 1936): "I wish one of them would come out with something hot and strong on the radical side (if he wants my assistance he can have it), so that we could make a test case of it with the Censor."

It is not my purpose in this article to discuss the need for censorship or the supersession of the present system in this country by some other kind of control. Quite apart from its present apparent tendency to prevent controversial opinion reaching the screen, the present system is weak in that it is designed for dealing only with the widespread distribution of films on a commercial scale. Its clumsy and anomalous regulations assume that all films are intended for unrestricted public circulation, and there is no power—whether or not there is the inclination—to license a film for limited exhibition to groups of societies specially interested in its subject or technique.

Thus a tantalising obstacle is placed in the way of developing a specialist cinema movement on the lines of similar movements in the theatre. If, for example, a film of serious social interest is submitted to the Board and rejected as unsuitable for general and indiscriminate exhibition, not only is there very little chance of the film receiving even limited exhibition but a damaging blow is struck at the production source. As I have pointed out, members of the K.R.S. have agreed to rent only those films which carry the Board's certificate, and while this agreement is considered to refer only to the public exhibition of films, it has had an intimidating effect and the members now hesitate to handle any uncertificated film for private exhibition.

If the renter is not a member of the Society, there remains the possibility of appeal to the local licensing authority, which is, however, too often prepared to accept without question the judgment of the Board. In this latter respect, a more progressive attitude was reported recently (March 1937) on the part of the licensing committee of the Surrey County Council, which, while refusing to permit the exhibition of *Sex Ignorance* (rejected by the Board), decided to place it in a special educational category. On application being made by a responsible society or body of persons, it was intimated, permission would be given for its exhibition to selected audiences. From the long-distance point of view, the refusal of a certificate is a serious matter for the producer. In its 1932 Report the Board stated with ironical satisfaction: "There is no case on record of a film, after its rejection by the

Censorship and Film Societies 273

Board, proving a commercial success." The outlook for any producer of advanced films is thus grim.

Despite this and other handicaps, there has grown up a movement devoted to securing exhibition for advanced social and artistic films. It began in London in 1925 when the Film Society was formed. As Ivor Montagu records in *Cinema Quarterly* (Autumn, 1932), the founders of the Society assumed that there would be the same freedom for private performances of films as there is for plays, being at the time unaware that "the clumsy wording of an incompetent lawyer has not only established a film censorship, but given it powers over private shows as strict as over public." Two days before its first performance, the Society got the London County Council sanction it needed to show films not submitted to the Censor. Since that time it has played a vital part in the development of the movement, both through its introduction into the country of films of special interest and by its function as a protective agent against censorship. Its lead has been followed by other groups and societies in different parts of the country.

Outside of London, however, the movement has been handicapped by "the whimsies and perversities" of local licensing councils; by opposition from strict Sabbatarians who disliked the thought even of private groups witnessing films on Sundays; and to some extent by the intervention of the trade. As an illustration of the first, I need only refer to the case of the Manchester and Salford Workers' Film Society which, after a period of opposition from the Salford Watch Committee over the early Soviet films, removed to

K

Manchester where, though the Watch Committee there refused permission to show *The Blue Express* and *The New Babylon*, the Society has enjoyed greater freedom. Its difficulties were increased by pressure brought to bear on licensees by the Watch Committees, and on one occasion an exhibitor was fined for an infringement of the regulations. Now, after having been forced to change cinemas on seven occasions, the Society has settled down in Manchester. A case such as this, however, reveals some of the difficulties encountered by those wishing to see films of educational value and artistic distinction not shown in the ordinary cinema.

Chief opposition seems to have come from Sabbatarian sources in the case of the Leeds Film Group, which has made a long and fruitless attempt to obtain the Watch Committee's permission for a monthly Sunday performance. By the Cinematograph Act of 1909, as has been pointed out, all exhibitions of inflammable films must be given in licensed premises. Cinemas, however, are not normally available on week-days; and the licensing of ordinary halls for film performances is bound up with complicated regulations dealing with safety against fire, the use of music and other details. The only practical method for the film society is to hold its private performances on Sundays, when the cinema is not in use. In Leeds, opposition to such a course came also from the local branch of the Cinematograph Exhibitors' Association, who argued that as cinemas in the Yorkshire area did not have Sunday opening, there was no reason why one cinema should. By such nauseous narrow-mindedness is a potentially valuable movement restricted.

A recent review of the film society movement in this country placed its strength at over a hundred groups. This includes the large and comparatively important exhibiting societies organised on the model of the Film Society, and combined in the Federation of British Film Societies and the Federation of Scottish Film Societies; the societies affiliated to the Film Institute, which combine courses of lectures with exhibitions, given for the most part on sub-standard stock; and the many unaffiliated societies less firmly established in practice and policy. Standards vary among the different major societies: there are diverse interpretations of their common aim—"The study and advancement of film art." Some societies, such as Edinburgh, have concentrated on experiment and technique, with specialised programmes on colour and music in films; others, including Glasgow, have arranged repertory seasons in addition to the ordinary programmes; one or two, notably the Tyneside Society, have provided the initiative for amateur production; many have considered it enough to provide local exhibition for the films shown in the specialised theatres in London. The different standards, however, may very well represent various stages of development. In general the film societies represent a growing interest in the more progressive applications of the film, and they have already contributed much to a better understanding of the potentialities of the medium. The influence of the movement is wider than its numbers represent. It has stimulated an intelligent appreciation of the art of the film in circles formerly unresponsive and raised critical standards all over the country. It has been so successful in building up a new audience that more and more cinemas are devoting themselves to specialised programmes on the lines of the Academy in London.

The work of the film societies, however, is just beginning. According to John Grierson, "the movement will not have achieved its aim till the new audience is strong enough to warrant specialised production as well. In that day the present rule of cinema will certainly be broken and the film directors who are also artists will find their first positive encouragement since cinema began." In the early years, the Film Society in London did what it could to assist and direct the young societies struggling into existence and they will always be grateful. The first attempt to found a Federation of British Film Societies (Welwyn, September 1932) did not produce the service and stimulus the movement so urgently needed. The second attempt, at a conference at Leicester (April 1936) was also unproductive, though the chaotic state of affairs it revealed had the effect of forcing the Scottish societies to take action independently and form their own Federation. Since then the English societies have collaborated in forming a new Federation of British Film Societies which, though its plans are not completed at the time of writing, has already made a workmanlike approach to the problems facing the movement.

The Scottish Federation, whose first year of independent working has been remarkably successful, recognises the desirability of a strong national body to speak for the whole movement and, at a later stage, will probably co-operate with the British Federation as one of the units into which it is proposed to divide the country. A central organisation for the introduction and booking of films and for the supply of information is a vital necessity, and this is appreciated by those sponsoring the new British Federation which will presumably take over much of the work done in this connection by the Film Society in London. The desirability in principle of co-operation has always been appreciated by the more progressive societies, but so far it has proved difficult to achieve in practice. The future of the movement, it is clear, lies with the greater power which nation-wide organisation of this kind can give.

At a time when there is a widespread impression that the producers are playing down to an ignorant audience which does not in fact exist, the film societies represent the only articulate demand for a better type of film than that which normally fills the screens. It seems intolerable that needless obstacles should be placed in the way of its meeting that demand. If the societies continue to be regarded with apathy by the trade, and if the Board of Censors makes difficult the circulation of films of serious purpose, then they must turn to the local authorities and seek their active co-operation. The local authority still retains responsibility for the films shown in its area, and an enlightened exercise of its legal right would allow the film societies, representing as they do intelligent and advanced opinion in the film-going world, a more reasonable latitude in the matter of censorship than the trade's Board, concerned with indiscriminate exhibition, is able to do. The local authorities must recognise by now that the cinema is as vital a medium of public address and information as the Press and broadcasting. They must ask themselves if its development is to be retarded by the power with which they have indirectly invested the Censor Board. They may ask themselves also if the censorship is justified in stepping over its vaguely defined limits and attempting to prevent the free discussion on the screen of the real issues affecting the life of British people.

If local authorities help to off-set this restrictive influence they will be assisting in the development of an independent British cinema, vitally concerned with the production of films of social importance. The film societies offer one medium for encouraging the development of such a cinema. They represent a vital constructive force in the matter of raising film standards. Censorship at best is restrictive. It may remove obscenity, but it is never very effective in raising the standard of taste. It is surely desirable that any agency by which a progressive influence can be brought to bear on the cinema should have the support of every public-spirited man, or body of men.

CONCLUSION:
ARE FILMS WORTH WHILE?

By Charles Davy

ANYONE who gets as far as here may be feeling he has read more than enough about films. Are they worth so much paper and print?

Footnotes to the Film exists to answer this question: it ought to justify itself, if at all, as it goes along. Yet its separate chapters, by authors with various special qualifications, are confined naturally to particular aspects of the subject. The general question of what the cinema is doing with all its technical resources may still be asked. What is the effect of films on the film-goer? What sort of experience do they offer him when he has bought his ticket at an average box-office and sat down for his two hours' show?

The most obviously new capacity of the cinema, as a source of entertainment, is its immense descriptive power. It can penetrate in and out of doors; it ranges through city slums and Western prairies; it sails the sea and explores every kind of landscape; and all these aspects of the world's daily life it renders in the peculiarly vivid terms of the pictorial image, reinforced now always with dialogue and natural sound and sometimes with attempts at natural colour.

However, film audiences certainly don't pay simply to have the world set before them. They want romance, adventure; they want to identify themselves with the glamorous behaviour of their favourite heroes and heroines; they pay to escape from their own dull lives and too familiar selves. It is because the cinema is able to satisfy these desires that it becomes a subject for criticism. If all it could do was to mirror the world there would be no point in writing books about it. Actually, it is occupied constantly in interpreting the world. Most films preach the worship of success and teach that success is the reward of virtue. They teach that life's supreme felicity consists in the winning of a desired woman. They teach that good intentions plus muddled thinking are lovable and will do no harm. They teach that our present society brings the best man to the top. They teach that luxury is an art and art a luxury. To all these charges exceptions could be found—more easily now than five or ten years ago. But the mere fact that the cinema has the power of telling emotionally effective lies is enough to make it worth writing about. It is evidently something quite different from a mirror; we could say it is more like a lens, able to distort and clarify and magnify. No scientific simile, however, is adequate, for the cinema acts upon the observer as well as upon the thing observed, establishing a new relationship of perception between them. Whatever nonsense films may talk about art, they are marked with the character of a potential art themselves.

Of D. H. Lawrence, Aldous Huxley says:[1]

> To be with Lawrence was a kind of adventure, a voyage of discovery into newness and otherness. For, being

[1] *The Letters of D. H. Lawrence.* Edited and with an Introduction by Aldous Huxley (Heinemann: 1932).

himself of a different order, he inhabited a different universe from that of other men—a brighter and intenser world, of which, while he spoke, he would make you free. He looked at things with the eyes, so it seemed, of a man who had been at the brink of death and to whom, as he emerges from the darkness, the world reveals itself as unfathomably beautiful and mysterious. For Lawrence, existence was one continuous convalescence; it was as though he were newly reborn from a mortal illness every day of his life.

This is the eyesight of the artist which he gives to others through his work. So often, our relation to the world of nature is determined by purposes and needs. Either we stand apart from nature and try to understand it by means of analytical thought, or we reach after it with lust to gain power over it, to devour it and make it our own. When through a work of art we experience a part of nature we are neither separate from it nor is it consumed in the flame of our demands. We experience it by entering into it and sharing its life—by experiencing it for what it is, not for what it means to us. We have something like an experience of love without desire.

All arts reveal harmonies in nature, but their methods of doing so are conditioned obviously by their respective tools. At one extreme is sculpture, whose harmonies are revealed purely in space and stand there, visible and changeless, as long as stone endures. At the other extreme is music, whose harmonies are revealed purely in time and cease to exist perceptibly as soon as the time occupied by a performance is over. Cinema, the art of *moving pictures*, expresses itself in time and in space, uniting both on equal terms. There is a sense in which poetry does this also, for the content of its time-patterns consists of images which may be of scenes or objects extended in space. There is always a radical difference, for cinema presents its images directly to the physical eye, not to the mind's eye, and their arrangement is governed by the rectangular frame of a picture-theatre screen. Nevertheless, I think that poetry is the art most nearly related to cinema; and I am sure that film technique has been handicapped by nothing so much as by the automatic assumption that it must somehow resemble the quite different technique of the stage play.

It is true that the art of the theatre, like the art of cinema, uses time and space together, and true also that it is possible to produce a film of sorts—and one which may not be entirely devoid of dramatic interest —simply by recording photographically the action and dialogue of a play. But the space used by a play is physical, three-dimensional space—"real" space. Whatever the audience are to see through the proscenium arch must be of such a size and character that it can be rendered, or suggested, in terms of material scenery, for the space is there and cannot be altered. The audience cannot be made to look first at tiny figures far off in a landscape and next moment at nothing but a single actor's face. In its use of time the theatre has rather more freedom; its time is less "real", for years are made to pass by dropping the curtain for a few moments. But while a scene is actually playing its time must be "real"; if there is a clock on the stage its hands will move at the same rate as those of a clock outside. In the theatre there is no way of presenting motion speeded up or slowed down; no way of weaving past, present and future events together into a single dramatic sequence.

These limitations of the drama are not a handicap to the drama itself; they are its natural working tools which it uses for conveying its particular effects, with the essential assistance of living players. Intimate contact between players and audience is indispensable to the theatre; indeed, the rendering of a play on any given night is a creative activity to which players and audience both contribute. The cinema is denied this powerful resource; and by imitating stage technique it accepts the limitations of the theatre without enjoying its advantages. When a stage play is photographed nothing is created *on the screen*; all the creative work has been done beforehand and is merely copied, flatly, in an alien medium wherein its own expressive powers are crippled and starved. (See Alfred Hitchcock's article, where he refers to the drawbacks of photographing long scenes without a break. "The camera . . . is simply standing there, *hoping* to catch something with a visual point to it.")

There used to be a Russian theory which said that the cinema ought to avoid as far as possible all theatrical material. There were to be scarcely any studio sets and no trained actors. If a director needed a peasant in the cast he got hold of a real peasant of the right type and found some way of photographing his behaviour, piece by piece, just when he was registering the right expressions. The classical example of this method is Pudovkin's use of a conjurer, out of camera range, to get a crowd of Mongols to show excited interest during the fur sale in *Storm Over Asia*. Certainly it is a valuable method, but to make a universal doctrine out of it is to turn one of the distinctive freedoms of the cinema into a limitation. Could a Chinese peasant woman have given as much as Luise Rainer does to *The Good Earth*? There is indeed no acting skill which the cinema does not need, but its need is always for separate pieces of acting which it can take and build into its own visual pattern, never for a complete, consecutive performance, however brilliant, played in front of a passive camera.

Similarly, there is need in film production for all possible skill in designing sets and costumes and lighting schemes—for skill and care and patience in all the innumerable tasks concerned with preparing material for the camera. Only it must never be forgotten that the purpose of these tasks *is* simply to prepare material—raw material: not to create complete scenes and finished effects which then have merely to be photographed and shown. The quality of a film's material gives it only potential value: nothing critically relevant can be said finally about whatever may have existed in real space in front of the camera, but only about whatever appears within the rectangle of the screen. The danger of theatrical preconceptions is that they are always tempting a director to forget the screen and to think instead of real objects and events which the audience never actually sees.

I don't want to seem to minimise story value or the film's power of rendering human character and talk

Are Films Worth While?   285

and action. No technique can change bad material into a good film. But how are we to tell what is good material? Only when we have seen what the director makes of it on the screen.

Now let us consider the relationship of cinema to poetry. In Mrs Virginia Woolf's latest novel, *The Years*,[1] the following passage occurs at the beginning of the second section, headed *1891*:

> The autumn wind blew over England. It twitched the leaves off the trees, and down they fluttered, spotted red and yellow, or sent them floating, flaunting in wide curves before they settled. In towns coming in gusts round the corners, the wind blew here a hat off; there lifted a veil high above a woman's head. Money was in brisk circulation. The streets were crowded. Upon the sloping desks of the offices near St Paul's, clerks paused with their pens on the ruled page. It was difficult to work after the holidays. Margate, Eastbourne and Brighton had bronzed them and tanned them. The sparrows and starlings, making their discordant chatter round the eaves of St Martin's, whitened the heads of the sleek statues holding rods or rolls of paper in Parliament Square. Blowing behind the boat train, the wind ruffled the channel, tossed the grapes in Provence, and made the lazy fisher boy, who was lying on his back in his boat in the Mediterranean, roll over and snatch a rope.

This passage, I believe, could be used without much change as the shooting script of a film—though a film we should be lucky to see made. An autumn wind is blowing over England, marking the end of summer, the turn of the year. This coming of autumn has been often described by poets and novelists, and there

[1] *The Years.* By Virginia Woolf (Hogarth Press: 1937).

are many ways of describing it more or less effectively. For instance, its quality may be concentrated into a single scene, watched by a single person—a person, perhaps, who stands on the edge of a wood while the wind sweeps through it, blowing down the leaves. Whether Mrs Woolf's method is superior, for the purpose of a novel, need not be considered here. What I want to emphasise is that the further her method gets away from straightforward reporting—from the description of a single scene from a single fixed viewpoint—the nearer it comes to another kind of description in which the cinema excels.

What is Mrs Woolf's method? The scenes she evokes are scattered through space and time: her total picture is of something which does not and cannot exist as an entity in the physical world. It is a picture of something created by herself, which comes into being for the first time as she writes. And in order to create it she has first to break down the given unity of the physical world and choose from it certain elements which are brought together into a new unity designed to convey a particular experience—an experience which could not be had from directly observing the physical world itself.

It is from a precisely similar selective approach to nature—an approach which breaks down and chooses and rebuilds—that the cinema derives its own creative power. Imagine this passage from Mrs Woolf put on the screen. (I am not suggesting that an *exact* translation would be possible: certain effects would lose and perhaps some others would gain.) First, a windy landscape: the floating leaves dissolving into hats blowing along city streets. The view widens to show the crowds passing the shop windows: people stopping to look at the windows and going in to buy. A view of money crossing the counter, of the writing of bills, and so of a pen writing in a ledger, and of the pen pausing while a clerk looks up through a window at St. Paul's and sees waves breaking on a beach. But in the wind is a sound of the chattering of sparrows in London; and now, chattering discordantly round the eaves of St Martin's, they are blown away to cast their droppings on the statues in Parliament Square. Following them, the view rises; smoke is blowing off chimney-tops, blowing from the engine of the boat train over fields, from the Channel steamer over the sea, whose waves are the waves of grapes tossed by the wind in Provence and are again the sunlit waves of the Mediterranean, where the lazy fisher boy feels his boat heave and rolls over snatching at a rope.

Translating Mrs Woolf into other *words* is a sorry business: its sole purpose is to suggest how this passage could be translated into *images* on a cinema screen. Why I have dwelt on it is to suggest that film technique will find its nearest models in the novel, not in the theatre. Not, certainly, in any kind of novel, but in the poetic novel, by which dangerous phrase I do not mean a novel written in that fearful hybrid, prose-poetry, nor a novel vaguely "romantic" in content. I mean simply a novel which conveys an experience of values and does not merely report events. The reason why the cinema is so much nearly akin to the novel than to the theatre is that in the theatre everything must happen in real space and time, whereas the cinema and the novel are alike free to move to and fro in time and space and to mould both to their own needs.

So far, it may have been noticed, I have spoken only of silent screen imagery, and I believe that all the essentials of screen technique derive from this realm of visual silence. But there are important reservations to be made. First—as Maurice Jaubert has noted in his contribution to this book—films never have been strictly silent. A need has always been felt for sounds of some sort—to begin with, musical sounds—not only to support the action and to cover incidentally irrelevant noises, and not only to induce in the audience a relaxed mood of emotional acquiescence, but also to emphasise and to *comment upon* certain aspects of the action.

When the talkies first arrived, various theories were put forward—notably by some of the leading Russian directors—as to the right way of blending dialogue with visual imagery. Some of these theorists went so far as to argue that an image must *never* be accompanied on the screen by the sound associated with it in nature. Sound and dialogue, they said, should be used as a kind of counterpoint, striking in precisely so as to convey an impression *not* emanating from any object visible at that same moment on the screen. It was never found possible to carry these theories far into practice, chiefly, I think, because, once sound and dialogue are admitted into a film, a disturbingly artificial effect will be created if you show a person talking without allowing his words to be heard. I can see no way round this difficulty, and yet I believe that in these theories—although they cannot be applied literally—there are valuable germs of truth capable of a development which as yet they have scarcely at all received.

The trouble is that the talkies, while supplying this new possibility, acted as a severe handicap on the general progress of screen technique. A performance recorded before microphone and camera was so realistic, so theatrical, that producers were deceived further and further into the use of stage methods, not only when they were filming stage plays with a minimum of alteration—as they quickly began to do—but equally when they were handling original stories or stories derived from novels. Talkie technique, since those early days, has improved immensely in mechanical efficiency—in quality of recording, in command of swift action, and in renewal of the camera's freedom to move about as it likes, indoors and out of doors—but the assumption still prevails that the business of a talkie is to record a series of acted scenes which could be observed and listened to just as well off the screen as upon it. Only the strength of this assumption can explain the chorus of praise bestowed last year on *Dodsworth*, Hollywood's version of the novel by Sinclair Lewis.

Dodsworth had the advantages of an intelligently conceived story dealing with interesting issues, social and personal, and of excellent acting from Walter Huston and Ruth Chatterton, but scarcely for a single moment did it give me the impression that I was watching a *film*. The effect was always of looking at a record of events which had happened somewhere in real space and time, with camera and microphone present simply as recording agents. And an immense amount of time was spent on the realistic acting and talking through of scenes whose essential points, crystallised into expressive visual terms, could have been given to the eye in a few moments.

The Russian theorists were, I believe, quite right to feel instinctively that the sound content of a film must be considered and treated separately from its visual content. This separation is in fact present already in the mechanism of talkie recording, with its separate sound-track, and of talkie production, with its battery of loud-speakers behind the screen; and to me it always seems surprising that we are able to accept so easily the queer mechanical marriage of sound and image which occurs when a film is shown. It is a marriage of life-like voices with quite unlife-like black-and-white images on a flat screen — an extraordinary mixture of conventions found in no other art. We do accept it, and yet I feel that in accepting it we fall victims to a kind of temptation. Because we like realistic effects we accept a conjuring-trick union of sound and image when this very need for trickery ought to rouse us to declare the *marriage* void—to unmask it as merely a business association between two partners whose powers of useful co-operation will be made clear only when they are no longer allowed to pose before the public as man and wife.

By accepting this marriage at face value the screen is again submitting to theatrical limitations without enjoying in return any of the essential advantages of the stage, where the marriage of sight and sound is genuine and indissoluble. What, then, is the right line of co-operation between sound and image on the screen? This is a problem which could be fully solved only by experiments of which very few have yet been made. It is true that film sounds and voices are used occasionally with a freedom impossible in the theatre. There is the device of synchronising a view of one person's listening face with the sound of another person's speech, and the device of allowing someone to hear audibly the voice of his own thoughts. But there has been so far no conscious, concerted attempt to treat sounds and images as separate elements from the start—as elements which must certainly be brought into association, but whose association should be governed by the needs of artistic expression and not derived automatically from their conjunction in nature. I am not suggesting a forced, arbitrary rule of invariably dissociating sound from images: there must obviously be passages of dialogue recorded quite naturally while the person speaking them is visible on the screen. But there is no less need for a clear understanding that film sounds and images *are* separable, and that the cinema will continue with tied hands until the possibilities of this separation are fully explored. Probably the most fruitful starting-point would be to assume that the essential function of sound and dialogue is to act as a *commentary* on the visual action; but it is experiments that are wanted here, not dogmatic theories. There have been some valuable experiments, chiefly in documentaries—notably in Grierson's and Wright's *Song of Ceylon*—

but there is great need for work with ordinary story-pictures on a larger scale.

A fundamental mistake of many commercial producers, I believe, has been to assume that talkie resources, once the initial mechanical difficulties were overcome, would make screen story-telling easier. They certainly have obviated the laborious sub-title, but actually the technique of any art becomes more exacting in proportion to the material complexity of its medium. The more of the objective world it tries to handle, the harder will be its task of subduing its subject-matter to its expressive purpose. The delightful silhouettes of Lotte Reiniger are an example of screen art at its freest. Miss Reiniger, manipulating her shadow figures against her exquisite paper backgrounds, can do with them just as she likes: neither her figures nor their settings are bound by the laws of a solid world inhabited by human beings. Walt Disney, drawing his cartoons, enjoys a very similar freedom, and it is not surprising—except that the gifts of an original artist are always surprising—that he should have gone farther than any producer of ordinary talkies in developing an expressive technique peculiar to the screen.

However, the cinema cannot rest content with silhouettes and cartoons. It has to plunge into the midst of the human world of men and women, and I doubt whether it can refuse any technical innovation which enables it to bring more of this world within its scope. At present there have been, I should say, no talkies so aesthetically satisfying as a few of the best silent films—Pudovkin's *The End of St Petersburg* or

Dovshenko's *Earth*—but the microphone, once invented, could not be barred from the film studio. Similarly, the cinema is now being driven to accept colour, and will probably have to accept it for regular use as soon as it becomes less expensive. Producers—see Paul Nash's article—are attracted towards colour mostly because they again suppose that it will make their task *easier*. That is, it will help them to reproduce realistically the external world. But to the art of the cinema, it seems to me, colour is offering no easy opportunity but an onerous new problem. More onerous, indeed, in some ways, than the new problems created by the talkies, for a talkie can have periods of silence, in which the old, purely visual technique may still hold good, whereas a colour film almost certainly must be coloured all through, which means that black-and-white technique is excluded from the start.

Nevertheless, the cinema has to bear these burdens of sound and colour, for its distinctive power, as an artistic medium, consists precisely in combining the most vivid physical realism with a treatment *not* limited by physical space or time. As Professor Allardyce Nicoll has said:[1]

> The film has the power of giving an impression of actuality and it can thrill us by its penetrating truth to life: but it may, if we desire, call into existence the strangest of visionary worlds and make these too seem real. . . . To the cinema is given a sphere, where the subjective and objective approaches are combined, where individualisation takes the place of type characterisation, where reality

[1] *Film and Theatre.* By Allardyce Nicoll (Harrap: 1936).

may faithfully be imitated and where the utterly fantastic equally is granted a home.

One way of combining subjective with objective on the screen is by using visual imagery to symbolise states of consciousness. This is a resource which the cinema has taken up occasionally but has never consistently explored. *The Cabinet of Dr Caligari* showed the world as seen by a madman; and *Raskolnikov*—the German silent version of *Crime and Punishment*—employed distorted scenery to illustrate the emotional conflicts in Raskolnikov's mind. The use of magic in *The Student of Prague* had a similar tendency (much more evident in the silent version than in the recent talkie version): visual expression was given to the interplay between a world of objective events and the subjective world of Balduin's tormented inner life. Further possibilities of the same order are offered by the use of subjective sound—as in the knife episode in Alfred Hitchcock's *Blackmail*, referred to in his article—but here there has been even less experiment than in the use of subjective imagery.

I am not sure how far films can wisely go in this symbolising of states of mind, for there are likely to be many difficulties in blending purely subjective images with objective ones. Here, again, many more experiments are needed. But I am certain that the future of the cinema lies in the cultivation of every one of its peculiar poetic powers, which are much more varied and far-reaching than any one might suppose from regularly visiting picture theatres to-day. Most certainly the cinema has also its legitimate realm of prose: here are found—or should be found—newsreels, scientific films, and the more directly instructive types of education film: in fact, all films concerned with conveying the plain bread of accurate information. But the main energies of the cinema will probably continue always to be devoted to story-films, together with documentaries which set out to convey experience as well as facts; and in this main field of its work it is as an art—a distinctive art, with a technique of its own—that the cinema must succeed or fail.

At this point objections may be expected from several quarters. It may be that Mr Basil Dean, to judge from certain passages in his trenchant article, would accuse me of emphasising technical theories at the expense of subjects. But I agree with Mr Dean that cinema and theatre should both "draw their inspiration from humanity", and I agree that theories of technique are useless unless they can help the cinema to deal expressively with the human material it finds in daily life. I believe strongly—as will be seen later—that the cinema should be, and can only be, a popular art, not a recondite one, and that indeed one of its chief sources of strength lies in its power of handling a wide range of richly human, solidly familiar subject-matter. What I wish to emphasise is not at all the importance of technique as an end in itself, but the importance for the cinema of a technique which will give it a maximum of expressive freedom in mediating between the world outside picture theatres and the public within.

However, let us consider some further likely criticisms. There are Left Wing social reformers to whom the word "art"—and it is a word which has become fearfully debased—is suspect because it suggests to them a desire to escape from the urgency of social problems into a world of beautiful dreams. And there are the commercial dealers in films who regard the cinema *solely* as a business: who feel quite honestly that their position is no different from that of any other sellers of a commodity wanted by the public. To them it seems silly to think of measuring the merits of a film by any standard except that of its box-office receipts.

Those Left Wing reformers who view with suspicion the word "art" are eager to seize hold of the cinema and use it for the one task which appears to them important—the task of promoting social revolution. Well, I am all for social revolution—of course, on my own lines, not exactly those of Moscow or Berlin—but I am not in favour of using the ordinary storytelling cinema as a vehicle for social propaganda. I mean that I am not in favour of using it, under a cloak of entertainment, to stir people to action by a presentation of screen material designed deliberately to work on their emotions. Let there be any amount of plain truth-telling by the cinema—far more in the newsreels, for instance, than there is to-day: that should be enough to provide plenty of pungent arguments for social reform. In this propagandist age, too, a place must be allowed to propaganda films which are made quite openly as weapons in a recognised campaign. But when the subtle power which art has of working on human consciousness is used to drive people unawares towards a certain course of action—or even towards certain conclusions which carry a demand for action—then I believe the result will always deceive those who expect by this means to build a better world.

The experience of a work of art is of values resident in the world here and now, in sorrow equally with joy. And if this were the *whole* truth about art, it might be necessary for social reformers to banish art from any society not already perfect. But it is not the whole truth, any more than "The Kingdom of Heaven is within you" is the whole truth about religion. To this saying must be added its paradoxical companion, "Thy Kingdom come." The question is —if a man has found the Kingdom within, in what way will he wish to change the world without? He must still wish the Kingdom to come, but I think he will not expect it to come in the form of a *permanent* social paradise on earth, for the ceaseless dialectic of history, keeping the forces of destructive change active in society equally with the forces of constructive growth, will appear to him as the counterpart of a dialectical conflict inherent in human nature. His revolutionary vision will look forward to no preordained Utopia; rather will it demand, perhaps, a condition of social life, assuming different external forms at different periods and in different places, in which the experience of the "Kingdom within" will be realised not only in solitude but in community.

The artist is concerned with values experienced to-day, the social reformer with goals attainable to-morrow: but they need one another. I doubt whether fruitful social reforms can be carried through by any one who thinks only of to-morrow, for when that to-morrow comes he will be thinking of to-morrow still; he and those whom he leads will never have time to live. Their eyes, fixed on a goal which recedes as fast as they approach it, will be blind to the world around them although it includes themselves. Yet the social reformer, if he is to help his fellow human beings, must be aware of them; he must understand the need of the human spirit for that contemplative experience which alone can give significance to the tension of action. The value of human life is measurable only in terms of experience—"where man is not, nature is barren"—and therefore the value of social reforms has to be measured in terms of the quality of experience which is made possible within the new society they create. But unless the experiences which give value to social life are known to-day, no measure is given for judging the value of any new social life to-morrow. As a source and inspirer of value-judgments the work of the artist is indispensable to the social reformer, and in order to act as such an inspirer art must be left free, not made to lose its integrity in the service of propaganda. This is what the social reformer must ask of the artist and all that he may ask—that the artist should devote his heart and soul to doing his best work, in freedom; and what is asked of him in return by the artist is that he should devote himself heart and soul to removing some of the social obstacles—there are plenty of them in our time—which prevent the artist's best work from getting freely done.

Perhaps this will not satisfy the social revolutionaries, but it is all I can say here, briefly, on a difficult subject. There remain the commercial film men who ask why talk about art should interfere with their business. But is theirs quite an ordinary business? Compare the faces of a crowd coming out of a suburban cinema at closing time and the faces of a crowd coming out of a big store or a tea-shop in the lunch hour. The product handled by the film trade is highly charged with emotional force; it exerts a profound influence for good or evil—see Mr Bernstein's article—on the feelings and attitudes and aspirations of thousands of men and women in most countries every day. In fact, whether film dealers like it or not, their product has always some of the characteristics of an art. The question is whether it shall be the whole art which refreshes or the shoddy art which drugs.

If a producer, however, were to agree with this outlook, he might still declare that he was constantly handicapped by having to sell his films to mass audiences in order to get back his production costs. And it is true that this necessity does act as a tremendous handicap on the cinema's artistic progress: it can scarcely ever afford to engage in experiments which only a small proportion of its total public will at first appreciate. Yet from this very handicap the cinema derives a status and a social importance of its own. It can only be a popular art and could be the first truly popular art in history—if we take art to imply a relationship between individual artists and a public, for in anonymous folk-art artist and audience are indistinguishable. (Alistair Cooke's article is relevant here.) The work of a great artist who made *successful* films would reach simultaneously an audience of unprecedented size, and for this reason alone would strike into popular consciousness with unprecedented force. But the cinema has the opportunity to become the first popular art not only because it is enabled by its mechanical facilities—and indeed compelled by its financial requirements—to multiply its products over wide areas. It has this opportunity also because it combines a power of compelling attention by appealing forcibly to the physical senses with a power of using its most vividly realistic effects as a source of poetry for eye and ear.

The bringing together of these two powers, the realistic and the poetic, is the purpose of film technique. Most certainly, the peculiar technique of cinema can be abused, just as the technique of any art can be abused, and is abused as soon as it is made a means of self-glorifying display instead of a self-effacing means of expression. (See Basil Wright's remarks on the abuse of camera tricks.) But the technique of cinema is simply its native language, and it must have a language if it is to say anything about the world beyond reporting it literally. At the first moment when Griffith cut from a long-shot to a close-up, without interrupting the action, the cinema began to speak a language of its own, and the most recondite experiments in Russian montage, or the most daring uses of subjective imagery, are no more than a development of this same language. They are not a new tongue demanded by cliques of aesthetes for their private pleasure.

It is because the cinema is thus endowed with a power of vigorous poetic language that it can afford to take its subject-matter from the most realistic aspects of daily life. "To exploit the powers of natural observation; to build a picture of reality; to bring cinema to its destiny as a social commentator, inspirator and art; to make it bite into the time, and, from its independent vantage, contribute to the articulation of the time"—this, as John Grierson says in his article, should be the ambition of film producers who understand the possibilities of their medium, for the cinema is not one of those minor arts or crafts which can handle only delicate, fragile, exquisite material—material already half-way towards poetry before any work upon it starts. But it is just here that the average producer falls between two stools. He knows that his audiences want something more than a reporting of the objective world, and at the same time he is suspicious of anything *called* art—so what does he do? He first constructs in his studio a prettily unreal world of sentiment and fancy, or a luridly unreal world of sensation, and then photographs his studio world with little alteration. Whatever artifice he uses goes into the building of a world unreal from the start, so that his audiences are given neither the plain bread of honest reporting nor the good wine of poetry. They are given a sort of synthetic mineral water, frothy with sentiment, highly coloured with cheap romance and strengthened with a dash of adulterated passion.

Nevertheless, film producers are quite right to feel that they are not free to decide what films they shall make. Nothing is more futile than to tell a producer he *ought* to make pictures which he knows cannot pay their way. Film standards are determined by the public; it is audiences, rather than producers, who should be blamed for bad pictures. But is it fair to blame audiences without asking who or what produces *them?* The film public in any place and time is a function of its social environment: if bad films are desired it is because the desire for them has been bred out of starvations and distortions encountered habitually in daily social life. On the whole, a society gets the films it deserves; but here one must add that it gets also the films which many of its more influential members think desirable for other people.

It is not the purpose of this book—I repeat—to tell producers what they ought to do, for their own business is something American producers, at any rate, do know—see Maurice Kann's article—and the answer to idealistic exhortations will always be: "Only too glad—if you'll show us how to pay for it." The purpose of this book is to suggest not *oughts* but *mights* —to suggest what the cinema might do and to give reasons for believing that what it might do is something worth writing books about. And what it might do is to become an art realistic, poetic and popular— realistic in its subject-matter, poetic in its final utterance and popular in its range of appeal. If its desire for realism were strong, it would be forced to achieve poetry in order to justify its separate existence; and because it is free to follow a desire for realism into the darkest and brightest corners of the world and the heart, indoors and out of doors, wherever human beings are, it has the power to write on the screen some of the new poetry of the future.

POSTSCRIPT: THE FILM MARCHES ON

By Charles Davy

LOOKING back over the short interval of time since the first edition of this book was planned, what is there to catch the eye? No masterpiece, certainly, which has given the cinema a new direction. No startling new talents. But there have been some important changes, with fruit still to bear.

How will the British film industry react to the new Cinematograph Films Act, passed after terrific negotiations in the spring of this year to renew the quota protection first given to British films under the expiring Act of 1927? The new Act was determined to kill the "quota quickies"—the films which were made as cheaply as possible by American renters to meet their quota obligations, and which helped Hollywood further by serving as a usefully bad advertisement for British production. And so the Act declared that only films on which a certain sum had been spent—a minimum of £7,500 for labour costs alone—should rank for quota in future. A queer arrangement, reached probably with reluctance only after it had been decided that any scheme for granting quota on a quality test basis would never work—for by whom and on what grounds could the quality judgments be passed? However, the Act does also provide—for whatever it may be worth—that a film "of special entertainment value" may be granted exemption from the cost clause by the Board of Trade on the advice of the Cinematograph Films Council, and that a film which satisfies the cost clause may be similarly disallowed for quota on the grounds of "insufficient entertainment value". The Cinematograph Films Council, set up by the Act, consists of twenty-one members, of whom eleven (including the chairman) must be persons independent of the film trade. Its functions are to "keep under review the progress of the British Film Industry and report to the Board of Trade; to advise the Board of Trade on all subjects relating to the industry and to submit an annual report to the Board of Trade". Since the middle of June the Council has been at work under the chairmanship of Sir Frederick Whyte.

For American renters the Act means first and foremost that they have now got to undertake—or at least to finance—the production here of a certain number of fairly expensive films every year. Metro-Goldwyn, for instance, with their own unit set up at Denham, have already a programme of first-line features in view; they began with *A Yank at Oxford* and at the moment are working on Cronin's novel, *The Citadel*, directed by King Vidor, with Robert Donat and Rosalind Russell in the leads. This kind of enterprise is preferable on most counts to the making of "quota quickies"; but a no less obvious weakness of the Act is its failure to distinguish between British films and films made in Britain. However, the problem of how to define a British film, except in strictly legal terms, has always been somewhat obscure. *Farewell Again*, one of the best pictures to come from a British studio recently, was sponsored by Alexander Korda, Hungarian born; produced by a German, Erich Pommer, from a story by another German, Wolfgang Wilhelm; directed by an American, Tim Whelan, and photographed by a Chinese, James Wong Howe.

A more important question for the future, perhaps, is whether the Act will do anything to bring some kind of order and sobriety into the gold-rush business of financing British production. Are the men who can make the best films going to get the money for them, or will most of the money continue to go to the men who can tell the best bedtime stories in City lunch-rooms? Here, it may be, the Government missed an opportunity suggested by the Moyne Committee, appointed precisely to survey the ground for the new Act. One of the recommendations in the Moyne Committee's report was that "the Government should, as soon as may be, take such steps as may be practicable to encourage financial interests to constitute one or more organisations to finance British film production, in approved cases, on reasonable terms". The Moyne Committee recommended also that the whole administration of the Act should be entrusted to a new body, the Films Commission, with far-reaching executive powers. This proposal was fought for strongly in the House of Commons, partly because of the hope it seemed to offer of financial reform. Indeed, John Grierson, writing in the *Kinematograph Weekly*, has said:

> When we started the big push for a Films Commission which so nearly succeeded—till Mr Stanley's—or Mr Burgin's—prestige as a Bill promoter was so sorely at

stake that he put on the Whips—all that some of us were concerned with was the creation of such an intermediary between production and capital. We saw the Commission as a means by which capital and film production could at last get together on sensible terms with some guarantee of discipline on both sides.

Well, the Government decided otherwise. Instead of a Films Commission, the Act created merely the Cinematograph Films Council, a quite different type of body, with purely advisory powers. Nor was any definite step taken under the Act to encourage the constitution of "one or more organisations to finance British production, in approved cases, on reasonable terms". However, we may still retain a faint hope that the financing of British production will not continue for ever on just the same bad old lines. In the past we have tried to build up a producing industry more or less on the Hollywood plan; perhaps we have made a mistake and should now look rather to an alternative plan, less familiar but no less valid.

The Hollywood plan is based on permanent companies owning their own studios and occupied with long-term production programmes. This method has obvious advantages; it provides for continuity of policy, for planning ahead and the nurturing of stars and directors; it may allow an inspiring tradition of team-work to grow up. But it is an expensive method. Overhead costs, including the salaries of stars under contract, go on all the time; and usually it means that the company, to meet its engagements and its overhead, has to keep on continually producing pictures, whether good subjects are available or not. Hollywood can afford all this, chiefly because the American producer has a huge home market safely in his pocket, covering his production costs at least, plus the prospect of clear profit from foreign markets thoroughly explored and organised while European film-producing countries were at war.

In England it has always been difficult for a producing company to keep going on a big scale, even with the backing of an exhibiting circuit. John Maxwell, of Associated British, has done it, but only by confining himself to comparatively low-cost pictures of a popular type, aimed chiefly at the British home market. Efforts to break into the American market with lavish features have either failed, or have needed such American support as London Films enjoy through Korda's membership of United Artists. But we are not compelled to imitate the Hollywood method of the big permanent company, owning its own studios. We have had a long and dazzling dream of a "British Hollywood" in Middlesex or Hertfordshire, the palatial offices, the high-powered executives, the bevies of beautiful stars, everything except the climate and the scenery and the vital assurance of a home market covering nearly three million square miles. We might look now instead across the Channel. Is there perhaps something we could learn from France?

Particularly during the past year there has been reason to look respectfully at France. Following *Mayerling*, *Pépé le Moko*, *La Kermesse Heroïque*, she has sent over a succession of pictures of rare quality— *Un Carnet de Bal*, *La Grande Illusion*, *Gribouille*, *La Belle*

Equipe, Orage, Le Roi S'Amuse, L'Homme du Jour. These films, showing in London at the Academy, the Curzon, the Berkeley, Studio One and the Forum, have provided far and away the best film-going of the last twelve months. For intelligence, humour, subtlety of acting and finish of style they deserve, I think, to be greeted with something of the same excitement, the same sense of a new stage in cinema accomplishment, which greeted the German "classics" soon after the War, and the silent Russian revolutionary pictures. The best of them stand to even the better type of Hollywood production as a hand-made article stands to a mass-production commodity.

France has passed lately through a series of social-economic difficulties, which still persist. Governments have fallen, the franc has slumped, across the frontiers have sounded echoes and rumours of war. Yet this impoverished, harassed country has begun to make the best films in the world. I asked Miss Elsie Cohen how it was done, and now pass on her replies.

First, production costs in France are much lower, and the French producer can expect a much better return from his home market. He can make a high-quality feature film for £20,000–25,000 and may reap a profit of £10,000 from the French-speaking market alone, with extra profits often from Great Britain and a little extra sometimes from America. The main reason is that he has to meet comparatively little competition from American films in his own country. The more popular American pictures are shown in Paris and in the large cities, but French audiences like their own films and support them without any of that condescension which audiences here have come —not without cause—to feel for British pictures. Further, French films are at present made almost entirely by independent production units, brought into being and financed perhaps for a single job of work. Most of the leading stars are free-lances; they are paid fees, not contract salaries. Hence the producer has few continuous overheads; he hires studio space, hires his players, and when a film is finished his commitments are mostly finished too. Nor is he compelled to keep on turning out films to carry out a schedule promised to renters and exhibitors in advance. The booking of films to cinemas is much less elaborately organised; a good new picture will probably get shown on the boulevards soon after it is ready and will run there as long as it continues to draw. And this freedom from time pressure gives producers a chance to plan their pictures carefully in advance; they are able to work as craftsmen, not as mechanics on an assembly line.

This simplified picture of the French film industry may be too idyllic, like most miniatures. Yet I think we can see in it a true picture of an industry which has grown up in happy remoteness from the haste and fever and money-intoxication of Hollywood. A French star thinks himself rich—and by French standards he *is* rich—on £10,000 a year. Sooner or later he may be tempted to Hollywood by dreams of £10,000 a week: and there is a steady drain of French talent—Boyer, Danielle Darrieux, and, among directors, Duvivier—across the Atlantic. But there are some French stars—Jean Gabin, for instance—who prefer to be comfortable and happy in their own country. The French are a sober, realistic, thrifty people; they are not very easily persuaded that films can be made only in an atmosphere of golden exaggeration, high-powered executives living in luxury suites and throwing money about to keep themselves feeling important.

What could we learn from France? Hardly how to bring production costs down to French levels, for Britain is a country living at present on an altogether more expensive scale. And the new Act is framed precisely to encourage the making of expensive films or none. In our home market, too, there can be no language barrier to keep Hollywood competition at bay. All the omens are for increasing Anglo-American co-operation, and we have to face the fact that probably not very many strictly independent British films, outside the educational and documentary fields, are going to be made in the visible future. But it may still be possible for production in this country to be either grandiloquent, wasteful and artistically dull, or modest, sensible and artistically enterprising. And one hopeful tendency, I think, more or less in line with French practice, is the recently increased number of independent production units, as distinct from studio-owning producing companies. Not long after the first edition of this book appeared, for instance, Charles Laughton joined with Erich Pommer to form the Mayflower Picture Corporation so that he could act in pictures of his own choice. Under this arrangement he has made two films so far— *Vessel of Wrath* and *St Martin's Lane*—and is just now at work on a third, *Jamaica Inn*, from Daphne du Maurier's Cornish smuggling novel, directed by Alfred Hitchcock. Leslie Howard, too, found independent backing for the version of Shaw's *Pygmalion* which he has been finishing this summer at Pinewood, acting the lead himself and sharing the direction with Anthony Asquith.

As a rule, the first step for an independent producer is to contract with a renting company to distribute his films, when they are made. (The Laughton–Pommer Mayflower productions are distributed by Associated British; *Pygmalion* will go out through G.F.D.) It is a system which may develop considerably, I think, but will it give any encouragement to young directors, young writers, producers with original ideas? John Grierson, in his article from which I have quoted already, discusses this question in the light of his own position (he has now left the G.P.O. Film Unit and set up as an independent producer):

> Let me put an example, and it is an example that others will parallel. As a producer, I have a certain reputation in my own field. I don't need to go into big films for I have enough to keep me going in documentary shorts. But this British film business is on my conscience, and it should be. I want to make my minor contribution to the development of the British films, and to produce, say, three or four films a year of a dramatic, realistic, or epic sort, near to my own style of thinking.
>
> I am humble about it.
>
> I would be glad to make them at the £10–15,000 level, and content myself with a second feature spot. Not only that, but I think, rightly or wrongly, that I could contribute something relatively sensible.

After discussing various possibilities, Grierson continues:

> What emerges is this. The producer already established in large-scale production must go his way, pursuing his policies as he thinks fit, and bringing men in who will fit his policies. The independents among us must help ourselves, pursuing our own schemes, building our own teams, either seeking a combination with an existing renter who can be trusted or setting out with crossed fingers to create our own odds-and-ends selling establishment.
>
> It follows that any renter who can build a reputation for giving his independent producer a first-rate service of salesmanship will command a certain attention in the next period of development. It follows that any established producer who has the imagination to ally himself with new ideas and new production forces, and knows how to maintain their spirit of independence, will command a certain loyalty in the next period of development.

Finally, Grierson speaks of "two profound weaknesses in British production." One is lack of co-ordinated team work: "a gang working together, who know how to hand it out, and also take it—and especially take it—is a vital necessity in the exacting business of film-making". The other weakness is in scripts: "The only first-rate British script that has been seen recently was the one for *Farewell Again*, the only one, in fact, that has had the sense of timing, the sense of filmic bits and pieces about it, necessary to story-telling on the screen." We have got to find or train new writers, and for the present, Grierson concludes, we had better not indulge too ambitiously in lavish dreams:

Clearly there are preliminaries before we start throwing our hats into the international rings. It seems to me the Ring, Blackfriars, would do excellently well for a year or two. British production needs to learn, first, a few essential tricks of the trade, and a few of the simpler secrets of stamina.

After that it can proceed.

All this seems to me excellent advice. On how far Grierson's ideas can be realised, by himself and by others, will depend the answer to the questions I have already asked. Is the British film industry to be yoked strictly to Hollywood ambitions, occupied mainly in turning out lavishly Americanised features under American control? Or will opportunities be found for the making of pictures genuinely British in style and spirit, with good ideas, careful preparation and enthusiastic team-work keeping production costs down to a level which encourages experiment and enterprise? The new Act obviously does little to encourage the producer with good ideas and not much money; in fact, it positively discourages him, for a film made economically will not rank for quota unless it satisfies the Board of Trade that it possesses "special entertainment value." And so he is left wondering, rather dubiously, just how the Board of Trade and the Cinematograph Films Council intend to interpret this obscure phrase. Will they bring to its interpretation a generously discerning spirit? More, will they show themselves actively anxious to interpret it favourably for the independent producer with something of original value to contribute to the development of British cinema? If they do not, the independent producer in this country has little to hope for under the new Act, and much to fear.

Well, so much for the background of British production in the light of current events. Now it is time to look at a few of the positive achievements of the cinema in various countries. During recent months, France apart, there is not much to report from the Continent. Two Jannings films have come to London—*Der Herrscher* and *Der Zerbrochene Krug*. They were full of careful detail and well acted by Jannings himself, but both were rather heavy and slow; in their whole style and colouring they were obviously not much concerned with international appeal. We shall soon be seeing Leni Riefenstahl's enormous documentary record of the last Olympic Games in Berlin; but German studios are nowadays occupied mainly either with commonplace comedies or with patriotically inspired dramas intended to drive home some aspect or other of the Nazi "idea". Mussolini is said to have ordered a grand revival of Italian production, but only one Italian feature film has found its way here at all lately—*The White Squadron*, a naïve story, with good desert scenery, of Kiplingesque empire-building in North Africa.

I have seen fairly lately three Russian films—*Son of Mongolia*, the adventures of a young shepherd in territory where Russian and Japanese ambitions clash; *The Last Night*, a drama of the October revolution in Moscow; and *The Thirteen*, a "lost patrol" tale of Red Army troops at issue with bandits in the Central Asian desert. All three have good qualities of vigour and graphically rendered episode;

but it is no use looking nowadays to Russian films for bold originality of technique. In Russia, as in Germany, the artist plays for safety; there is no free creation within the threatening boundary of a "party line".

Turning now to recent British, French, and American pictures, I feel the beginnings of a certain *malaise*—or, perhaps, the right name for it is film critic's sloth. When one is constantly seeing and writing about films, a peculiar effort is necessary—I always feel—to go back and sort out one's memories into categories of best, better, good, bad. And when I try to think back over a certain period, it is not the titles of films which occur to me, but separate scenes and episodes which have somehow left a lasting impression and can be recalled with pleasure. I will put down a few of these, in no particular order, and with no pretension to anything approaching completeness.

Most vivid, I think, are certain scenes from Duvivier's *Un Carnet de Bal*. Christine is looking for the admirers of her youth, now grown much older, and in a little room of the choir school at Chartres she sits talking to the master of the school, kindly and stout in his monk's cassock—and so perfectly played by Harry Baur—while snow drifts down outside the window and the voices of the boys at singing practice are heard from another room. Again, she is talking in a night-club to Louis Jouvet, the promising young solicitor who now has the watchful smile of the man likely at any moment to be wanted by the police, and to revive their old relationship she quotes a few lines of French poetry, something about lovers who meet in the wintry solitude of a park. Yet again, she is in Marseilles—and there is no difficulty in remembering that grim scene, the shabby consulting-room, with cranes on the water-front rattling ceaselessly just outside, and Pierre Blanchar as the epileptic doctor, home from the East, who fails to recognise her and thinks she has come as a patient for his illegal abortion practice. And I remember Louis Jouvet in other parts—as the elegant young baron who, with the air of an untroubled philosopher, takes up his quarters in the doss-house in Renoir's *Underworld*; and more recently as the formidably polite detective in *L'Alibi*, setting his traps for von Stroheim as a vaudeville telepathist and murderer. Yes, for me Jouvet is decidedly the actor of the year. I have other memories of French films—of von Stroheim, again, in tight Prussian uniform, moving stiffly from war wounds, as commandant of the fortress whence the French officers escape through the snow in Renoir's *La Grande Illusion*; of Michèle Morgan as the heroine of *Gribouille* and *Orage*—but enough, perhaps, of these.

When I think now of American films, I find my impressions sorting themselves naturally into certain categories. Hollywood has continued to show an intermittent uneasy concern with social issues—particularly, just lately, with prison problems. I remember Sylvia Sidney and Henry Fonda driving interminably through the rain after Fonda's prison break in Lang's *You Only Live Once*—a nightmarish film, poignant in spots, mechanically melodramatic in others. And the queer impressionism of Lang's later picture, *You and Me*—crime again in social perspective, the realism of back streets most oddly mixed with a fairy-tale morality. And the gang of street-boys, with their young-old faces, like the faces of sad, precocious monkeys, in *Dead End*—perhaps the best American treatment of a social problem, the slums and the fashionable apartment block side by side on the river bank, the hot weather and the boys bathing in the greasy water. First in this social-theme category many people, probably, would put *The Life of Emile Zola*, but to me this picture, in spite of Muni's brilliant individual performance, seemed too long and laboured, too plainly American in manner for its French subject, too often an example of what happens when—in Herbert Read's phrase—"art becomes, not a mode of expressing the life of the imagination, but a means of illustrating the concepts of the intelligence".

There was more of the spontaneity of art, I think, on the humbler level of the "crazy comedies" which Hollywood suddenly took to turning out one after another—*Easy Living, Woman Chases Man, Nothing Sacred, It's Love I'm After, Bringing Up Baby*. They represent a trend—predicted in Hitchcock's article—away from the individual comedian in comic clothes towards an exploitation of the absurdities lurking under the precariously balanced surface of everyday life. They have some connection with surrealism and psycho-analysis; though it is an odd reflection that Dr Freud, that uncompromising scientist, should be even partially responsible for Miriam Hopkins climbing a tree in her nightgown or Katharine Hepburn and Cary Grant crawling nocturnally after a baby leopard in the garden of a sedate country house. Another American trend—not dissimilar—has been towards the showing-up of Hollywood—dramatically in *A Star is Born*, uproariously in *Stand-In*. Stars, there is no doubt, are less sacred than they were; and it is not for nothing that child players have risen to the top of popularity—Shirley Temple is the best box-office draw in the world—and that Deanna Durbin and Sonja Henie are among her nearest rivals. The seductively sophisticated vamp seems to be almost dead; singing schoolgirls and skating flappers, appealing with their youthful wholesomeness to maternal instincts, are rapidly driving her from the field.

And what is the secret of the prodigious, unfailing popularity of Walt Disney's cartoons, and particularly of his first feature-length production, *Snow White and the Seven Dwarfs*, which has been beating all records at the New Gallery in London, and will probably do the same in most places where it is shown? Perhaps, in this mechanised, war-distraught world, which often seems to be rushing backwards towards a new night of cruelty and barbarism, there is an increasing desire to escape from such nightmares by experiencing again something of the fairy-tale innocence of childhood. But I am not sure that it is always quite this experience, in its pure form, that Disney has to offer. In *Snow White and the Seven Dwarfs* the animals, the birds, the deer, the chipmunks and the persevering old tortoise, are as usual masterly and delightful creations, seen and rendered with intimate sympathy, full of humour and affection; but Disney's touch is not nearly so sure with Snow White herself, who is far too doll-like and pretty-pretty, nor with the dwarfs, needlessly ugly with their bulbous red noses; they belong to the realm of pantomime far more than to the realm of mother earth. Disney has an extraordinary talent; he and his multitudinous helpers are marvellous craftsmen, incredibly skilful and patient, but a touch of mechanism is difficult to avoid in the queer illusion of the animated cartoon, and I am doubtful whether traditional fairy-tales are the best field for its development.

No such clear-cut tendencies are discernible in recent British films. With chief pleasure I remember Flora Robson's masterly acting as the Colonel's ailing wife in *Farewell Again*, a film of brilliant episodic sketches, so fluently woven together, of troopship life; Carol Reed's equally brilliant direction of *Bank Holiday*—a British picture which would have received much louder acclaim had it been put over with a louder noise of publicity behind it; and the warm Eastern colour of Korda's *The Drum*, in spite of its conventional frontier-intrigue story. (I think Paul Nash might have written more kindly of colour if he could have waited to see *The Drum*, *Nothing Sacred*, and *A Star is Born*, all very creditable achievements for the Technicolor process. But there is no sign yet of a general rush into colour: its box-office value seems to be too small—except perhaps in spectacular open-air productions—to off-set its extra trouble and expense.) Then there was Hitchcock's *Young and Innocent*, a most agreeable entertainment, one of his best in a light style—a not very credible story packed with acutely noticed detail and told with that visual fluency which not many other directors can equal. Hitchcock sees his pictures before they are made and works thoroughly on his own script; and I think that the only directors worthy of a special reputation in future should be those who do this, who create a film where only it can be truly created, in the visual imagination. It was different when pictures were shot "off the cuff" from primitive scripts, or from no scripts at all; then films were really made from start to finish by the director as he went along. Nowadays the man who does most to make a picture is the man who invents it and writes it down, shot by shot, in terms of clearly conceived visual detail. The director who merely translates another man's script into film lengths on the studio floor is at best a fine craftsman, not a creator. How strange it is that Derrick de Marney and Nova Pilbeam, a delightful young couple in *Young and Innocent*, are apparently to be given no further chances together! This is a great commercial weakness of British production methods—no consistent policy of star-building. On the other hand, if British studios had managed to rival Hollywood in commercial prosperity, they might possibly have attracted—and perhaps misused—some of the talents and energies which have given Britain a world lead in the documentary field. But there may also be something about the documentary style which suits our native temperament and outlook. Anyway, it often happens that British entertainment films are at their best when they approach a documentary style.

Two recent examples are *The Challenge* and *Owd Bob*. The Alpine scenes in *The Challenge*—Whymper climbing the Matterhorn—are excellent; and the sheep-dog trial sequence in *Owd Bob*, directed by Robert Stevenson, deserves to be remembered as a classical example of how a familiar activity of the countryside can be brought faithfully, vividly and dramatically on to the screen. Yet both these pictures had conventional stories; they were convincing only when they were dealing directly with matters of fact. And how much these matters of fact can in themselves yield to the cinema has been magnificently shown this summer in a straight documentary—*North Sea*, produced for the G.P.O. Film Unit by Alberto Cavalcanti and directed by Harry Watt, which for me ranks as easily the best British picture of the year, so far. I have found very little in ordinary film dramas so exciting and so moving as this record—drawn from life, without the aid of a single professional player—of a North Sea trawler's battle with a gale and the help she receives from the G.P.O. coastal wireless stations.

A few days later it happened that I went to see a Metro-Goldwyn production, *Yellow Jack*—Robert Montgomery and Virginia Bruce in a story taken from the struggle against yellow fever in Cuba just after the Spanish-American war. The tracing of yellow fever to the *stegomyia* mosquito and the subsequent work of Gorgas in clearing the death-stricken Panama zone for the building of the Panama

Canal, is one of the epics of medical history—fine material, surely, for the screen. But for some reason—the star system, perhaps, or simply economy—*Yellow Jack*, though in many ways a creditable production, introduced Gorgas as a comparatively minor figure, and showed only the beginnings of his work, with no mention of the Panama Canal enterprise, the natural climax of the story. And this made me wonder whether drama and documentary might not be able to draw closer together. I should like to see the building of the Panama Canal, for instance, treated in a style which, while keeping strictly to facts and introducing no fictional characters, would at the same time bring the characters to life as named individuals; for as long as documentaries deal in types rather than in persons they must remain somewhat restricted in popular appeal. *March of Time*—that most effectively enterprising American development of the newsreel—is, I believe, planning a feature-length production soon; it might turn out to be rather what I have in mind. The need always is for more realism *and* more imagination—for more of both, in ever closer union; this is how the film marches on.

CONTRIBUTORS' WHO'S WHO

BERNSTEIN, SIDNEY L. Chairman of Bernstein Theatres, Ltd., controlling thirty-five cinemas in suburbs of London and the provinces. One of the founders of the London Film Society. Has paid many visits to foreign film studios; returned recently from three months spent studying production methods in Hollywood. Issues periodically a comprehensive film questionnaire to 500,000 regular patrons of his cinemas.

BETJEMAN, JOHN. Formerly Film Critic of *The Evening Standard*. Wrote *Ghastly Good Taste*, a book about the decline of architecture in England. Editor of *Shell Guides*.

BOWEN, ELIZABETH. Daughter of Henry Cole Bowen, barrister-at-law, of Bowen's Court, Kildorrery, Co. Cork. Born in Dublin. Educated at Downe House. Married in 1923 Alan Charles Cameron, now Secretary to the Central Council for School Broadcasting and a Governor of the British Film Institute. Author of *The Hotel, The Last September, Friends and Relations, To the North, The House in Paris* (novels); and *Encounters, Ann Lee's, Joining Charles, The Cat Jumps* (short stories). Has travelled in France and Italy and visited America. A member of the London Film Society; has done only one piece of film criticism and has no technical knowledge of the cinema.

CAVALCANTI, ALBERTO. Born 1897. Started in films as an art director. Later, as a director, became a leading member of Avant-Garde movement in France. Made *En Rade* and *Rien que les Heures*. Went into the big commercial studios to direct *Capitaine Fracasse*. Lately has joined the documentary and realist film movement in England, working with John Grierson. Has done pioneer work in exploiting the use of sound in films. Produced *North Sea* for G.P.O. Film Unit, 1938.

COOKE, ALISTAIR. Born Manchester, 1908. Graduated Jesus College, Cambridge, 1930. Research in dramatic criticism, 1930-2. Elected to Commonwealth Fellowship for research at Yale, 1932-3; Harvard, 1933-4 (work on American language). Film Critic to British Broadcasting Corporation, October 1934 to April 1937. Film Critic of *Sight and Sound*. London commentator for National Broadcasting Company of America, 1936-7. Emigrated to United States, April 1937.

DAVY, CHARLES. Literary Editor and Film Critic of *The Yorkshire Post*. Film Critic of *The London Mercury* since 1935. Formerly Film Critic of *The Spectator* (1934–5) and of *The Bookman* (1933–5).

DEAN, BASIL. Born in London; intended for the diplomatic service; trained as an analytical chemist; at the age of seventeen appeared on the stage in *The School for Scandal*. Joined Miss Horniman's Manchester Repertory Company at its beginning in 1907 and stayed with it four years. Spent two years as director of the Liverpool Repertory Theatre, and one at Birmingham. After war service with the Cheshire Regiment, and as head of the entertainment branch of the Navy and Army Canteen Board, became responsible for a long series of stage productions in London. In 1928 turned his attention to films, becoming head of Associated Talking Pictures with studios at Ealing. Among the films he has directed are *The Constant Nymph*, *Escape*, *Nine Till Six*, *The Sign of Four*, and *Lorna Doone*. Producer of many of Gracie Field's pictures and of George Formby's comedies; himself directed Miss Fields' in *The Show Goes On*.

DONAT, ROBERT. Born Manchester, 1905. First stage appearance, 1921, as Lucius in *Julius Caesar*. Member of Sir Frank Benson's company, 1924–8, interspersed with seasons of modern repertory in the North. Leading man at the Playhouse, Liverpool, 1928–9, and at the Festival Theatre, Cambridge, 1929–30, where he also produced *The Kingdom of God* and *The Medium*. At Embassy Theatre, London, 1930–1, appearing notably as Gideon Sarn in *Precious Bane*. Played Dunois in *St Joan*, His Majesty's, 1931. At Malvern Festival, 1931 and 1934, creating part of Charles Cameron in *A Sleeping Clergyman* and playing it later at Piccadilly Theatre, London. Entered films 1932; appeared in *The Private Life of Henry VIII*; took lead in *The Count of Monte Cristo* (at Hollywood); returned to take lead in *The Thirty-Nine Steps*; *The Ghost Goes West*; and *Knight Without Armour*, playing opposite Marlene Dietrich; and *The Citadel*.

GREENE, GRAHAM. Born 1904. Went from Oxford to work as subeditor of *The Times*, 1926–30. Novels include *The Man Within*, *Stamboul Train*, *It's a Battlefield*, *England Made Me*, *A Gun for Sale*, *Brighton Rock*. Travels in West Africa, 1935, described in *Journey Without Maps*. Film Critic of *The Spectator* since 1935. In collaboration with Walter Meade wrote the screen play and dialogue of Galsworthy's *The First and the Last*, directed by Basil Dean for Alexander Korda, at Denham, 1937.

GRIERSON, JOHN. Born Deanston, Scotland, 1898. Entered Glasgow University as Clark Scholar. Three and a half years' war service in Navy, auxiliary patrol and mine-sweeping. Graduated in philosophy, Glasgow University; appointed to a Rockefeller Research Fellowship in Social Science. Three years in the United States studying the Yellow Press and other instruments affecting public opinion. After a meeting with Sir Stephen Tallents, joined staff of Empire Marketing Board. Made *Drifters* to demonstrate the documentary theory without knowing one lens from another. On the abolition of the E.M.B. formed the G.P.O. Film Unit. Founded *World Film News*. Has been responsible as Film Officer of the E.M.B. and G.P.O. for a hundred and fifty films. In 1937 left G.P.O. and is now an independent producer.

HARDY, FORSYTH. Film Critic of *The Scotsman* since 1933, after four years as critic of *The Evening Dispatch*. With Norman Wilson founded *Cinema Quarterly* and ran it for three years before it was incorporated in *World Film News*. Founder member and first vice-president of Edinburgh Film Guild. Secretary of Federation of Scottish Film Societies. Member since its inception of Scottish Film Council (representative body in Scotland for the British Film Institute). Has broadcast on Scottish films.

HITCHCOCK, ALFRED. Born London, 1900. Education at a Jesuit college; trained as engineering draughtsman. Worked as artist for advertising agency, writing film captions in spare time. Employed as caption-writer by Famous-Players-Lasky at Islington studio, afterwards taken over by Gainsborough, for whom, promoted to director, he made *The Pleasure Garden*, *The Lodger*, *Downhill* and *Easy Virtue*. Married Alma Reville, scenario writer. Moved to Elstree, where his silent films for British International included *The Ring*, *The Farmer's Wife*, *Champagne*, *The Manxman*. In 1929 made his first talkie, *Blackmail*, followed by *Juno and the Paycock*, *Murder*, *The Skin Game*, *Rich and Strange*. Joined Gaumont-British to direct *Waltzes from Vienna*, with Jessie Matthews. Turned to thrillers and for Gaumont has since directed *The Man Who Knew Too Much*, *The Thirty-Nine Steps*, *The Secret Agent*, and *Sabotage*, Has since made *Young and Innocent;* is to direct Laughton in *Jamaica Inn* and later a *Titanic* disaster film at Hollywood.

JAUBERT, MAURICE. First among the leading young composers in France to make a serious study of music in films. Started by writing concert music and had his most important work, *Le Jour*, performed by the Orchestre Symphonique de Paris. First work for the films in *Le Pays du Scalpe*, in collaboration with Cavalcanti. Has been throughout a supporter of the French documentary movement and has worked with Vigo, Painlevé, Lods and Storck. Chief work for the cinema in René Clair's *14 Juillet* and *Le Dernier Milliardaire*. Collaborated with Honegger in the music for *Mayerling*, and has on his own account adapted Offenbach's *La Vie Parisienne* for the screen.

KANN, MAURICE. Editor of *Motion Picture Daily*, New York, a Quigley publication. Worked first on *New York Journal of Commerce*; joined *Film Daily* in 1918 and became editor in 1926. Was editor of *Motion Picture News* in 1929; took up present post when the *Motion Picture News* was amalgamated with the *Exhibitors' Herald-World*. Writes in *Motion Picture Daily* a tri-weekly feature, "The Insider's Outlook." Has paid many visits to Hollywood; in the summer of 1936 was over here studying British film production.

KORDA, ALEXANDER. Chairman and Managing Director of London Film Productions, Ltd. After working as a newspaper reporter, began directing in 1916 in Budapest, later going to Vienna, Rome and Berlin, where he directed for UFA. In 1926 went to Hollywood and made many films for Fox and First National, notably *The Private Life of Helen of Troy*. Returned to England to make *Service for Ladies*, his first British picture, before forming London Film Productions in 1932. Scored an international success with *The Private Life of Henry VIII*, following this with *The Scarlet Pimpernel*, *Sanders of the River*, and *The Ghost Goes West*, directed by René Clair. In August 1935 elected an owner member of United Artists and in 1936 opened his own studios at Denham, Middlesex. His recent films include *Things to Come*, made with the collaboration of H. G. Wells; *Rembrandt*; *Fire Over England*; Robert Flaherty's *Elephant Boy*; *Knight Without Armour*; and *The Drum*.

NASH, PAUL. Born 1889. Educated St Paul's and Slade School. First exhibited group of drawings, Carfax Gallery, 1911. War service with Artists' Rifles and Hampshire Regiment, and as an official artist, Western Front, 1917. War paintings and drawings exhibited at Leicester Gallery, 1918. Instructor in Design, Royal College of Art, 1924–5. Paintings, water-colours, and wood engravings shown at numerous galleries in later years. British Representative Carnegie International Exhibition Jury, 1931. Exhibitor at First International Surrealist Exhibition, London, 1936, and at first exhibition of Artists' International Association, London, 1937. Author of *Room and Book* (Essays in Decoration), 1932; contributor of art criticism to *Week End Review*, *The Listener*, *Architectural Review*, *Decoration*, etc. Most recent exhibition at Leicester Galleries, May 1938.

WRIGHT, BASIL. Aged 31. After leaving Cambridge began work for John Grierson in 1929. Under Grierson's producership directed *Country Comes To Town*, *O'er Hill and Dale*, *Liner Cruising South*, and a West Indies series for the Empire Marketing Board. Later directed *Song of Ceylon*, photographing most of it himself, and co-directed *Night Mail* with Harry Watt for G.P.O. Film Unit (Grierson producing). Now making documentaries with Realist Film Unit.

INDEX

(i) TITLES OF FILMS

Accused 59
Alibi, L' 316
Alpine Climbers (Mickey Mouse) 85
Aren't Men Beasts 59
Arroseur Arrosé, L' 71
Assassination of the Duc de Guise, The 72

Bank Holiday 318
Becky Sharp 89, 124
Beggar's Opera, The (Dreigroschenoper) 103
Beloved Enemy 59
Ben Hur 241
Berlin 149
Birth of a Nation, The 38, 66, 156
Blackmail 3-5, 11, 294
Blue Express, The 274
Broadway Melody 103

Cabinet of Dr Caligari, The 99, 294
Carnet de Bal, Un 307, 315
Casta Diva 103
Cavalcade (stage) 20
Challenge, The 321
Chang 148
Chapayev 155
Charge of the Light Brigade, The 93
City Lights 82
Colour Box 133
Coming Thro' the Rye 138
Congress Dances 103
Covered Wagon, The 156
Crime and Punishment 294

Dante's Inferno 97, 139
David Copperfield 97, 168
Dead End 317
Deserter, The 155
Devil Take the Count 59
Dodsworth 58, 61, 64, 289
Downhill 14
Dreaming Lips 54, 60
Drifters 150, 151
Drum, The 318
Duck Soup 64, 65

Earth 155, 293
Elephant Boy 97, 147, 148
End of St Petersburg, The 155, 292
En Rade 149
Ernte 59

Farewell Again 304, 312, 318
Farewell to Arms 111
Felix the Cat 81
Forty Days of Musa Dagh, The 201
Forty-second Street 104, 157
Fury 66, 68, 225, 236

Garden of Allah, The 124
General Line, The 42, 155
Ghost Goes West, The 16, 26, 95
Girl I Love, The 73
Girls' Dormitory 59, 60
Gold Diggers of Broadway 104
Good Earth, The 157, 284
Good Morning, Boys 59
Go West 79
Grande Illusion, La 307, 316
Great Barrier, The 59, 160
Great Train Robbery, The 139, 240
Great Ziegfeld, The 172
Gribouille 307, 316
Guardsman, The 81

Hat Trick, The 71
His Lordship 59
Herrscher, Der 314
Hortobagy 61, 62

I am a Fugitive from the Chain Gang 67, 225
Industrial Britain 151
Informer, The 108, 215, 236
Iron Horse 156
Isn't Life Wonderful 156
Italian Straw Hat 80
It Happened One Night 214

Jazz Singer, The 103

328 Footnotes to The Film

Kameradschaft 150
Kermesse Héroïque, La 59, 307

Last Night, The 314
Libelled Lady 15
Little Lord Fauntleroy 168
Lost Horizon 259
Lost Patrol, The 107, 108
Louis Pasteur 66, 236

Mädchen in Uniform 236
Magnificent Obsession 59, 60
Maid of Salem 59
Man of Aran 61, 62, 97, 147, 236
Man Who Knew Too Much, The 6
March of Time, The 142–4, 154, 322
Mary of Scotland 168
Mayerling 307
Mazurka 59, 60
Men and Jobs 66, 156
Mickey Mouse 85, 131
Midsummer Night's Dream, A 97
Mr Deeds Goes to Town 236, 260
Mr Wu 67
Moana 146, 236
Modern Times 82
Monte Cristo 16, 20
Mutiny on the Bounty 168
Mutt and Jeff 81
Mutter Krausen 150
My Man Godfrey 214

Nanook of the North 146, 148, 149
New Babylon, The 274
Night Patrol, The 264, 268
North of '36 156
North Sea 321
Nothing Sacred 317, 319

Old Curiosity Shop, The 97, 99
O.H.M.S. 59
Orage 308, 316
Outward Bound 264
Owd Bob 321

Paths of Glory 201
Peace of Britain, The 264, 266
Pépé le Moko 307
Peter Ibbetson 111
Pilgrim, The 79
Plainsman, The 59
Polo Match (Mickey Mouse) 132
Pony Express 156
Popeye the Sailor 85
Potemkin 155

Private Life of Henry VIII, The 16, 158, 191, 236
Prologues 104

Rainbow, The 134
Ramona 59, 116, 119, 121, 124, 125
Raskolnikov 294
Rien que les Heures 149
Ring, The 10
Road to Life, The 155
Road to Paradise, The 103
Roi s'Amuse, Le 308

Sabotage 6, 7
Safety First 79
St Martin's Lane 310
Scarface 225
Secrets of Nature 41, 227
Sex Ignorance (censored) 272
She Married Her Boss 214
Shipyard 57
Simple Case, A 155
Silly Symphonies 128, 131
Sleeping Clergyman, A (play) 33–5
Snow White and the Seven Dwarfs 318
Son of Mongolia 314
Song of Ceylon 57, 62, 63, 291
Song of Freedom 63
Sous les Toits de Paris 96
Spy, The 68
Star is Born, A 318, 319
Storm over Asia 155, 311
Storm over Mexico 155
Student of Prague, The 294

Tabu 146, 147
Ten Days that Shook the World 155
Texas Rangers, The 59
These Three 66
Thirteen, The 314
Thirty-nine Steps, The 15, 16, 26
This'll Make You Whistle 59
Three Songs about Lenin 244
Turn of the Tide 97

Underworld, The 316
Unfinished Symphony 103

Vaudeville 156
Vessel of Wrath 310

We from Kronstadt 68, 155
White Shadows 146, 147
White Squadron, The 314
Wings of the Morning 116–21, 125, 126–8
World Melody 114

Index

Yank at Oxford, A 304
Yellow Jack 321, 322
You and Me 317
You Only Live Once 316
Young and Innocent 319, 320

Young Madame Conti, The (play) 27
Zerbrochene Krug, Der 314
Zéro de Conduite 42, 253
Zola, The Life of Emile 317
Zoo in Budapest 45

(ii) PERSONAL

Annabella 124
Asquith, Anthony 217, 311
Astaire, Fred 91

Bakshy, Alexander 241
Baur, Harry 315
Baxter, John 158
Bennett, Charles 13
Berkeley, Busby 43
Bernstein, Sidney L. 221–37, 299
Betjeman, John 87–100
Borzage, Frank 111
Boyer, Charles 209
Bridie, James 33–5, 159
Brinton, Ralph 127
Bruce, Virginia 321
Bunny, John 241

Capra, Frank 224, 254, 259, 260
Carroll, Madeleine 15
Cavalcanti, Alberto 71–86, 145, 149, 150, 154, 321
Chaplin, Charles 22, 65, 77–80, 82, 83, 93, 128, 180, 224, 260
Chatterton, Ruth 289
Claire, René 26, 80, 98
Cohen, Miss Elsie 123, 308
Cooke, Alistair 238–63, 299
Coward, Noel 19, 58
Crosby, Bing 65, 66
Cruze 156
Cummings, Constance 27

Darrieux, Danielle 309
Dean, Basil 172–84, 295
Delluc, Louis 80
de Marney, Derrick 320
de Mille, Cecil B. 87
Depinet, Ned 147
Dietrich, Marlene 124, 196
Disney, Walt 84–6, 91, 128–31, 292, 318–19
Donat, Robert 16–36, 72, 304
Dovshenko 293
Dressler, Marie 79, 198
Dufay, Louis 126
Durbin, Deanna 318
Duvivier, Julien 309, 315

Eggert, Martha 103
Eisenstein 42, 46, 74, 145, 150
Elton, Arthur 154

Fairbanks, Douglas 75
Farrell, Glenda 79
Fauré, Elie 240
Fazenda, Louise 79
Feyder, Jacques 60
Field, Mary 145
Fields, Gracie 158, 160, 209
Fields, W. C. 93, 94
Fiesinger 105
Fisher, Bud 81
Flaherty, Robert 46, 49, 53, 62, 145–9, 154, 156
Fleischer, Dave 84
Fonda, Henry 316
Fontane, Lynn 81
Ford, John 108
Formby, George 158
Francis, Eve 73

Gabin, Jean 309
Gable, Clark 124, 224
Garbo, Greta 24, 74, 224
Gilkison 97
Goldwyn, Samuel 65, 75, 85, 147
Grant, Cary 318
Grierson, John 137–60, 146, 227, 276, 293, 301, 302, 311–13
Griffith, D. W. 38, 138, 240, 300

Hardy, Forsyth 264–78, 302
Hart, Bill 21, 75
Hepburn, Katharine 317
Henie, Sonja 318
Hersholt, Jean 24
Hitchcock, Alfred 3–15, 26, 76, 94, 160, 217, 283, 294, 311, 317, 319
Hopkins, Miriam 124, 317
Howard, Leslie 311
Howe, James Wong 53, 305
Hubert, René 128
Hunter, Ian 14
Huston, Walter 289
Huxley, Julian 227

Iwerks, Ub 129

Jannings, Emil 314
Jaubert, Maurice 101-15, 288
Jeans, Isabel 14
Jennings, Humphrey 122
Jouvet, Louis 315-16

Kalmus, Mrs Natalie 126
Kann, Maurice 185-202, 302
Keaton, Buster 77-9, 82
Keeler, Ruby 91
Korda, Alexander 87, 147, 162-71, 192, 305, 319

La Marr, Barbara 75
Lang, Fritz 46, 68, 316
Langdon, Harry 78, 156
Laughton, Charles 310
Laurel and Hardy 65, 81-3, 215
Leenhart, Roger 106
Legg, Stuart 154
Linder, Max 79
Lloyd, Harold 78, 79
Lotinga, Ernie 83
Lubitsch 157
Lumière Brothers 71, 137
Lye, Len 116, 133-4

Maxwell, John 307
Marx Brothers 79, 83, 85, 208
Miller, Max 158
Mix, Tom 75
Montagu, Ivor 273
Montgomery, Robert 321
Morgan, Michèle 316
Muni, Paul 317

Nash, Paul 116-34, 293, 319
Nazimova 73
Nervo and Knox 83
Nilsen, Asta 73
Normand, Mabel 79
Novello, Ivor 14

O'Casey, Sean 159

Pallette, Eugene 24
Pickford, Mary 75
Pilbeam, Nova 320
Pitts, Zasu 79
Pommer, Eric 305, 310
Ponting, Herbert 146
Powell, Michael 97
Powell, William 15
Pudovkin 42, 67, 74, 145, 283, 292

Rainer, Luise 284
Ray, Charles 73
Reed, Carol 319
Reiniger, Lotte 292
Rennahan, Ray 127
Renoir, Jean 316
Riefenstahl, Leni 314
Riskin, Robert 260
Robson, Flora 319
Robson, May 198
Rogers, Ginger 91
Rotha, Paul 57, 154
Russell, Rosalind 304
Ruttman, Walter 114, 145, 149, 150

Shaw, Alexander 154
Shaw, Bernard 265, 268; *Pygmalion* 311
Sennett, Mack 76
Sidney, Sylvia 316
Skipworth, Alison 198
Smith, Percy 145
Spice, Evelyn 154
Sternberg, von 87
Stevenson, Robert 321
Stroheim, von 316
Sullivan, Pat 81

Taylor, Donald 154
Temple, Shirley 224, 318
Thalberg, Irving 262
Tissé 46
Tracy, Spencer 97

Vane, Sutton 264
Victor, King 304
Vigo, Jean 42

Wakefield, Douglas 83
Walker, Norman 97
Watt, Harry 154, 321
Weil, Kurt 103
West, Mae 224
Whelan, Tim 305
Wilhelm, Wolfgang 305
Wilkinson, J. Brooke 141
Woolfe, H. Bruce 145, 294
Wright, Basil 37-53, 57, 62, 154, 291, 300

Young, Loretta 124

Zanuck, Darryl 142
Zukor, Adolph 139

Index 331

(iii) GENERAL

Academy Cinema 123, 276, 308
Act, Cinematograph (1909) 266, 274
Act, Cinematograph Films (1927) 169, 186*ff*
Act, Cinematograph Films (1938) 303, 313
acting (film) 6, 16-36, 19, 58, 72, 83, 224, 284 *See* characterisation
actor 3, 6, 9, 19, 24, 38, 71, 139, 148, 157, 163, 173, 178, 283
actuality *See* realism
adaptations 33-4, 61, 92
advanced films *See* experimentalists, surrealism
advertising 233*ff*, 241, 246
America 14, 58, 85, 157, 205
American market 167, 185*ff*
American production 27, 73, 75, 79, 91-4, 97, 98, 103, 110, 125, 139, 141, 143, 156, 158, 166, 169, 177, 182, 185*ff*, 215*ff*, 225*ff*, 242, 255*ff*, 313, 316 *See* Hollywood
angles 38, 45, 49-51
animated diagrams 43
architecture 92
art 165, 207, 219, 229, 232, 239*ff*, 261, 265, 271, 275, 279*ff*
art director 47
Associated British 307, 311
Association of Cine-Technicians 270
audiences 302
Austria 94, 96

backgrounds 6, 26, 43, 78, 87-100, 139, 214, 227
back-projection 43, 138
ballet 104, 105
Berkeley Cinema 308
black-and-white 11, 90, 116, 214, 290, 293
Board of Film Censors, British 66; Report (1932) 272 *See* censorship
Board of Trade 304, 313
Board of Trade Committee (Moyne Report) 161, 169, 190, 305
box-office 13, 18, 87, 88, 196, 208, 223, 236, 254, 296 *See* finance
British Film Institute 235, 275, 296
British International Pictures (B.I.P.) 97
British production 94, 141, 150, 151, 157, 158, 162-71, 187*ff*, 226*ff*, 304, 313, 319

broadcasting 178, 278 *See* radio
business 89, 187, 229, 296, 299 *See* finance

camera 6, 8, 10, 21, 29, 30, 32, 37-53, 72, 77, 91, 92, 179, 284, 289
cameraman 25, 37-53, 58, 63, 122, 127
cartoon 43, 84-6, 104, 128-30, 234, 292
censorship 66, 67, 141, 232, 264-78, 302
characterisation 24, 175, 204, 284
children 234
Cinecolor 125
Cinema Quarterly (quoted) 273
Cinematograph Exhibitors' Association 274
Cinematograph Films Council 304, 306, 313
ciné-plastics 240
close-up 8, 9-10, 25, 27, 29, 31, 32, 35, 38, 40, 47, 74, 138, 178, 300
colour 11, 43, 85, 89, 90, 116-34, 220, 275, 279, 293, 319
Columbia Pictures 91
comedy 14, 15, 22, 71-86, 93, 96, 183, 215*ff*, 259, 260
comic 14, 42, 72, 78, 215
commentary, sound as 291
commentator 116
commercial film 5, 17, 27, 63, 89, 158, 165, 245, 271, 292, 299
competition 164, 199
Continental films 226, 283 *See* France, Germany, etc.
controversy 264, 270, 302
costume 88, 128, 284
coteries 253
countryside 95 *See* naturalism, outdoor
crime 268
crime story 3-4, 91, 94
criticism 165, 168, 173, 207, 230-1, 238-63, 276, 279
criticism of life 60, 62, 68
cutting 5, 26, 38, 61, 74-5, 77, 82, 115, 222, 244, 261
Curzon Cinema 308
custard pies 241

Danish films 79, 138
décor 90, 91
Denham studios 61, 95, 117, 147, 192*ff*, 307

detail 49, 98-9
dialogue 88, 252, 288
Dickens 96, 139, 240, 249
direction 3-15, 45, 224, 253
director 3, 9, 24, 26, 29, 32, 58, 63, 75, 76, 83, 102, 105, 106, 109, 122, 147, 152, 167, 195, 221, 259, 284, 288, 309, 320
director and cameraman, relation between 45, 46, 63, 262
dissolves 42, 252, 261
distance 49, 50
distortion 11, 40, 294
distributing 185
documentary 57, 62, 78, 137, 148, 150, 152, 155, 158, 160, 215, 218, 222, 227, 229, 291, 295, 322
double-exposure 252
double image 43
drama 15, 71, 168, 283, 322
dubbing 114
Dufaycolor 125
Dutch films 166

economics of cinema industry 227-8
editing 5, 261 *See* cutting, montage
education *See* instructional
electrician 47
Empire Marketing Board 152-4
Empire Theatre 211
English scene 13, 168, 216, 226
entertainment 166, 174, 189, 218, 222, 242, 251, 254, 303, 319
excitement 65, 66, 232
exhibitor 148, 151, 163, 185*ff*, 221-237
Exhibitors' Association, Cinematograph 190
experimentalists 243, 245, 254, 273 *See* surrealism

facial expression 8, 22, 23, 73, 77, 82
fades 42
farce 158
feature films 222
Federation of British Film Societies 275, 276
Federation of Scottish Film Societies 275, 276-7
film-fan 224, 255
Film Institute, The *See* British
Film Society, The 154, 156, 273, 276
filters 41
finance 48, 78, 140, 146, 148, 160, 190, 305 *See* box-office
flash-back 240

focus 49
folk art 254*ff*, 299
Forum Cinema 308
France 73, 96, 98, 124, 139, 149, 201, 205, 218, 240, 242, 255, 307, 315-6
future of the film 173

gags 80, 104
Gasparcolor 132, 133
Gaumont British Instructional 90
Gaumont British studio 192
gauzes 41
Germany 38, 73, 79, 96, 103, 132, 145, 150, 200, 218, 294, 314
General Film Distributors (G.F.D.) 311
glamour 213, 306
Government control 245 *See* Act
G.P.O. Film Unit 90, 133, 134, 154, 311, 321

Hollywood 42, 61, 94, 147, 156, 157, 168, 181, 183, 185-202, 213*ff*, 226, 244, 299, 303, 306, 310, 313, 317
humanity 175, 178, 208, 295, 303
humour, national 200, 217
Hungary 61, 132

imagination 97, 98, 117, 240
industrial films 150
industry, film (Part III) 135-202, 241, 254, 261, 303
inflammable films 266, 274
instructional films 295
interest films 53, 71
interiors 6, 98
Italian films 314

Japan 260
jazz 85, 256, 259
Jewish character 79, 82

Kinematograph Renters' Society 267, 272
Kinematograph Weekly 305

labour, contact with 159
lens 32, 40*ff*; multiple-prism 43 *See* camera
licensing 266, 273
life 7, 57-62, 67-9, 75, 89, 139, 140, 142, 152, 160, 215, 251, 279, 290, 295
light, lighting 29, 39, 45, 47, 53, 128, 138, 219, 284

Index 333

local cinema 230
Local Government authorities 265, 272*ff*; Education 234
London County Council 273
London Film Productions *See* Denham
long-shot 25, 29, 40, 77, 261, 290
love-stories 91, 94

magnate 163 *See* finance
make-up 24, 29, 73, 120, 123, 127
man in the street 165
markets 167, 171, 177, 187*ff*, 228, 307
masks 41
mass appeal 200
Mayflower Picture Corporation 310
melodrama 21, 42, 102
Metro-Goldwyn-Mayer (M.G.M.) 12, 15, 193*ff*, 211, 304
microphone 32, 112, 289, 293
minority, catering for 228
montage 91, 243, 244, 300
morals 265
movement of camera 52, 53, 69 *See* pan, tilt, shot
Moyne Committee *See* Board of Trade Committee
Museum of Modern Art Film Library 233
music 88, 101-15, 134, 275, 281
musicals 87, 91-2, 94, 158, 226
music-hall 59, 78, 83, 158, 159, 239

national life 161, 226
natural colour 132
naturalism 58, 119, 120, 125, 131, 138, 142, 241 *See* realism
nature films 145
newsreel 71, 142-4, 154, 222, 227, 294, 296
New Gallery Cinema 318
New World Pictures 117 *See* Denham
novel 33, 174, 285*ff*, 299

opera 104
orchestra 102
outdoor (countryside) 93, 94, 97, 126, 139 *See* naturalism

panning 43, 52
panorama 38
Paris 149, 308 *See* France
pattern 3, 105, 111, 219
period 88, 92, 219
photography 224 *See* camera
"pictures, the" 219

Pinewood studios 193*ff*, 311
play, stage 20, 23, 174, 281, 289
player *See* actor
poetry 57, 61, 64, 68-70, 105, 109, 281*ff*, 300, 303
politics 265, 268
popularity 5, 64, 65, 208, 227, 303
producer 27, 97, 105, 148, 162-71, 241, 261, 271, 301, 302
progress 14, 20, 25, 229
prohibited categories 267
projection 32 *See* studio
propaganda 74, 88, 162, 174, 222, 229, 296-8
psychology 8, 28, 123, 131, 164, 252
public, the 163 (Part IV), 203*ff*, 232
publicity *See* advertising

questionnaire 223
quotas 158, 171, 186*ff*, 303

radio 154, 235, 257 *See* broadcasting, television
Radio Pictures 91, 193
"reaction shot" 9
realism 66, 102, 106, 108, 115, 119, 137-60, 290, 293, 300, 308
recording 112, 117, 289
rehearsal 30
religion 268
renter 151, 163, 186, 272, 304
rhythm 74, 82 101, 105, 109, 111, 133
Russia 38, 67, 74-5, 90, 96, 152, 155, 157, 174, 205, 213, 218, 229, 242, 283, 288, 290, 300, 314

salesmanship *See* box-office, finance
scenario 5, 18, 26, 75, 105
scenery *See* backgrounds, setting
schools 234
scientific films 295
screen material (Part II) 55-134
script 5, 6, 26, 47, 115, 269
sentiment 76, 83, 158, 224
set, setting 5, 6, 72, 76, 78, 87-100, 200, 208, 284
sex 268
Shakespeare 61, 97, 139
shorts 90
shot, shooting 6, 25, 29, 40, 75, 77, 115, 320
showmanship 230
silent film 9, 18, 22-4, 78, 82, 101, 106, 115, 180, 236, 288, 292, 294
silhouettes 292

sincerity 27, 29
slapstick 15, 83, 139
slow motion 42, 53, 145
slow pace 182, 200 *See* speed
societies, film 154, 229, 264-78 *See* Film Society
sound 75, 81, 83, 85, 102, 114, 150, 220, 235, 279, 288, 294
sound department 48
sound-track 113, 290
Soviet 74, 93, 264, 273 *See* Russia
speed 41-2, 53, 72, 77, 82, 88, 200, 219, 261, 283
speeded-up motion 42, 145
stage 6, 15, 18, 28, 68, 83, 91, 172-84, 216, 281, 289, 291 *See* theatre
stars 14, 73, 76, 79, 87, 120, 124, 157, 167, 183, 193*ff*, 208*ff*, 224, 306, 309, 318
stories 3, 12, 26, 33, 57-70, 78, 88, 165, 193, 197, 205, 218, 261, 284, 289, 295
Strand Films 90
studio 3, 6, 26, 29, 32, 139, 146, 148, 160, 181, 192, 242, 283, 293, 301, 306
Studio One 308
studio work (Part I) 1-53
subsidised films 63
sub-titles 77, 292
subtlety 10, 29, 36, 64, 75
Sunday opening of cinemas 232, 273*ff*
surrealism 83, 91, 122, 132
Swedish films 138
swing music 255
synchronisation 47, 83, 85, 101, 103, 108, 291

talkies *See* sound
taste (popular) 14, 233, 236, 278
Technicolor 117*ff*, 319

telephoto lens 49
television 18, 239
tempo 182, 251 *See* speed
tension 8, 208
theatre 16, 18, 34, 174, 240, 241, 252, 272, 279, 287 *See* stage
thriller 67, 219
tilting 52
top-lighting 47
town life 98
travel 13, 116, 119
trick films 240, 300
trucking 38, 50, 52
truth 30, 240, 241 *See* life, naturalism, realism
Twentieth-Century Fox 97, 116, 118, 193
type-casting 24, 283
Tyrrell, Lord (Film Censor) 264, 270

units 83-4
unit staff 32
United Artists 307
United States *See* America

Variety (magazine) 246
verisimilitude *See* truth
visual imagery 294; metaphors 62
Vitaphone Sound Films 172

Wardour Street 141, 270
Warner Brothers 87, 91, 193
Westerns 75, 139, 219, 234, 240, 279
Whyte, Sir Frederick 304
wireless *See* radio, television
wisecracks 205
writer 12, 163, 167, 176
wipes 252
World Film News (quoted) 266, 270
Wurlitzer 19